An Ethics of Biodiversity

An Ethics of Biodiversity

Christianity, Ecology, and
the Variety of Life

Kevin J. O'Brien

Georgetown University Press
WASHINGTON, D.C.

Library of Congress Cataloging-in-Publication Data

O'Brien, Kevin J.
    An ethics of biodiversity : Christianity, ecology, and the variety of life /
Kevin J. O'Brien.
        p.   cm.
    Includes bibliographical references and index.
    ISBN 978-1-58901-645-3 (pbk. : alk. paper)
    1. Human ecology—Religious aspects—Christianity. 2. Biodiversity.
I. Title.
    BT695.5.O27 2010
    261.8'8—dc22

                                    2009026933

Cover image is from "Francis and the Wolf" by John August Swanson, used by
permission. Los Angeles artist John August Swanson is known for his finely
detailed, brilliantly colored paintings and original prints. His works are found in
the Smithsonian Institution's National Museum of American History, London's
Tate Gallery, the Vatican Museum's Collection of Modern Religious Art, and the
Bibliothèque Nationale, Paris. www.JohnAugustSwanson.com.

♾ This book is printed on acid-free, 100% recycled paper
that meets the requirements of the American National Standard for
Permanence in Paper for Printed Library Materials.

14 13 12 11 10 9 8 7 6 5 4 3 2
First printing

Printed in the United States of America

Contents

Part IV
Political and Morally Formative Conservation   111

Part V
Social Justice and the Conservation of Biodiversity   151

Preface

Human beings are degrading Earth's ecosystems, creating serious problems for all creatures and causing unknown long-term changes to our planet. This is not a controversial statement in most circles. However, it is not a particularly clear statement, either. Which ecosystems are most degraded and what are the most urgent threats to them? Which human beings and human behaviors in particular are causing the degradation? What sorts of studies are necessary to learn more about the long-term consequences of this degradation? What can concerned people do to mitigate or solve this problem? Which moral and intellectual traditions can be helpful in responding to this effort, and which need to be rethought or abandoned in light of it? These are enormous and challenging questions, questions that will take generations to answer.

An Ethics of Biodiversity aims to move toward some answers, focusing on a particular example of environmental degradation, the destruction of biodiversity, and demonstrating that even one example presents a hugely intricate and complicated set of challenges. I emphasize the particular role that humans in the industrialized world are playing in driving populations, species, and ecosystems to extinction, and I call for change and reform among privileged peoples. Learning from the ecologists and conservation biologists who have studied biodiversity most closely, I hope to capture the wonder of life's variety as they understand it and the mystery revealed by the vast amounts they do not understand. As a teacher and scholar of Christian ethics, I particularly work to develop a perspective from my own religious tradition, offering a set of guidelines and tools that will help people of faith to think about and relate to the variety of life as creation and recognize its degradation as sinful.

The goal of this book is to help students and scholars to think critically about biodiversity as a natural phenomenon, a scientific enterprise, and an object of religious attention. I hope that readers concerned with environmental issues will be better equipped to wrestle with the moral dimensions of conservation and to appreciate the role religious beliefs and communities can play in responding to the loss of biodiversity. At the same time, I hope Christians will be better equipped to recognize the need to take ecological science seriously if we are to live morally in God's world, and to appreciate how the moral and theological traditions we have inherited can adapt and evolve in light of biodiversity loss.

We human beings are degrading Earth's ecosystems, creating serious problems for all creatures and causing unknown long-term changes to our planet. A crucial step in dealing with this problem is to study it carefully, to bring multiple perspectives to bear that help us cope with the vast complexities of this world and our own cultural systems. This book aims to model such an approach by focusing on the loss of biodiversity and offering a Christian argument about how conservation should be understood and undertaken. With this argument I hope to contribute in a small way to the difficult and uncertain work of trying to ensure that a diverse world endures.

Acknowledgments

I have been deeply fortunate in the company that has kept me over the long process of writing this book.

First thanks go to my teachers. The religion faculty at Earlham College deserve enormous thanks for teaching me how to take human faith traditions seriously while I first learned to think critically about the diversity of life in our world. The faculty and students at Union Theological Seminary taught me what it means to thoughtfully engage Christian faith as a response to the suffering and injustices of our world, a lesson I am still struggling to learn and by which I remain deeply humbled. The faculty at Emory University taught me what it means to study Christian ethics in and amid a social context, and they helped me to find my own scholarly voice. I thank all who have taught me, and I hope that those who care to will recognize some fruits of their labor in this book.

Particular thanks are due to those who nurtured this project: Liz Bounds supervised my research and writing of the initial draft with diligence, care, and phenomenal insight. Also reading, questioning, and improving the project were Jon Gunnemann, Rusty Pritchard, and Larry Rasmussen. These four teachers found value in what I wrote and pushed me to think and write better at every stage. Each also offered an inspiring example of scholarship, teaching, and engaged citizenship, a combination I strive to emulate in this work and throughout my career.

I am blessed to have written in two collegial professional contexts. While I was enrolled in the Ethics and Society Program of Emory's Graduate Division of Religion, my colleagues offered support, friendship, and critical engagement. Darryl Stephens and Jill Weaver were particularly invaluable, and both read far more words than I could fit into this book and offered thoughtful feedback on every one of them. I completed and revised this book in my first three years teaching at

Pacific Lutheran University, and my colleagues in the Religion Department and Environmental Studies Program have welcomed me and nurtured my desire to teach and write about Christian and environmental ethics from interdisciplinary perspectives while also helping me to navigate the complexities of this task. Thanks are also due to my students, who always challenge me to think more clearly about and to respond more immediately to the world's problems.

I am grateful to Laurel Kearns and Catherine Keller of Drew University who organized the *Ecospirit* colloquium in 2005 and published my contribution, "Toward an Ethics of Biodiversity," in the 2007 volume of the same name, offering a chance to share the ideas at the foundation of this book early on. I am also grateful to Bron Taylor and the helpful anonymous reviewers at the *Journal for the Study of Nature, Culture, and Religion*, which published my first argument about the ethical implications of ecological scale, "Thinking Globally and Thinking Locally," in 2008. The ideas and text of those essays have been considerably reworked for the present volume thanks to the chance to share them in those venues.

Kathryn Blanchard and Ulrike Guthrie both read parts of this manuscript early on and helped me understand what I was trying to write. The anonymous readers who reviewed the project for Georgetown University Press made thoughtful and constructive observations that improved the book. Richard Brown, the director of Georgetown University Press, showed faith in this work from our earliest correspondence and nurtured it to completion.

A number of institutions provided support. Emory University's Graduate Division of Religion offered years of aid and many opportunities for research and teaching about Christian ecological ethics. The Aquinas Center of Theology at Emory provided a fellowship, an office, and invaluable chances to share my ideas with the local community. A Summer Fellowship from the Wabash Center for Teaching and Learning in Theology and Religion offered the time to complete and substantially revise the manuscript in the summer of 2008.

Last and most I thank my family. They offered support when I asked for it and distraction when I didn't realize I needed it. My mother, Mary Lou McCloskey, first taught me what a scholar is and why scholarship matters, and she still affirms my work unflaggingly while challenging me to do better. My brother, Sean O'Brien, has helped me to think more deeply all my life and continued that tradition by reading and responding to this book in draft form at a critical time. My father, John O'Brien, inspired my love of texts and of thinking that does not fit into any single category. Joel and Tom Reed joined in supporting me and talking about this project—and so much else—at regular family dinners on Sundays in Atlanta.

Finally, I thank my wife, and greatest teacher, Mary, to whom I dedicate this book. She supported me in every way as I worked on this project, and believed in me throughout. Words cannot express my gratitude and love for who she is and all she does, but I will nevertheless keep trying.

Introduction

Christian Ecological Ethics and Biodiversity

In the Pacific Northwest, the corner of the world where I live, the U.S. Fish and Wildlife Service proposes to shoot owls in order to save owls.

The birds to be shot are barred owls, a species native to the eastern side of the continent that has expanded its range, becoming particularly numerous in the Pacific Northwest in the 1990s. The birds to be saved are northern spotted owls, one of the most famous subspecies protected by the Endangered Species Act and an icon of environmental conflicts in the Pacific Northwest and across the nation. Spotted owls make their homes in the old-growth forests of this region, into which barred owls have moved.

When northern spotted owls were listed as a threatened species in 1990, the chief danger to their survival was the timber harvesting in western Washington, Oregon, and northern California. This sparked a contentious national debate in which many citizens understood the economic interests of logging communities as diametrically opposed to the environmental interest of preserving the subspecies and its habitat. After numerous controversies and compromises, the federal government set aside a critical habitat of 6.9 million acres of old-growth forest for the owl, and logging was forbidden on those lands. This changed the economic structure of many communities and created a symbol of the perceived division between human and environmental interests for decades to come. Years later those divisions have not fully healed, and many questions remain about whether habitat conservation and economic prosperity can coexist.

Unfortunately, something else that remains is the threat of northern spotted owl extinction. Already weakened by a reduced habitat, the owls face new threats, including mutating viruses such as West Nile, an increased risk of forest fires because of climate change, and an invasive species. This last threat is among the most severe: barred owls have the same nesting and dietary needs as their spotted cousins, and they are much more aggressive when competing for breeding ground.

Researchers have found extensive evidence that the competition between the two species is reducing northern spotted owl habitat and thereby making breeding and survival less likely.[1]

The Endangered Species Act charges the Fish and Wildlife Service with protecting most threatened species, and it is under this authority that the agency proposed in 2008 to expand an experimental program to capture and kill the invasive owls. Since they are not members of a threatened species, it is entirely legal to shoot barred owls in order to help northern spotted owls survive and, one hopes, return to a viable and self-sustaining level of population. The Fish and Wildlife Service argues that something must be done to control the invasive barred owl to prevent the threatened spotted owl "from declining irreversibly in the foreseeable future."[2]

This case is deeply complicated: the economic interests of some human beings clash with the interest of a subspecies of bird, and the interests of that subspecies clash with those of another group of owls. These conflicts are an unintended consequence of industrialized human society in North America, but the nonhuman world around us forms their context. As a society we must make difficult choices about what we value, what we should do, and how much we are willing to act and sacrifice on behalf of—and against—other creatures with whom we share this planet.

Of course, the northern spotted owl is just one of almost two thousand species listed by the Endangered Species Act, and these represent only a small sample of the variety of life threatened with destruction and extinction across our world.[3] Each threatened species, community, and ecosystem poses moral challenges as difficult as those raised by the spotted owl. Clearly, the project of protecting the variety of life on our planet—the conservation of biodiversity—is a complicated and difficult one. These complications and difficulties are the inspiration for and a subject of this book, which is about the global epidemic of biodiversity loss and its primary cause: human beings in industrial societies. *An Ethics of Biodiversity* calls for changes in the ways we think and act toward the variety of life, beginning with the premise that the decline in the variety of life on our planet can be halted only by significant changes in human behavior.

Life on Earth today is wildly diverse but the future of that diversity is increasingly domesticated. Through monoculture farming, expanding energy consumption, and the development and homogenization of land, wealthy and powerful human beings have caused unprecedented reductions in the variety of life around us. Estimates suggest that species extinctions now occur at up to one thousand times the natural rate and that one of every twenty species on the planet could be eradicated by 2060.[4] Each of these species is the product of thousands of years of evolution, plays a vital role in healthy ecosystem functioning, and represents countless individual creatures with an enormous wealth of genetic diversity.

As a Christian ethicist I understand each threatened life as a creation of God, loved by God, and so to be loved by human beings. From my perspective the dwindling numbers of northern spotted owls and the worldwide decline in biodiversity it represents are not just biological, economic, political, and moral challenges. They are also a theological challenge, a sign of disorder in the ways people like me are relating to God, God's world, and one another.

This one book of course cannot resolve all the questions raised by biodiversity loss and conservation. Its task is slightly more modest: to explore the moral and theological lessons to be learned from the conservation of biodiversity and to make some proposals about what Christian theological ethics might contribute to such efforts.

Environmental Degradation, Environmental Injustice, and Christian Ecological Ethics

We are past the point that we *can* or *should* consider living differently. We *must* learn how to live differently, because the ways many of us now live—particularly those of us who are materially comfortable in the industrialized world—make it more difficult and sometimes impossible for the rest of life on Earth to live at all. Our habits, choices, and social structures drive other species extinct, destabilize ecosystems, and take resources and sustenance away from the poorest peoples of the world, who frequently live closest to their immediate natural environments. Ultimately, the ways we live are degrading all life on this planet—our own lives included.

Broadly understood, this set of problems can be called environmental degradation, a catchall phrase for the myriad and expanding ways human beings are negatively affecting this planet. As recorded in a 1997 article from the journal *Science* by Peter Vitousek and his colleagues, humans have become the dominant force shaping our living world. "No ecosystem on Earth's surface is free of pervasive human influence," they write, and they go on to quantify the extent of the land humans have developed, the productivity of oceans altered by our actions, our enormous impact on global and local biogeochemical cycles, and the fundamental adaptations to life and its distribution for which humanity is responsible. Human beings have made substantial and lasting changes to at least half of the planet's land surface and fundamentally altered the flow of almost two-thirds of its rivers. Atmospheric carbon levels had increased to 130 percent of preindustrial levels by 1997, and that number has continued climbing exponentially since. Other environmental problems are better represented by the information we do not have, such as the untested and relatively unmonitored environmental impact of the one thousand new compounds created and distributed by the chemical industry each year.[5]

Such scientific analysis offers clear evidence that human activity is having a serious and troubling impact on the systems and structures of our planet. The most popular example of this impact is global climate change, the shifts in our planet's systems created by the atmospheric by-products of industrial society. Human beings have become numerous and powerful enough that the world's weather is no longer a topic for idle conversation but a worrying example of our dominance and the uncertainties that dominance creates for our planet's future.[6] We are degrading the capacity of our world to stably support life without fully understanding what we are doing.

However, climate change is just one example of our impact upon the planet and of the fact that this impact is not fully under our control. The same trend is evident in a variety of other environmental problems: toxic and nuclear waste disposal, polluted air and water, depleted soil, and dangerously scarce food, fossil fuel, and raw materials for human life. All of these complicated and deeply rooted problems call for attention.

The loss of biodiversity interacts with each of these other examples of environmental degradation. Many fragile species are endangered as the changing climate alters their ecosystems faster than they can adapt. As we develop land so that it can house human beings or otherwise indulge our desires, the animals that lived, fed, and bred there must find new habitat or die off. As we turn fertile ground into large-scale, industrial farms growing only a single crop, the variety of plant life in our ecosystems shrinks. Pollution of the air, water, and soil profoundly affects the millions and billions of other creatures with whom humanity shares this planet. In sum, declines in biodiversity are the product of a degraded global environment.

All these examples of environmental degradation are problems because of what they do to the nonhuman world: other species are being hurt, ecosystems are being destroyed, and our planet as a whole is changing in fundamental ways that we cannot fully understand or control. Environmental degradation is a moral issue because human beings are relating immorally to the nonhuman world around us. However, it is crucial to also note that environmental degradation is a problem for human beings: the ways we treat our planet, its ecosystems, and its species degrade human lives, and the distribution of that degradation occurs within oppressive and inequitable social systems.

To recognize that the ways human beings relate to our environments are connected with the ways we relate to one another is to recognize the reality of environmental injustice. The degradation of the nonhuman world is inseparable from the racism, sexism, and exclusion that poison our communities, because oppressed peoples tend to bear the burden of a depleted resources and polluted ecosystems. As liberation theologian Leonardo Boff puts it, "The poor and the oppressed belong to nature and their situation is objectively an ecological aggression."[7]

Strong evidence suggests that the global climate is changing primarily because of the actions of wealthy, industrialized people who burn the most fossil fuels and consume the most energy and resources. However, these changes will be felt most severely by people living in poverty who cannot afford to build sea walls against rising oceans, move away from dry and inhospitable areas, or otherwise adapt to the changing world.[8] Similarly, toxic pollution is distributed unevenly, and people who are poor and marginalized face vastly disproportionate burdens and threats. In the United States, this phenomenon is most clearly demonstrated by a series of reports from the United Church of Christ on "Toxic Wastes and Race," which conclusively show that people of color in this country are far more likely to live near hazardous waste facilities and thus to bear a disproportionate burden of worsening health created by our industrial society.[9]

Biodiversity loss, too, causes environmental injustices. When species are driven extinct and ecosystems are weakened, when crop diversity is replaced by monocultures, when environments can no longer support life, the effects are felt most by those who cannot afford or would not want to substitute one species or one place for another. The destruction of native plant and animal species is a threat to us all, but it is a far more immediate threat to those who depend upon and define their culture based on particular local places. Indigenous communities with long ties to particular ecosystems and powerful cultural associations to its species are affected in profound ways by extinction, a fact that is sometimes difficult to understand for those of us who can move easily and import our food and cultural heritage from far distant places. Thus, when biodiversity is degraded, those who are least responsible for its destruction tend to suffer first and to suffer worst.

The central topic of this book is a study of diversity, and awareness of environmental injustice dictates that this must include cultural as well as biological diversity. Our species, a part of the natural world, is incredibly diverse, made up of billions of individuals and thousands of diverse societies, and it is vital to respect and learn from this diversity, which is declining alongside the variety of nonhuman life. The loss of diversity is a fact of our world, a fact for which we are responsible because we have become unique among the species on Earth in having so much power over the rest of life. However, the reality of environmental injustice demands an immediate definition of the "we" being discussed: degradation is not caused by all human beings but rather by certain human beings with power in globalized and dominant cultures. The "we" in question is therefore made up primarily of people in industrial societies. So the story of biodiversity's decline is not just about humans dominating other creatures, it is also about humans with wealth, privilege, and power dominating other humans and the natural systems upon which we all depend.

My own attention to environmental injustice and environmental degradation occurs within the context of Christian ecological ethics, a scholarly field that draws on the resources of the Christian tradition to respond to the vast environmental threats currently facing our species and our world. It is for theological reasons that I assume environmental degradation is a problem: I believe that all life is created by God, that it is declared good by God, and that the responsibility of human beings is to live with rather than degrade the creatures with whom we share this planet. It is also for theological reasons that I pay special attention to the social injustices created by environmental degradation:

I feel called as a Christian to love God by loving my neighbors and so to pay attention to and empower those who are marginalized and dismissed by mainstream society. It is therefore as a Christian that I am troubled by the declines in diversity across our world and my own location within the culture that is primarily responsible for those declines.

However, as a Christian I also bring a theological hope to my discussion of these trends: hope that it is not too late to live differently with the variety of life on Earth, and hope that we can learn from that variety itself about how to structure our societies. I believe that a different way of life on Earth is possible because of a faith that God created us in and through this world and intends for us to live as part of it. I believe that the diversity of our world can teach us to live differently because it is sacramental, a sign of and connection to the mysteries and workings of God.

By calling my particular approach to Christian ethics "ecological," I aim to signal two things. First, I will be paying substantial attention to the science of ecology, learning from ecologists about what biodiversity is, how it is threatened, and what we can do in response to that threat. Based on the doctrine of creation, I believe that theological insight can be found from studies of God's world, and the studies to which this book pays the most attention are ecological. Ecology as I refer to it in this book is a branch of biology that studies living organisms while paying special attention to their relationships with the living and nonliving world around them.[10] Inherent in this definition is the second implication of ecological ethics: we should not study or concern ourselves with an "environment" as if it were distinct from ourselves. Rather, we are organisms who live in, are dependent upon, and are fully included within our environments. Ecological ethics stresses this interconnection, refusing to distinguish human beings in any absolute way from the rest of the world with which we coexist.[11] An ecological ethics of biodiversity is therefore holistic, emphasizing that we care for the variety of life on Earth in part because we are participants in that variety and dependent upon it for a healthy future. To understand ourselves we must understand the biodiversity from which we emerge.

This book is a work of ethics because it seeks to offer a set of tools for analyzing moral arguments. The Christian and ecological starting points just discussed offer a clear moral case for the conservation of biodiversity, and the job of an ethicist is to reflect on such moral arguments and develop perspectives and tools that help to make sense of them.[12] My assumption is that conservation is a vital moral task calling for rigorous and extensive ethical reflection, and I aim to offer such reflection and suggest the tools with which it might continue.

The conservation of biodiversity can be understood as one aspect of the broader environmentalist goal of sustainability, a goal defined by one Christian ecological ethicist as "the capacity of social and natural systems to survive and thrive together, indefinitely."[13] This goal includes a hope that human beings can stop carelessly changing our atmosphere, can control the expansion of our population and our development of land, and can find a way to justly distribute the benefits and burdens of life among us. Sustainability is about developing an approach to life on Earth that is cautious, thoughtful, and adaptable enough so that future generations will have at least the same chance of thriving as have we. This goal expresses a particular hope for human existence that is compatible with and complementary to the rest of the variety of life. That hope is the focus of this book.

Ethics in Context

In sum, this is a work of Christian ecological ethics that reflects on moral responses to the degradation of biodiversity. That explains why and how this book develops, but it is also important to pay attention to who is developing these ideas. As Christian ethicist Dan Spencer argues, all responses to environmental degradation should be a product of the whole self, and he introduces the concept of "ecological location" to emphasize that the social and natural contexts of our ideas make a difference.[14]

My own most formative ecological location is suburban Atlanta, where I was born and raised and where I lived while researching and writing the majority of this book. This city is situated in the Piedmont at the foothills of the Appalachian Mountains, a region characterized by a vast diversity of heavily forested habitats. However, the Atlanta of my experience was dominated by paved highways, strip malls, and chemically well-tended lawns. My most regular encounter with forest ecosystems was to notice when they had been removed to make way for economic development. In Atlanta I saw the domination of ecosystems by human beings and witnessed the ways that degradation impoverishes human life by exacerbating social divisions and injustices.

This book was completed where I now live, in Tacoma, Washington, on the Puget Sound in the Pacific Northwest. Much of this region is identical to my old home: roads and strip malls cover the landscape; the same chain restaurants, big box stores, and corporations structure the social world. But here in Tacoma human development is visibly boundaried by natural barriers: the vast ocean, a majestic mountain range, and an enormous volcano. Constant awareness of these features makes it difficult to believe that human culture defines all of life, and my time in the Pacific Northwest is teaching me how inescapable and important the nonhuman context for human life really is. The Tacoma of my experience is a human settlement that cannot ignore its nonhuman surroundings, its dependence upon healthy ecosystems, and the enormity and ancientness of the nonhuman world around us. While I continue to learn here about the disastrous impact human beings have had on the nonhuman world, I am also beginning to learn about the power the natural world has over us.

As my homes in Atlanta and Tacoma indicate, I am a creature of cities. I have lived virtually all my life in urban settings, and I thrive in the cultural diversity and activity of such centers of civilization. This leads to a gap and a predilection in my environmentalism. The gap is in my relative lack of familiarity with the nonhuman world: most of the biological diversity that I know best is that which thrives in human cities—our species, those others we choose to live with, and those that thrive in the sorts of habitats we create. My attention to biodiversity is therefore in part an attention to something I am missing: I do not know well the variety of life with which I share this world, and this ignorance—particularly insofar as I am not alone in it—signals that something is wrong. That is one of the problems upon which this book reflects.

My urban life also creates a predilection toward a certain kind of solution to that problem: I hope to sustain such human settlements, to preserve the possibility of human cultures and of cities where those cultures can mix and thrive. Wilderness advocates abound in the environmentalist movement, and I respect them, but my own experiences leave me less interested in preserving the pristine nonhuman world and more interested in how human beings can live sustainably with our nonhuman contexts. I therefore come to the project of an ethics of biodiversity with the assumption that conservation should not simply be about protecting the variety of life from human beings.

Instead, the ecological morality to which I aspire is about convincing people that we represent one expression of the variety of life and then working together to craft human habitats that are hospitable to humans and the rest of nature.[15] While I recognize serious environmental problems with the way cities—particularly cities with sprawling suburbs like Atlanta and Tacoma—are currently designed, I hope that city life can be preserved, that humanity can continue cultural development while also learning to participate in the nonhuman world around us.

Of course, my ecological location is not just about the places on a map where I find myself. It is also important that I am a citizen of the United States; I understand environmental issues primarily within this country's political context and direct my moral arguments primarily to other citizens and residents of this nation. Furthermore, I come from relative privilege: being a heterosexual, white male with financial security and years of education gives me a status and authority in my social context. This leads me to a cautious awareness that I must pay attention to the conditions of others in different situations, and it also reminds me of the limitations I have in understanding their experiences, needs, and moral responsibilities. Thus, as I study cultural diversity and environmental injustices in this book, I must first be aware of my own complicity in degradation and the limits of what I can understand about others' perspectives. In that context, I hope to challenge those of us in positions of privilege to create a better and more sustainable world.

Finally, as a Christian ecological ethicist, it is important to be clear about my religious and academic location and the audiences to whom I am writing. I am a Roman Catholic trained at Quaker, interdenominational, and Methodist institutions, now teaching at a Lutheran university; I identify myself primarily as a Christian interested in thinking ecumenically about the beliefs and practices of Christian communities. I am trained in this work as a Christian social ethicist, predisposed disciplinarily to reflect on the moral ideas and practices of religious people in the contexts of the social institutions that shape us. Thus, I offer my primary ethical argument to other Christians who share my social context in the United States: our faith can and should take biodiversity seriously, and this will not only remind us of our responsibilities to the rest of life on Earth but also help us to better understand the Christian moral life as a whole.

My theological training is also important as a qualifier on my use of biological science. While I draw heavily on the writings of ecologists, I am not a scientist myself. My attempt to learn from science is the attempt of an ethicist to gain insight from and offer some modest suggestions to another discipline in service to the common project of conservation. I come to ecology as an outsider, offering an interpretation of the moral dimensions of this research and how committed Christians might act upon it.

I hope that this work will also be of use to environmentalists and to anyone interested in ethics, science, and theology. Biodiversity is a scientific, moral, religious, and political concept. It has much to teach us all, and a genuine understanding of it requires multiple perspectives. Thus, while my work is conditioned by my particular ecological, social, and theological location, it seeks to teach and inspire diverse groups of people in order to begin and continue a broad conversation about how human beings can live with the variety of life on Earth after we recognize that we—the species destroying that variety—are ourselves part of it.

Five Questions for an Ethics of Biodiversity

This book is structured by five questions that develop an ethical perspective on the variety of life, its decline, and the importance of a Christian theological response. The most basic question comes first: *What is biodiversity?* There are of course many possible answers, but this book focuses on three: two ecological answers that observe the diversity of genes, species, and ecosystems that make up life on Earth and a theological answer that identifies such diversity as a characteristic of God's creation. According to all these definitions, biodiversity is a characteristic of our world that is in decline and under threat from human activity.

This fact leads naturally to the second question of the book: *Why does biodiversity matter?* The answers of scientists in conversation with economists and philosophical ethicists are first reviewed and considered, forming the context for my own theological answer: biodiversity matters because it is a sacrament of God, a sign of and connection to the mysteries and workings of God and therefore a means by which we can better understand and grow closer to the creator. In other words, biodiversity matters not only because it has value to human society, because it teaches us about how the world works, and because it has intrinsic value. It also matters because God created it and intends for us to live among and as the variety of life.

Having developed an argument about how complicated biodiversity is and an argument about the importance of learning from it, I next ask *How and at what level should we pay attention to biodiversity?* Answering this question requires a model of the different scales at which biodiversity exists and at which we can observe it: from the very local and immediate experience of our own communities, through the broader scale of landscapes and nations, all the way to the global scale at which we observe worldwide trends. These scalar levels, drawn from the science of ecology, also have moral and theological implications, which become concrete when the efforts of particular local churches on behalf of local biodiversity are placed in the context of a worldwide Christian and environmentalist movement.

The book then turns to a fourth question: *How should politics and moral formation be balanced in the conservation of biodiversity?* The central observation here is that protecting the variety of life will not be encompassed by any single activity. More concretely, we must decide how to distribute our attention and energies between the task of reforming laws and social structures on one hand or of revolutionizing the ways we think about the variety of life and our place within it on the other. Of course, both political and morally formative efforts are a necessary part of any conservation strategy, but concerned individuals must decide how to balance the two. To examine political work I offer an analysis of the U.S. Endangered Species Act, observing the power and limitations of such a legislative effort. To present the contrast of morally formative conservation, I examine the practices and teachings of Christian churches, which reshape the ways believers feel and think about biodiversity.

A theme throughout these discussions is that, whatever the scales of our attention and however we focus our conservation efforts, we do well to understand biodiversity as a social issue, to attend to the environmental injustices inherent in biodiversity loss. Conservation inevitably takes place in the context of oppressive and dominating systems, and if it is done morally it should seek to resist these systems. Examining this challenge leads to the fifth and final question of the book: *What does the conservation of biodiversity have to do with human diversity and with social justice?* Conservation must be understood as an activity of human beings, and human activity is frequently motivated and limited by the power inherent in our relationships. Conservationists must carefully attend to the ways protecting biodiversity affects the diverse human cultures with a stake in conservation as well as the nonhuman species and ecosystems on whose behalf we act.

The answers to these five questions—What is biodiversity? Why does it matter? How should we pay attention to it? How should we conserve it? What does the conservation of biodiversity have to do with human diversity and with social justice?—contribute to the basic argument of this book: diversity surrounds and exists within all human beings, and Christians in the United States will be more ethical and more faithful when we accept, embrace, and learn from that fact.

It will not be easy for Christians, or for any human beings, to live sustainably with and as the variety of life, but we must nevertheless try, because such a life is what we were made for. We can live better in God's world if we can learn to live with and embrace its diversity.

Notes

1. Two helpful scientific articles that discuss the relationship between barred and spotted owls in the Pacific Northwest are Olson et al., "Modeling of Site Occupancy Dynamics for Northern Spotted Owls"; and Hamer, Forsman, and Glenn, "Home Range Attributes and Habitat Selection."

2. U.S. Fish and Wildlife Service, *Recovery Plan for the Northern Spotted Owl*, 36. www.fws.gov/pacific/ecoservices/endangered/recovery/pdf/NSO%20 Final%20Rec%20Plan%20051408.pdf.

3. The current numbers of species listed in the United States can be found at U.S. Fish & Wildlife Service, "Summary of Listed Species," http://ecos.fws. gov/tess_public/Boxscore.do. As discussed below, quantifiable measures of threats to biodiversity as a whole are much more difficult to come by and to defend but would certainly include thousands more species, subgroups within species, and entire ecosystems as endangered with destruction.

4. These particular estimates come from Pimm and Raven, "Extinction by Numbers"; and Reid and Miller, *Keeping Options Alive*. For a discussion of the difficulty of such measurements and some approaches to overcoming it, see Nigel Stork, "Measuring Global Biodiversity and Its Decline" in Reaka-Kudla, Wilson, and Wilson, eds., *Biodiversity II*.

5. Vitousek et al., "Human Domination of Earth's Ecosystems."

6. This book is not a theological and ethical reflection on climate change,

in part because that work has already been done quite well. See particularly Northcott, *A Moral Climate*. I offer this book as a complement to that work, however, and an implicit argument that environmentalists and ecological ethicists should pay careful attention not only to climate change but also to other examples of the complicated phenomenon of environmental degradation. I do not go quite as far as a 2006 commentary in *Nature* that argues that biodiversity presents an even more complicated set of problems and questions than climate change, but I do agree with that commentary's suggestion that there should be comparable international organizations of scientists and politicians organized to study and reflect upon the variety of life, to make recommendations, and to enact conservationist policies. See Loreau and Oteng-Yeboah, "Diversity without Representation."

7. Boff, *Cry of the Earth*.

8. See for instance David G. Hallman, "Climate Change: Ethics, Justice, and Sustainable Community" in Hessel and Ruether, eds., *Christianity and Ecology*.

9. Their most recent report is Bullard et al., *Toxic Wastes and Race*.

10. Of course, "ecology" can also be understood to represent all Earth sciences, or a broader philosophical worldview that extends beyond science. However, for purposes of this book I focus my attention on the particular scientific discipline of ecology that occurs within the broader frame of biology. For a discussion of the various uses of this term, see Kevin J. O'Brien, "Ecology." I am careful to specify what it means to call this ethics "ecological" because of Neil Evernden's observation that it is "a source of irritation to some ecologists that their discipline, which they endeavour to make as scientific and objective as possible, has become linked in the public mind with a rag-tag collection of naturalists, poets, small-scale farmers, and birdwatchers who constitute a visible part of the environmental movement" (Evernden, *The Natural Alien*, 5). I therefore do not mean to suggest at any point in this book that my ethics is self-evidently or purely derived from ecological science but rather that it is developed in conversation with ecology.

11. As philosopher Erazim Kohák puts it, "environmental ethics suggests that the point is how humans, the center of meaning, ought to manage a world which deserves respect only as their environment." Kohák therefore presents his work as "ecological ethics" to stress that human beings are in mutual "interaction with the nonhuman world." Kohák, *The Green Halo*, 2–3. Emphasis removed from original.

12. Christian ethicist James Gustafson articulates the distinction between morality and ethics this way: "Ethics is an activity of reflection upon the form or forms of moral activity, providing reasons for choices and actions, justifying a way of being moral in the world. Morality is the activity of engagement and forbearance in life in the world." James M. Gustafson, "Afterword," in Beckley

and Swezey, *James M. Gustafson's Theocentric Ethics*, 245.

13. Rasmussen, *Earth Community, Earth Ethics*, 168.

14. Spencer, *Gay and Gaia*, chap. 10. Spencer asserts that it is not only social patterns but also biophysical and ecological ones that influence how we act and see in the world, and so introduces the concept of "ecological location," which enlarges the idea of "social location" to recognize that "human epistemologies—how we see and interpret the world—are also shaped by our relationship with the land and other creatures in our broader biotic environment," 295–96.

15. I signal this by identifying the project of protecting and sustaining biodiversity as "conservation." This is in part inspired by the work of conservation biologists, but it is also important to recognize the philosophical and theological implications of the word. In environmentalist and ecological ethics, conservation has typically been contrasted with preservation, and a distinction has been made between the former as a wise use of resources while the latter is about keeping wildness free of all human influence. See for instance Hay, *Main Currents in Environmental Thought*, chap. 2. By adopting conservation as a generic term, I signal that in my view any environmentalist effort to preserve biodiversity is in a large part an attempt to shape the ways human beings live with the world around us rather than distinguishing the "natural" world or its "wildness" from our species. However, by using this term I do not mean to suggest that the nonhuman world should be protected only for the sake of human use or that it should be understood solely as a "resource."

Part I

Defining Biodiversity

Chapter 1

The Variety of Life

One of countless subjects to ponder at the American Museum of Natural History in New York City is the changing role its scientists and curators understand for themselves. Older exhibits tend to feature specimens and models in cases, with descriptions that offer fascinating insight into how scientists ask questions about the world. Newer exhibits intersperse artifacts the public is encouraged to touch along with interactive computer programs and attention-grabbing films. This generational contrast is particularly clear when walking from the North American Forests exhibit to the Hall of Biodiversity. In the former, visitors see models of leaf patterns and greatly magnified earthworms behind glass and are invited to study cross sections of thousand-year-old trees from the other side of a plastic wall. In the latter, the visitor is immediately greeted by a "Biobulletin" film about current research in field biology and invited into a replicated section of the Dzangha-Sangha Rain Forest, complete with sound effects and lighting appropriate to life under a heavy canopy.

These differences in the style and media of presentation are all the more striking given an equally sharp distinction in the two exhibits' messages. In the North American Forests exhibit, one walks through sections on "Weather in the Forest" and "Forest Soils"; the emphasis is very much on how forests work and how scientists investigate them. If this exhibit is intended to inspire anything other than a fascination with the flora and fauna of North American, the goal is hidden. In the Hall of Biodiversity, by contrast, the designers were quite openly motivated by moral urgency. There are not only sections demonstrating the "Spectrum of Life" and "Spectrum of Habitats" but also a "Resource Center" that discusses the anthropogenic sources of "Transformation of the Biosphere" on one side and "Solutions" to such transformations on the other. Interspersed around the hall are inspiring quotations from a diverse group of environmentalists and a somber plaque commemorating all animal species confirmed extinct at the time of the exhibit's installation. The message is clear: biodiversity is not only a fascinating natural phenomenon but also under threat and in need of serious moral and political attention.[1]

The Hall of Biodiversity is an appropriate starting place for this chapter because it shows that biodiversity is a subject of both careful research and impassioned activism, and that these activities often go hand-in-hand. The exhibit moves, as a great deal of discourse about biodiversity does, from the attempt to objectively represent the way the world works to explicit advocacy of certain moral attitudes and public policies. This chapter follows that move by defining biodiversity both descriptively and morally, a dynamic explored first through ecological definitions and second through Christian ethics.

Three distinct but compatible definitions emerge: a broad scientific definition that captures the reality of biodiversity, a more precise ecological definition representing the research goals of scientists who study and measure the concept, and a third definition linking the biodiversity of this planet to the Christian doctrine of creation. Understood together, these definitions reveal how much is contained in the concept of biodiversity and how complex a thoughtful response to it must be.

Two Scientific Definitions of Biodiversity

Most ecologists who study biodiversity see themselves as seeking not only to understand it but also to contribute to its protection. Some of these scientists have taken to identifying themselves within a related academic field, conservation biology, to emphasize that they apply their research to a particular environmentalist agenda.[2] However, even among researchers who agree that biodiversity must be conserved, there are important disagreements about whether it serves their research and cause better to articulate a narrow, clear, and quantifiable definition or a broad, inclusive, and adaptable one.

These distinct approaches to a scientific definition are introduced well by E. O. Wilson in a 1997 book of essays about biodiversity:

> So what is it? Biologists are inclined to agree that it is, in one sense, everything. Biodiversity is defined as all hereditarily based variation at all levels of organization, from the genes within a single local population or species, to the species composing all or part of a local community, and finally to the communities themselves that compose the living parts of the multifari-

ous ecosystems of the world. The key to effective analysis of biodiversity is the precise definition of each level of organization when it is being addressed.[3]

Given that the term "biodiversity" has been in use since the mid-1980s and the significance of nature's variety was widely discussed even before then, it might be somewhat surprising that the question "So what is it?" would still be asked, but there was in 1997 and remains today no standard and widely accepted definition.[4] Still, as Wilson makes clear, the fact that the term has broad and wide-ranging implications need not be an excuse to surrender any attempt to understand it, and so he offers two definitions: On one hand, biodiversity is "everything." On the other hand, biodiversity is a carefully delineated measurement of particular phenomena at different scales of attention. One ecological definition seeks breadth and comprehensiveness, the other precision and measurability.

A Broad Ecological Definition

Those who advocate a broad and sweeping definition of biodiversity frequently begin with basic etymology: biological diversity straightforwardly means "the variety of life." In this sense the concept reflects an observation about the character of our world, noting that the planet displays a wide array of living things and that evolutionary processes and ecological systems seem to be structured by and dependent upon this variety. Biodiversity is a way to talk about the vast variety of life, a way to note the differences and distinctions between individuals, species.

This broad and vague concept exceeds the capacity of any one research program or number to quantify, a fact emphasized by the most familiar measurement of biodiversity: the number of species on Earth. Thus far, taxonomists and researchers have identified and at least partially catalogued more than 1.75 million species, but no one realistically claims that this represents even half of the species that exist, and a common estimate suggests that there may easily be 10 million or more distinct species, the vast majority of which have not been classified.[5] The variety of life is clearly bigger than contemporary science can measure, catalog, or understand.

Even this uncertain number of distinct species—which ecologists call species richness—is at best a synecdoche and at worst a gross simplification of biodiversity and its complexity because it ignores the diversity within each species and the diversity of systems in which species are organized. Thus, biodiversity is generally expanded to include at least three levels: species, genetic, and ecosystemic variety. Genetic biodiversity refers to the variety within a stock of particular organisms. For example, while human agriculture cultivates only two domestic species of rice, included within these are 120,000 distinct genetic varieties.[6] While few species are studied and cataloged as comprehensively as rice, all are incredibly genetically diverse. Ecosystemic diversity observes that life has evolved within a vast variety of communities and biomes, and so biodiversity must also be recognized in the systems into which species are organized. Some authors seek to rename these levels or add others to the list, but the central, widely agreed-upon point is that the variety of life crosses multiple levels and scales.[7]

When understood as including not only species but also genes within species and the ecosystems in which species are organized, the vastness of the variety of life is clear. This also reminds ecologists about how much they do not know: the enormous number of uncataloged species, unexplored genetic diversity, and ecosystems not fully understood.

For many ecologists, the broad definition of biodiversity is ideal precisely because it emphasizes the vastness of life's variety and the limits of human knowledge about it. For example, Reed Noss and Allen Cooperrider write that "biodiversity is not just a numbers game" and then applaud the fact that "simplicity is not one of the virtues of biodiversity. Ecosystems are more complex than we can imagine."[8] Noss elsewhere defines biodiversity broadly as "the variety of life and its processes" and argues that this definition can serve as "an appropriate organizing concept for what it is we're interested in protecting."[9] The virtue of biodiversity understood this way is that it expresses the vastness of the natural world.

A broad definition also emphasizes that biodiversity is not merely a characteristic of distant rain forests or scientific labs but a fundamental part of the world as a whole, a characteristic of life wherever it exists. This is a phenomenon almost as broad as nature itself, more focused only because it calls explicit attention to the variety therein and marks out living creatures as uniquely important.[10] It is therefore impossible to ignore the vast complexity of biodiversity and the fact that if we care about life—life on Earth, the life of the natural world, human

lives—we must care about biodiversity. Biodiversity in this broad definition is clearly a moral concept, and it serves to increase attention on
the complexity and degradation of the natural world as a whole.

Measuring Biodiversity: A Precise Ecological Definition

While a broad approach to biodiversity signals human participation
in the complexity and vastness of the variety of life, such a definition
lacks clarity, cannot be quantified, and therefore cannot be uncontro-
versially identified. These disadvantages lead some ecologists to seek a
more precise definition, one that can be objectively studied and measured according to careful and rigorous scientific standards. These researchers argue that the authority of ecology comes from its status as a
science, and such expertise requires a narrow and careful classification
system. To this purpose, Ian Swingland argues in the *Encyclopedia of
Biodiversity* that "an unequivocal and precise meaning of biodiversity
that is scientifically sensible and universally applicable" is required if
ecologists hope "to help guide the design of policy and programs for
the future, as well as to make critical decisions in the present."[11]

In this spirit, wildlife manager Don DeLong undertook a literature review of eighty-five scholarly definitions in order to develop the
most "objective and sound" one possible. His definition is intricate but
worth citing at length for both its content and its style: "Biodiversity is
a state or attribute of a site or area and specifically refers to the variety
within and among living organisms, assemblages of living organisms,
biotic communities, and biotic processes, whether naturally occurring
or modified by humans. Biodiversity can be measured in terms of genetic diversity and the identity and number of different types of species, assemblages of species, biotic communities, and biotic processes,
and the amount (e.g., abundance, biomass, cover, rate) and structure
of each."[12] This definition is careful and involved, presenting biodiversity as quantifiable and concrete. Biodiversity is not simply the variety of life; it is the variety of organisms in an array of configurations,
measured within a specific area. Like the previous definition, this understanding of biodiversity is explicitly multiscalar, paying attention to
genetic, species, and ecosystemic diversity. But this definition is different because it specifies that biodiversity should be measured at each of
these levels, emphasizing a number of factors that must be delineated
in such measurements.

A more technical definition like DeLong's allows ecologists to more clearly and consistently identify biodiversity, a process important not only for the standards of their science but also for the conservationist purposes to which their work will be applied. Those who seek such a precise definition are committed to ecological research that serves the cause of conservation, but they argue that conservation is best when it is informed by rigorous and careful science. Political leaders and society as a whole will be more likely to respect and act upon clear and quantified findings rather than vague and broad assertions. Ecologists have unique access to information about biodiversity, and they should offer concrete accounts of how Earth's living systems work and how biodiversity fits into it. Richard Tracy and Peter Brussard, for instance, argue that what distinguishes ecologists from others who advocate on behalf of biodiversity is precisely their commitment to scientific rigor and their authority as "open-minded and objective" students of environmental problems.[13] Other environmentalists might make sweeping claims without careful substantiation, but ecological researchers must take a different approach.

One reason for a technical definition is that biodiversity raises difficult questions that require careful answers. For instance, there are many questions about whether human activity can actually *increase* biodiversity: When human beings genetically engineer new organisms, does this make the world more diverse? Does it make a difference whether the new organism can sustainably survive as part of a healthy ecosystem? When human attempts to suppress fire across North America create a forested habitat that serves as a pathway for species like the barred owl, does this increase biodiversity? When barred owls threaten to drive spotted owls to extinction, does this reduce local biodiversity, or does the exchange of one owl for another maintain the status quo? Does it make a difference which changes in ecosystems are caused by human beings and which happen despite humans?[14] These questions will not have straightforward answers if biodiversity is defined solely as "the variety of life." By contrast, a more precise definition, such as Don DeLong's, offers relevant resources: he stresses that "biotic processes" must be measured and attended to alongside simple counts of species or individuals, but he is careful to note that these biotic processes contribute to biodiversity whether they are naturally occurring or have been changed by human beings.

Ecologists who advocate a broad definition might reply that it is less important to stake out ecological expertise and clear answers than it is to invite nonspecialists into the project of biodiversity conservation to encourage the general public to ponder, explore, and recognize ourselves as a part of the vast and ancient variety of life on Earth. For my purposes it is not vital to settle this disagreement within the ecological community; both definitions are instructive and helpful in understanding what biodiversity is. Furthermore, the existence of multiple definitions among scientific experts makes possible the contribution of other definitions from other approaches, such as the one to which I now turn.

The Variety of Creatures in God's Creation: A Definition from Christian Ecological Ethics

Biodiversity is not merely of interest to scientific ecologists but is also a religious and theological concept. In my own faith tradition this is particularly evident in a 1991 pastoral letter from the United States Conference of Catholic Bishops, *Renewing the Earth*. The bishops assume the goodness and order of creation and look to it "for indications of God's existence and purpose," for direction on how human beings should live with our fellow creatures.[15] They call special attention to biodiversity: "The diversity of life manifests God's glory. Every creature shares a bit of the divine beauty [because] the divine goodness could not be represented by one creature alone."[16] Biodiversity is here a religious concept, a part of God's creation and a path to better understanding God. Building on this statement, I offer a third definition of biodiversity: the variety of creatures in God's creation that manifests God's glory.

Biodiversity as Creation

An exploration of biodiversity as a manifestation of God's glory occupies the third chapter of this book, but it is important here to emphasize the basis of that claim and the definition I derive from it in the doctrine of creation. Because I take my inspiration in large part from a Catholic source, my definition reflects a Catholic emphasis on the importance and enduring goodness of God's creation. This is exemplified in Pope John Paul II's 1990 message for the World Day of Peace, titled "Peace with God the Creator, Peace with All of Creation." The pope characterizes environmental degradation as an expression of human sin, the result of human beings abandoning their place within creation, losing sight of the fact that God made a world "with its own integrity, its own internal, dynamic balance."[17] This message asserts that creation itself is good and moral, and that when human beings live as fully committed participants in this world, we will live rightly. My definition of biodiversity is based upon this core belief in creation.

However, it is important to emphasize that I am not appealing to an exclusively Catholic belief. Indeed, the view of the world as the creative work of divinity is common to many traditions. In broad, ecumenical terms it is fair to say that Christians believe God made this world and all life within it, and that what God has made is good. To assert that biodiversity is an aspect of God's creation, then, is to make a very basic but a very important claim of Christian faith.

This claim can be grounded in the shared witness of the Christian Bible, starting with an interpretation of the first chapter of Genesis. This book begins by dividing and categorizing life-forms based on an order in which they are created, and at each stage of this creation God declares what has been made "good." Upon completing this task, God reflects upon the order and interdependence of all that is and declares, "Indeed it was very good." This is followed by another creation story in Genesis 2, in which humanity is instructed to "till and keep" the Garden of Eden, a command frequently interpreted as a still-relevant call for human beings to serve as stewards of the environment, caretakers of the other species with whom humans share God's world.[18]

Other biblical texts celebrate the majesty and variety of God's creation not to call human beings to stewardship but to humble our species as just one among many of God's creatures. At the end of the book of Job, for instance, God responds to the questions of a blameless and upright man by putting them into the context of the wild world beyond human experience. God describes lions, mountain goats, deer, donkeys, oxen, ostriches, horses, locusts, and hawks, celebrating the unique characteristics of each species and painting a picture of the world as rich and complicated beyond human understanding. Particular attention is paid to two mysterious and powerful creatures: behemoth and leviathan, both of whom God suggests are beyond human control. In Job the variety of life is celebrated as something beyond and bigger than our experience or capacity, a message that characterizes biodiversity as part of God's creation rather than a resource for human convenience.[19]

It would be simplistic and anachronistic to suggest that the Bible makes a single and coherent argument about biodiversity; that is not what I am arguing. I take seriously the caution of ethicist James Nash, who notes that many parts of the Bible are "oblivious, ambivalent, or even antipathetic on the protection of wildlife in wild lands and waters."[20] The Bible is an incredibly diverse collection of texts and views, and it is not accurate to say that the book as a whole advocates an ethics of biodiversity. However, the texts mentioned above suggest that there are resources available to the Christian tradition in parts of our sacred scripture, resources that can be used to argue that biodiversity is an important part of God's creation.

Inspired by such sources, many contemporary Christian thinkers have affirmed the theological importance of biodiversity. Despite his questions about the witness of the Bible on biodiversity, Methodist ethicist James Nash writes, "All God's creatures are worthy of moral consideration, as a sign of the worthiness imparted by God and, in fact, as an expression of the worship of God."[21] The Ecumenical Patriarch Bartholomew told a 1997 Orthodox Environmental Symposium that the entire universe participates in "a cosmic liturgy," which we humans witness "in the symbiosis of life's rich biological complexities."[22] Evangelical ethicist Steven Bouma-Prediger argues that Christians must care for the creation out of gratitude for God's grace, an attitude that "presupposes both belief in God as Creator and some degree of knowledge of the Earth as the intricate, interdependent, and truly amazing system it is."[23] These examples from three different Christian traditions have in common an appreciation for the variety of life on Earth as God's good creation. This is the basis for my definition of biodiversity and the foundation upon which this book's Christian ethics of biodiversity will be built.

A Conversation about Biodiversity

By defining biodiversity as the variety of creatures in God's creation that manifests God's glory, I do not intend to replace, compete with, or abandon the two scientific definitions discussed above. Rather, I hope that my definition makes it possible to engage in a conversation with scientific perspectives—to learn from ecological research and to explore what Christian ethics might contribute to the project of understanding and conserving biodiversity.

A fruitful conversation requires enough difference that each party can learn from the other and enough respect that each will listen thoughtfully and openly. The difference that motivates this conversation is methodological. Ecologists seek to understand the world by careful scientific observation, experiential and mathematical analysis, and results that can be tested and verified by repeated experiments or studies. Christian ethicists, on the other hand, analyze the world in the context of scriptures and theological traditions, offering perspectives to communities who share their faith and testing their findings with the insights and goals of fellow believers. These are two drastically different ways to develop ideas, and it is this difference that makes a conversation between scientific ecology and Christian ethics so necessary.

As an ethicist I have defined biodiversity in the context of God's creation. This definition is compatible with the ecological definition of biodiversity as the variety of life but it is far more specific. I stipulate a theological interpretation of the natural world as God's good work, an interpretation that I would never suggest could be established or tested on scientific grounds. The language of "creation" implies a creator and, as I use it, a particular worldview and attitude toward that creator, the nature of the creation, and the ways in which we human beings can and should honor our maker.

The difference between Christian ethics and ecology is even more apparent in light of the second, more precise ecological definition, which understands biodiversity as the variety of living organisms, assemblages, biotic communities, and biotic processes within a specific area. This is an explicitly and uniquely ecological definition, and so it has much to teach us about the nuances of life's variety, the multiple scales at which it can be studied, and the complexity of the ways life on Earth is organized. I find conversation with scientific ecologists fruitful precisely because this definition is so different from any that I could develop on my own.

A fruitful conversation also requires a baseline of respect between different perspectives, and this respect is possible between ecologists and people of faith. While some assume an inherent and intractable conflict between scientific and Christian perspectives, such conflict is not necessary. The appropriate Christian stance to take toward scientists is one of respect for researchers who seek to understand reality, and such respect for research can develop out of a faith that God's creation is both important and good. If God made this world, made us to live within it, and intended us to seek and find our place within it, then we should honor the work of those who are attempting to understand how this world works. Ethicist Dan Maguire expresses this idea well when he writes that "morality is based on reality," explaining that it is crucial for Christians to develop our ideas about what we ought to do based on the best possible understanding of the truth through naturalistic means.[24] As such, it is appropriate to turn to ecologists for a scientific perspective on how the world works and, in particular, how living beings function and interrelate in this world.

We can better understand God and God's purposes for us when we better understand our world. As ethicist Charles Curran puts it: "The shadow of God is present in all creation, and we can see something of God in all that is. God not only tells us something about creation and the human, but creation and the human tell us something about God."[25] Fueled by such belief, I respect and value the contributions of ecologists because I believe their work sheds light on the fundamental character of creation.

Of course, this does not mean that scientists have sole and unfiltered access to absolute truth about the natural world. Science is the work of human beings, and human beings are fallible and limited. Scientists make mistakes, get things wrong, and have misunderstood basic facts about the world in the past; they almost certainly also misunderstand basic and important facts today. What's more, there are other vital ways of understanding the world around us, such as traditional forms of knowledge from indigenous cultures and the powerful interpretations of naturalist writers and poets. However, I do not believe that the imperfections or incompleteness of natural science is reason enough to dismiss it, and so the focus of my own work is on the insights of scientists. I understand science as industrialized society's most deliberate and careful attempt to understand reality. This is not the only way to pay attention to the world, and it is not a perfect way, but it is a very important way and so is a worthy conversation partner for Christian ethics.

Some ecological scientists have similarly called for a respectful conversation with theologians and ethicists. One such call came clearly in 1990, when a group of scientists wrote an "Open Letter to the Religious Community" stressing that environmental degradation "must be recognized from the outset as having a religious as well as a scientific dimension" and proposing that "efforts to safeguard and cherish the environment need to be infused with a vision of the sacred."[26] A similar attitude was clearly expressed by many of the scientific experts interviewed by David Takacs, who captures the ways conservation biologists understand and work on behalf of the variety of life in his book *The Idea of Biodiversity*. While some of his subjects appealed only to non-Western or nontraditional religions, a clear theme was the need for religious attitudes as part of the conservation of biodiversity. Takacs summarizes the idea this way: "If the value of biodiversity were felt not merely in the pocket or in the brain but in the *soul*, then the most effective, permanent conservation ethic imaginable might result."[27] Many scientists clearly recognize the need for a conversation with religious ethics.

As an ethicist I make claims that are based in theological tradition and Christian communities. Ecologists make claims based on experimentation and analysis of organisms in their contexts. An ethics of biodiversity should not blur these two approaches to the world but rather nurture a conversation between them. I work with scientific data because I believe it teaches me about God's creation, and this effort requires a respectful attitude toward the work that scientists do on their own terms.

The Decline of Biodiversity: Perspectives from Ecology and Christian Ethics

The conversation I seek between ecology and Christian ethics has a clear opening topic: the history and contemporary loss of life's variety. Because biodiversity represents the vast variety of life to all people, a vital research subject for ecological scientists, and the character of God's creation for Christians, its evolution and its degradation are important topics that must be understood through the conversation of multiple perspectives.

The Evolution of Biodiversity

Aiming for a conversation that assumes mutual respect across difference, I distinguish my creation-based Christian ethics from a creation-*ist* approach that would insist upon a single story about the origin and history of the cosmos. I disagree with creationists about the literal interpretation of the biblical story of creation and the place of evolution in the history of the human species. However, the most fundamental and problematic mistake I see creationists making is the assertion that their resolutely theological claims should be normative in scientific discussions. In my view the sciences of cosmology, evolutionary biology, and ecology are and should be very different from the project of Christian ethics, and the best we can hope for is dialogue rather than uniformity between these very different methodological approaches.

Openness to the reality of evolution is particularly necessary for a Christian ethics of biodiversity because the contemporary variety of life cannot be fully understood unless we recognize that it is not only a vast present phenomenon but also unimaginably ancient. Paleontologists believe that the earliest organisms on this planet existed 3.5 billion to 4 billion years ago, with multicellular organisms taking shape about 1.4 billion years ago and animals appearing about 600 million years ago. Our own species is famously a latecomer in this history, with the fossil record showing the first modern human beings between 150,000 and 200,000 years ago.[28] Interestingly, throughout this history the dominant trend has been a steady increase in biodiversity: graphs showing genetic, species, or ecosystem diversity over the history of life on Earth tend to climb steadily upward. This is particularly clear over the last 200 million years, during which biodiversity has apparently spiked quite substantially.[29] Why this is the case, why life on this planet seems to have evolved steadily toward greater diversity, is so far not conclusively explained.

This does not mean, of course, that the evolution of life on Earth has always been about creation rather than destruction. The beginnings of life were followed very closely by losses of life, and nature as we now know it is the product of billions of years of deaths as well as births, requiring the disappearance of many species, genetic tendencies, and ecosystems along the way. In addition to these gradual changes, paleontologists trace five major extinction events in which enormous numbers of species disappeared in a very short period of geological time as diseases or environmental factors caused widespread genetic and ecosystemic changes. The most recent of these massive extinctions, marking the end of the Mesozoic era and the departure of the dinosaurs 65 million years ago, made room for the assent of mammals and the eventual arrival of our own species.

The evolution of biodiversity is a story of death as much as it is a story of life. Having asserted that God created the world and that God's creation is good, it is worth pausing over this fact. Billions of years of deaths and extinctions preceded the arrival of human beings on the planet. Violence and predation continue to be a normal and inevitable aspect of life on Earth. Christian faith and tradition might teach that creation is good, but there seems to be a great deal of contrary evidence. The natural world is, as Tennyson famously wrote, "red in tooth and claw."[30] The most serious challenge of evolution to faith is not, as the public debate implies, about a time line or the parentage of the human race. Rather, the major challenge is that evolution reveals a world characterized by what Charles Darwin called "the universal signs of violence."[31]

Christian ecological ethicists must face these signs of violence openly and honestly, a process continued in chapter 3. The most central answer to be offered is an appeal to mystery. The "goodness" of God and creation is not straightforward and simply explicable but rather must be beyond human understanding. Christians should be aware of the billions of years of violence and extinction that have characterized life on Earth as God's creation without seeking to make final and clear sense of it. Accepting such mystery and uncertainty may not be entirely satisfying, but it is consistent with the longstanding teaching of the Christian tradition that a great deal of God's work is beyond human understanding. It is also consistent with an advanced ecological understanding of biodiversity, which reminds us repeatedly about how much we do not, and perhaps cannot, know about the variety of life among which we live.

Despite all that we do not know, however, and despite the lack of any guarantee that creation will always be good from human perspectives, it remains possible to seek to live within God's creation. To define biodiversity as the variety of creatures in God's creation that manifests God's glory is not to say that all genetic tendencies, species, and ecosystems must survive to glorify God; it says, instead, that the variety of life among which we live is good according to God's perspective. This goodness should be enough to motivate Christians to worry about the massive extinction going on today, unquestionably caused by human beings.

The Anthropogenic Decline of Biodiversity

Given that life on Earth has already survived five major extinction events, it might not be immediately alarming to note that the planet is now in the midst of a sixth. However, this sixth mass extinction seems to be unique in that its cause is the activity of a single species: *homo sapiens*.[32] Biodiversity loss today is anthropogenic; it is caused by humanity. The actions of human beings are causing extinctions to occur one hundred to one thousand times faster than they otherwise would, which implies untold and unmeasured impacts on genetic and ecosystemic diversity as well.[33] A 2008 assessment conducted by the World Conservation Union determined that nearly 25 percent of all mammal species on Earth are threatened with extinction, and another 15 percent have not been adequately studied to know whether they are threatened or not.[34] This represents an alarming threat to the creatures closest to our own species, to the creatures we are most likely to protect and predisposed to care for.

Perhaps the simplest way to explain how human beings are destroying biodiversity is the expansion of the scale of our impact. Humanity is increasingly using more of the world's resources and occupying more of the world's space, leaving less for other creatures. Examples of this increase in the scale of human life include large-scale agriculture and land development that destroy habitat and deplete resources; spikes in pollution and human population that make ecosystems less hospitable to other species; and the invasive species human expansion has spread across the globe. As paleontologist Niles Eldredge explains, the common theme is an expansion in the scale of humanity's influence:

> We humans have transformed the very face of the planet. Agriculture has triggered the population explosion, enabling the rise of civilizations and the growth of towns and cities. Clearing forests and grasslands for agriculture and the spread of those towns and cities has meant the end for many ecosystems—and species—the world over. . . . As human beings have spread around the globe, we have taken other species with us, deliber-

ately transporting domesticated animals and plants as well as accidentally introducing a number of disease-causing microbes and other species to foreign ecosystems. . . . Alien species often cause great ecological disturbance and are a side effect of the growth and spread of human populations around the globe.[35]

Questions must be asked about whether it is fair to talk about the human species so monolithically, and what tools ethics can offer to morally analyze the expansion of the scope of human activities, but Eldredge's central claim is undeniable: biodiversity is declining as the scale of human influence on the globe increases. The human population of the planet, almost seven billion at the time of this writing, places a burden on the rest of Earth's ecosystems. Even more problematic is the consumption by those of us who live in the industrialized world and use resources at a global scale.

The clear intention of most human societies to continue extending the scope of their development and consumption leads ecologists to predict that biodiversity will drop even more sharply in the near future. Indeed, by measuring the rate at which human development is destroying existing habitats and the number of species likely to be dependent on those habitats for survival, one study predicts a shockingly sharp spike in extinctions, a loss of up to one of every twenty species by the year 2060.[36]

Thus, an essential part of any definition of biodiversity is a definition of the contemporary crisis of drastic, anthropogenic declines in the variety of life. The reality of biodiversity today is one of loss, with an expectation of much more drastic reductions in the near future if current trends continue. Biodiversity is a characteristic of nature increasingly at the mercy of humanity, and as such it is rapidly declining. While billions of years of history suggest that some life on Earth will survive our activities, there is no guarantee that our own species will survive or thrive in the new world we are creating. This is a crisis at least in part because a less diverse planet will be less able—perhaps even unable—to support human life.

As already noted, human activity need not be seen solely as reducing the variety of life on Earth. Hybridization in agriculture, genetic engineering in laboratories, and the transportation of species across the globe are three clear examples of the ways people can potentially increase biodiversity. To this one could add the argument that urban and suburban landscapes—which represent new kinds of natural systems and make space for different species and genetic traits to thrive—increase the variety of life as well. This is why the second ecological definition of biodiversity is important: while new species and ecosystems may be created, biotic processes are being degraded and biotic communities are becoming less capable of supporting varied life. Careful ecological measurements and analyses therefore show a sharp and unambiguous decline in global biodiversity.

If Christians understand biodiversity as an aspect of God's creation, this anthropogenic decline is even more of a crisis because it reveals the degradation and abuse of what God has given us. When we accept that human beings are creatures intended to live with and as God's creation, then it becomes truly disturbing that we are making it more difficult for God's creatures to thrive. The difference between this sixth extinction event and the previous five is also deeply significant for Christians. Mass extinction today is a result of human carelessness and ingratitude in the face of God's majestic creation. In degrading biodiversity human beings are undoing the work of the creator in a very real way. This suggests an arrogance on the part of human beings that can only be described as sinful, a problem that Christians must work to solve.

A first step in responding to the anthropogenic decline of biodiversity is to understand what biodiversity is, which this chapter has attempted to do through an analysis and reflection on three definitions of the concept. The next step is to determine how and why biodiversity is valuable: to explore why scientists and activists rally around the variety of life as a vital environmental cause, and to understand why Christians are increasingly seeing biodiversity as not only a characteristic of God's creation but also a sign and lesson of God's glory. Those explorations of the value of biodiversity are the project of the next two chapters.

Notes

1. That this message of political and ethical advocacy is explicit and intentional is further demonstrated by the title of the book that accompanies the exhibit: Novacek, *The Biodiversity Crisis: Losing What Counts.* For another theo-ethical reflection on this exhibit, see Larry Rasmussen, "Eco-Justice: Church and Community Together," in Hessel and Rasmussen, eds., *Earth Habitat,* 4–6.

2. Michael Soulé, one of the founders of conservation biology, describes it as a "crisis discipline," responding to an urgent problem and so "a mixture of science and art" that "requires intuition as well as information." Soulé, "What Is Conservation Biology?" 727. Conservation biology is not only more explicitly activist than ecology, it is also less exclusively scientific, frequently including social scientists and even philosophers and other humanists within its ranks.

3. E. O. Wilson, "Introduction," in Reaka-Kudla, Wilson, and Wilson, eds., *Biodiversity II*, 1.

4. The term "biological diversity" and the contemporary awareness of its importance is generally credited to two 1980 U.S. government reports: Lovejoy, "Changes in Biological Diversity"; and Norse and McManus, "Ecology and Living Resources." The words were first contracted into one by Walter Rosen during the organization of the 1986 "National Forum on BioDiversity," the proceedings of which became the 1988 volume, *BioDiversity*.

5. These figures come from Eldredge, *Life in the Balance*, vii. However, the same or similar figures can be found in many sources. See especially Heywood, ed., *Global Biodiversity Assessment*.

6. Secretariat, "Global Biodiversity Outlook 2,"10.

7. For instance, Noss and Cooperrider add a fourth and fifth level above the ecosystem—landscape and region—in their book *Saving Nature's Legacy*, 8–12. Paul Ehrlich and others advocate the recognition of population biodiversity between the genetic and species levels (see Hughes, Daily, and Ehrlich, "Population Diversity.")

8. Noss and Cooperrider, *Saving Nature's Legacy*, 3–4.

9. Quoted in Takacs, *The Idea of Biodiversity*, 48–49.

10. "Nature" itself is, of course, one of the most famously difficult to define terms in the English language, weighted with moral as well as conceptual complications and difficulties. I assume the goodness of "nature" on theological grounds, but by this I mean the scope of reality in its entirety, and I will not use the term in any other sense. On the difficulties of making sense about nature, see especially Soper, *What Is Nature?*

11. Swingland, "Definition of Biodiversity," 389.

12. DeLong, "Defining Biodiversity," 745. See his helpful chart of available definitions and their themes, 739.

13. Tracy and Brussard, "The Importance of Science in Conservation Biology," 918.

14. See Angermeier, "Does Biodiversity Include Artificial Diversity?"

15. United States Conference of Catholic Bishops, "Renewing the Earth," www.usccb.org/sdwp/ejp/bishopsstatement.htm.

16. Ibid.

17. John Paul II, "The Ecological Crisis: A Common Responsibility," The Vatican, http://www.vatican.va/holy_father/john_paul_ii/messages/peace/documents/hf_jp-ii_mes_19891208_xxiii-world-day-for-peace_en.html.

18. All biblical citations in this book come from the New Revised Standard Version (NRSV).

19. See Newsom, "The Moral Sense of Nature."

20. Nash, "The Bible vs. Biodiversity," 225.

21. Nash, *Loving Nature*, 96.

22. Ecumenical Patriarch Bartholomew, "To Commit a Crime against the Natural World Is a Sin," in Tal, *Speaking of Earth*, 205.

23. Bouma-Prediger, *For the Beauty of the Earth*, 179.

24. Maguire, *Death by Choice*, 78.

25. Curran, *Catholic Moral Tradition Today*, 11.

26. Sagan et al., "An Open Letter to the Religious Community," iii.

27. Takacs, *Idea of Biodiversity*, 256.

28. Wood and Constantino, "Human Origins," 526.

29. See especially Gaston and Spicer, *Biodiversity*, chap. 2.

30. Tennyson, *In Memoriam*, 41.

31. Quoted from *The Voyage of the Beagle* in Worster, *Nature's Economy*, 125. See chapters 6–9 for an extended discussion of Darwin's struggle with this reality and his contemporaries' reactions.

32. For accounts of the previous five major extinctions and justifications for the existence of a sixth, see especially Leakey and Lewin, *The Sixth Extinction*.

33. Reid and Miller, *Keeping Options Alive*.

34. Species Survival Commission, "State of the World's Species," International Union for the Conservation of Nature, http://cmsdata.iucn.org/downloads/state_of_the_world_s_species_factsheet_en.pdf.

35. Eldredge, *Life in the Balance*, x.

36. Pimm and Raven, "Extinction by Numbers."

Part II

Why Biodiversity Matters

Chapter 2

Valuing Life and Ecosystems

The 1992 Earth Summit in Rio de Janeiro was a milestone in the work of conserving global biodiversity, when leaders from 150 nations formally embraced the idea that the variety of life is both important and under threat. By signing the Convention on Biodiversity (Convention, hereafter) these leaders affirmed an incredibly broad list of reasons that biodiversity matters, with the preamble noting that the Convention's signatories were "conscious of the intrinsic value of biodiversity and of the ecological, genetic, social, economic, scientific, educational, cultural, recreational, and aesthetic values of biodiversity and its components."[1] This long list of biodiversity's values hints at the many reasons humans should commit to conserve it: the variety of life is valuable in and for itself, is necessary for healthy ecosystems, provides biological resources, helps create healthy societies, has monetary worth, inspires significant research, has much to teach us, is essential to many cultural traditions, and makes the natural world more enjoyable and pleasant for human activity and appreciation.

This wide-ranging list of values from the Convention on Biodiversity was no doubt meant to inspire commitment from leaders around the world and encourage cooperation from diverse cultures with diverse interests. This is an essential step for any ethics of biodiversity: to establish a broad consensus that the variety of life is worthy of consideration, that it has significant value, and that human beings have good reason to acknowledge and respect that value.

In the next chapter I discuss one of the qualities of biodiversity not included on the Convention's list: spiritual value, which I demonstrate by making a Christian argument about biodiversity's sacramental importance. Before moving to that constructive work, however, I here analyze four arguments included in the Convention's list that have also been developed and expanded by ecologists and conservation biologists: that biodiversity is essential to healthy ecosystem functioning, that it has economic value, that human communities can learn from it, and that it has an intrinsic value beyond human interest.

Ecosystem Functioning and Human Survival

When the Convention on Biodiversity begins its list of arguments for biodiversity with "ecological" and "genetic" values, it signals the importance of the variety of life as a necessary and irreplaceable characteristic of natural systems. This is perhaps the most basic argument on behalf of biodiversity: the world around us requires variety to function, and that variety is therefore precious and should not be tampered with. If it can be shown that biodiversity is essential to the health of natural systems, then a strong case can be made that conserving it is essential for protecting life on this planet—including, of course, human life.

Many activists assume a strong causal relationship between the diversity of a natural system and its health, and these assumptions have precedent in scientific work. No less foundational a figure than Charles Darwin makes this claim in *On the Origin of Species*, writing "it has been experimentally proved, if a plot of ground be sown with one species of grass, and a similar plot be sown with several distinct genera of grasses, a greater number of plants and a greater weight of dry herbage can be raised in the latter than the former case."[2] This calculation offers a clear argument in favor of diversity: the more diverse a system is, the more productive it will be.

However, the case is not as straightforward as Darwin presented. It is not clear what experiment he referred to, and many theorists have since argued that diversity can in fact degrade the functioning of an ecosystem. In the 1960s and '70s a series of mathematical models suggested that the complexity resulting from too much diversity could in fact make ecological systems less stable and therefore less productive.[3] The more competing entities and levels of organization exist within a system, these models suggested, the more likely it would be to break down. While this was not a suggestion to rid ecosystems of all diversity, it was an argument against protecting and increasing the variety of life without question or limit.

In contemporary ecology these questions have come to be discussed under the heading of "ecosystem function," which involves measuring the relationship between diversity and the stable productivity of natural systems. It remains debated whether or not increased diversity leads to higher ecosystem function. For example, community ecologist Shahid Naeem and his colleagues conducted a series of experiments in a carefully controlled, artificial environment called the

"Ecotron" in London, in which they monitored three replicated ecosystems with high, intermediate, and low species diversity. They found that those with lower diversity were significantly less productive and less stable.[4] However, other ecologists responded to publication of these findings by arguing that the productivity difference in Naeem's experiments could easily be explained by the rapid growth of a species that was planted only in the "high diversity" plot, questioning whether a conclusive statement could truly be made about the relationship between diversity and ecosystem functioning.[5] The lead author of this critique, David Wardle, had earlier published research on island ecology concluding that "ecosystem process rates were lowest on those islands with the greatest diversity."[6] Debate over this issue continues. While all agree that healthy ecosystems require some level of diversity, there is also widespread agreement that the relationship between diversity and ecosystem functioning requires further study.

Thus, ecological science cannot provide a conclusive claim that more diversity is always better for healthy ecosystems. This should come as no surprise: the method structuring scientific work is predisposed toward careful verification of every claim, and ecologists are trained to be cautious about what can be established by any particular line of research. With that noted, however, it becomes even more important to appreciate the broad consensus that has emerged in the field about the fact that the current anthropogenic destruction of biodiversity is dangerous. Along these lines the editors of a volume synthesizing both sides of the ecosystem function debate agree that although "there are many intricacies, uncertainties and questioning" remaining, it is clear that the current decline in biodiversity can "alter the functioning and stability of ecosystems and of the Earth system."[7] In other words, whatever disagreements may exist about the level of diversity required to maintain a healthy ecosystem, ecologists do not disagree about the fact that the current, drastic declines in biodiversity run a dangerous risk of causing irreparable harm.

Ecological science, with all its caution and care about what can be claimed, is quite clear that the destruction of biodiversity is a serious and urgent problem. There is more research to be done to understand biodiversity, but enough is now known to assert that the loss of biodiversity is a dangerous trend calling for immediate action. Population ecologist Paul Ehrlich makes this argument to fellow scientists in a book on diversity and ecosystem function, writing, "More research is badly needed," but quickly adding: "we already know enough about the manifold values of biodiversity (of which involvement in biogeochemical cycles is just one) *to take action now.*"[8]

The arguments within ecology about ecosystem function help us to see that the value of biodiversity emerges not only from what we know about it but also from what we do not. Ehrlich's famous metaphor making this point compares each species on Earth to the rivets attaching a wing to an airplane. The system is built with redundancy, so that some rivets can be removed without the wing falling off. However, if we are not sure which rivets are vital and how many are necessary, it is wise to minimize the number of rivets lost. Similarly, it may be that an ecosystem could continue to function after losing some of its variety, but it is unwise to test how much or which aspects of that variety can be taken away.[9]

Another way conservationists demonstrate this point is with the story of the Biosphere 2 experiment in which a giant, sealed greenhouse was built in an effort to support human life with no contributions, after initial construction, from Earth's external ecosystems, with Earth being dubbed Biosphere 1 for the purposes of the experiment. Preparation for this experiment took seven years and cost $200 million. The attempt was to create an artificial, life-sustaining world in which eight people could live for two years, beginning in 1991. The result was a failure. Residents were unable to stabilize the atmosphere, to consistently feed themselves using internal resources, or to keep a majority of the nonhuman species alive during the two-year experiment.

The lesson of Biosphere 2, according to ecologists David Tilman and Joel Cohen, is simple: "At present there is no demonstrated alternative to maintaining the viability of Earth. No one yet knows how to engineer systems that provide humans with the life-supporting services that natural ecosystems produce for free."[10] We depend upon Biosphere 1, the only functioning life support system available to us. For that reason the diverse ecosystems of our world and the variety of life that contributes to them are utterly necessary. The broad point here is the same as that of the rivet argument: we do not know how to survive without the natural systems around us, so we should be careful not to do anything that might degrade those systems. Any reduction in biodiversity is dangerous because we simply do not know how to live without it.

As David Takacs summarizes this view, "biodiversity keeps the world running," and for that reason it should certainly be considered morally valuable.[11] The variety of life is necessary for a thriving and functioning world, necessary for human survival. While experts may not yet know how varied nature's systems must be or how much biodiversity is required to keep ecosystems functioning, it is beyond doubt that all of life depends upon variety. This, for many, is the strongest argument about biodiversity's value.

Social Goods and Economic Value

The argument that the variety of life is necessary for our survival is a powerful one for establishing the value of biodiversity as a broad phenomenon. But many conservationists have noted that this argument is not always useful when it comes to *particular* decisions about how we treat the variety of life. We may recognize that we depend upon diversity across the globe, but that broad point is not always easy to connect to a local land-use decision or the attitude one takes to a particular pest in one's own house or field. Thus, many conservation biologists and ecologists also develop a more concrete argument about the value of biodiversity, seeking to prove that the variety of life has specific, quantifiable social and monetary values.

It is not difficult to demonstrate that biodiversity provides valuable benefits to human society. A great deal of the recreation and aesthetic pleasure of human societies depends upon the diversity of the nonhuman world, most directly through outdoor activities featured in popular recreation, literature, and art. Furthermore, our medicines are frequently extracted, derived, or inspired by naturally occurring species. Our physical habitats and possessions are built in large part from naturally occurring, biological materials that human beings have thus far been unable to effectively synthesize, such as wood, oils, and waxes. Our food is itself biological, and its quality is enhanced when the ecosystems that produce it are healthy.[12] These "ecosystem services" are based upon the diversity of life on Earth. Biodiversity is therefore not only a precondition for human life, as established above, but it also enhances human lives, brings people satisfaction, and creates countless benefits for human societies.

Economists have done the majority of work demonstrating this, and environmental and ecological economics have produced an array of theories, ideas, and findings calculating the value of biodiversity.[13]

Economics is the social science suited to measure the value of things and compare relative values when hard choices must be made. While this book focuses on dialogue with ecologists and conservation biologists, it is vital to note that these scientists are working alongside economists, using their tools to quantify the value of life's variety in order to stress its potential to enhance human prosperity.

In that spirit a group of ecologists and economists together published an article in the journal *Nature* in 1997 that sought to measure "the value of the world's ecosystem services." They determined that the natural world provides "at least US$33 trillion dollars worth of services annually." Among the many ecosystem services measured, they included the contribution of ecosystems to food production ($1.4 trillion per year), waste treatment ($2.3 trillion per year), a variety of recreational and cultural activities ($3.8 trillion per year), and nutrient cycling, which is the single largest ecosystem service ($17 trillion per year). In each case this value is created by natural systems but is not paid for by any human being because it is not included in economic markets. Indeed, one of the most interesting findings of the study was that the nonhuman world clearly creates more economic value than human beings do, as the best figures for global economic production per year are significantly smaller.[14]

Numbers this size are difficult to understand or make sense of, but of course that is part of the point: the diverse ecosystems of this planet do more to make our lives possible and our societies thrive than we understand, so to value them properly we must struggle to make as much sense of them as possible and to accept their importance even when it is beyond our ability to fully grasp. If the monetary value of ecosystems is a number so large that it is beyond our realistic experience, then we must embrace the diversity and variety of those systems as valuable too. This is a core economic argument on behalf of biodiversity.

Other analyses emphasize not only the value of ecosystem services but also the changes required in economic institutions to measure this value. This was the prominent theme in a 2008 report commissioned by the European Union on "The Economics of Ecosystems & Biodiversity," which argues that the variety of life within healthy ecosystems is degraded because "they are predominantly public goods with no markets and no prices, so are rarely detected by our current economic compass." What is required, then, is a change in economic structures and policies. As the report put it, the most urgent need is "to replace society's defective old economic compass and then to use the new one: to rethink today's subsidies, to design policies and market structures which reward unrecognized benefits and penalize uncaptured costs, and to share the benefits of conservation and protected areas in a more equitable manner."[15]

During the global economic crisis of 2008, the study leader of this report, Pavan Sukhdev, emphasized the economic seriousness of biodiversity loss by naming it a greater threat than any bank or market failures. In October of that year he told reporters that "whereas Wall Street by various calculations has to date lost, within the financial sector, $1–1.5 trillion, the reality is that at today's rate we are losing natural capital at least between $2–$5 trillion every year."[16] To recognize the value of biodiversity, Sukhdev argues, is to discover a drastic and unnoticed economic catastrophe.

In addition to the already-existing value extracted from the natural world, many biodiversity advocates frequently promise that there are considerably more social goods—and therefore more wealth—yet to be found in diverse, healthy ecosystems. E. O. Wilson, for instance, argues in *The Diversity of Life* that there are "tens of thousands of unused plant species" available for use as food and likely to be "demonstrably superior" to foods commonly eaten today. Wilson also claims that the pharmaceutical industry has discovered "but a fraction of the opportunities waiting" for medicinal applications of plant and animal compounds.[17] Making a similar argument, Andrew Beattie and Paul Ehrlich note that the world's tropical rain forests, the most diverse systems in the world, have produced at least forty-seven major pharmaceuticals, with "an accumulated net worth of $147 billion." When this fact is combined with the vast amount not yet known or explored about rain forest ecosystems and species, it leads to a clear argument that far more human health and wealth could be generated by conserving and studying the rain forest, producing a much more sustainable and fruitful harvest than habitat-destroying logging.[18]

So, biodiversity is socially and economically valuable because we depend upon it and use it and because there are vast and unexplored avenues of use still available to us. Such predictions of future economic value to be found in biodiversity are perhaps the most compelling arguments to be made in a society focused on progress and capitalist exchange because they emphasize the availability of more wealth to be gained from intact, diverse ecosystems. To pay attention to the economic value of biodiversity is to see that conserving the Earth's biodiversity is in humanity's economic interest.

Biodiversity as Instructive and Inspirational

Biodiversity is also valuable because scientists have so much to learn from it. Ecologists study biodiversity because of what it reveals about how natural systems work, organize themselves, and change over time. The variety of life matters to researchers, in part, because measuring, studying, and making hypotheses about it helps them to understand living organisms and the ways they relate to their environments. Conservation biologist Thomas Lovejoy made this point starkly in testimony before the U.S. Congress in 1991, informing legislators that the variety of life "is essentially the basic library on which the life sciences can build" and then comparing its degradation to "a form of bookburning and one of the greater anti-intellectual acts of all time."[19]

Ecologists and conservation biologists frequently build upon this idea to the even broader argument that all people could and should learn from the variety of life, particularly about the limits of our knowledge and the place of human beings within natural systems. The first of these lessons is humility: biodiversity reveals something about what human beings do not, and perhaps cannot, understand. Such limitations have already been demonstrated in this chapter and the previous one: ecological researchers who have devoted their lives to studying biodiversity still do not fully understand its role in ecosystem function. They have not cataloged the majority of species on the planet and can only approximate and estimate how many species there might be. They know even less about the genetic and ecosystemic diversity of life on Earth, which is perhaps too vast for human beings ever to comprehend fully. Furthermore, the 3.5 billion-year history of biodiversity is almost certainly beyond anyone's capacity to reconstruct in any but the broadest strokes, and the best understandings of the fossils we have found cannot tell us everything we might want to know.

The study of biodiversity is therefore not only a way of characterizing life on Earth as diverse but also a reminder of the vast and ever-changing processes of life and the limits of what we can understand

and control. David Orr makes this point in the journal *Conservation Biology* by urging his colleagues to accept the inevitability of not knowing: "we are ignorant because of the vastness of what is to be known relative to our intellectual and perceptual capacities." However, these limits in human knowledge can be used to caution against a more destructive kind of ignorance, the ignorance that leads some people to believe that they truly understand and can manage the world's ecosystems. When done well, Orr argues, conservation biology should be "so compelling as to displace once and for all the myth that humans can be the lords and masters of creation."[20] This argument applies a lesson from biodiversity—that human beings do not and perhaps cannot fully understand our world—to all people, hoping that everyone can learn humility from the variety of life.

Another broad lesson to be learned from biodiversity concerns the fact that we human beings are not separate from the rest of the natural world and so must find a way to accept our place as fully a part of it. The variety of life is a broad and encompassing concept, a concept that includes human beings as expressions, carriers, and participants in this variety. As E. O. Wilson tells his readers,

> You do not have to visit distant places, or even rise from your seat, to experience the luxuriance of biodiversity. You yourself are a rainforest of a kind. There is a good chance that tiny spiderlike mites build nests at the base of your eyelashes. Fungal spores and hyphae on your toenails await the right conditions to sprout a Lilliputian forest. The vast majority of the cells in your body are not your own; they belong to bacterial and other microorganismic species. More than four hundred such microbial species make their home in your mouth.[21]

Wilson recounts these facts not just to shock his readers and inspire a need to rub their eyes and brush their teeth but also to make it clear that human beings are part of the pervasiveness of biodiversity on Earth. We cannot fully understand the variety of life without understanding our own species, and we cannot fully understand our own species without understanding the variety of life. This is a lesson not just for scientific researchers but for all people, who must learn to see humanity and its future as intricately tied to the biodiversity in which we participate. If we understand ourselves as utterly distinct from the natural world, we will be less likely to recognize the degradation of biodiversity as a serious problem; but if we recognize ourselves as "rain forests," then the fate of diverse expressions of life becomes more personal. Biodiversity is valuable because it helps to teach this lesson.

It is important to recognize that this point about human beings as expressions of biodiversity is more than just an instructive lesson; it is also an attempt to use biodiversity to change people in more basic ways, helping us to feel as well as think differently. Wilson hopes that his readers will not be disgusted to learn about the microorganisms to which they play host because he trusts that understanding breeds familiarity, comfort, and even affection. In broader terms he writes that the best way to get people emotionally committed to biodiversity is to spread knowledge about it. Along these lines he asserts in *The Future of Life*: "To know this world is to gain proprietary attachment to it. To know it well is to love and take responsibility for it."[22] Biodiversity is not just a source of information but of inspiration, not just education but also transformation.[23] Conservation biologist James Miller picks up on the same argument, suggesting to fellow researchers that their most important and often-neglected task is to "convey the importance, wonder and relevance of biodiversity to the general public," primarily by providing experiences of naturally occurring biodiversity that will inspire people to care about it.[24]

These scientists clearly believe that exposure to biodiversity creates a moral commitment to it. Again, David Takacs offers a helpful summary, concluding his book by calling readers to follow the example of conservation biologists and to take biodiversity seriously as a characteristic of reality with much to teach us. Takacs argues that the best way to deal with the moral problem of biodiversity's decline is to learn from biodiversity itself:

> If some healthy, renewable chunk of biodiversity is to endure in the world, it must become part of world consciousness, part of the fundamental ethical core of each woman and man. Each of us must come to love it as deeply as do the biologists I portray here. When our basic needs are met, why shouldn't we selfishly devour more if we have not been transformed by biodiversity? And when government will fails and sacrosanct park boundaries fall, those surrounding biodiversity's remaining refuges will respect its sanctity only if they know and *love* what's inside.[25]

To know and to love biodiversity, Takacs argues, is to become a better and more moral person. This suggests that the variety of life is valuable because it is instructive and inspirational; it teaches us about our world, about how we should live within it, and about how we should feel about it.

Value beyond Human Interest

The arguments summarized above—that biodiversity maintains eco-system function, ensures human survival, enhances human societies, creates economic value, teaches important lessons, and can inspire new ways of feeling and thinking—all have in common the strategy of demonstrating biodiversity's value by proving that it contributes to hu-man well-being. The same is true of the list of values in the Convention on Biological Diversity: "the ecological, genetic, social, economic, scien-tific, educational, cultural, recreational, and aesthetic values of biodiver-sity" are all values for humanity. However, the Convention preceded this list by noting that its signatories were also "conscious of the intrinsic value of biodiversity" and so signaled that there are other reasons to con-serve biodiversity beyond the interests of the human species.

To argue that biodiversity has intrinsic value is to suggest, strictly speaking, that it matters for its own sake, without regard to its impact or effect on anything else. The idea of "intrinsic" value is famously com-plicated, and enormous energy has been spent in philosophical en-vironmental ethics debating what this idea means and how unique and influential it might be.[26] The core of the idea, however, is that if something is intrinsically valuable, its value does not depend on hu-man interests; we do not judge its worth based on its worth to our-selves. Outside of environmental ethics, this argument is frequently used about human life: we need not measure the contributions or exter-nal value of individuals or a people to declare that their lives matter and should be cared for. Many environmental ethicists make the same claim about biodiversity, as does the Convention on Biological Diversity.

A number of scientists have made this argument as well. Ecolo-gists Kent Redford and Brian Richter end their discussion of conserva-tion with the claim "that all biological entities and their environments have intrinsic value independent of their usefulness to humans. . . . The preservation of biodiversity for its own sake, in its entirety and in its component parts, is a legitimate objective in itself."[27] Biodiversity, they argue, need not be valuable *for* humanity to be valued *by* human beings. This could be interpreted simply as an argument that biodiversity need not be useful to human beings to be valuable—we may appreciate it for aesthetic or abstract reasons that do us no material good. However, the use of the phrase "intrinsic value" means something even stronger: regardless of whether human beings appreciate the variety of life in any way, it has value.[28] This means that we should conserve even species or systems that might hypothetically be shown to have absolutely no benefit to the human species or the ecosystems upon which we depend.

Michael Soulé, a conservation biologist who played an important role in founding the field, writes that the "most fundamental" normative commitment of conservation biologists is this: "*Biotic diversity has intrinsic value. . . .* Species have value in themselves, a value neither conferred nor revocable, but springing from a species' long evolutionary heritage and potential or even from the mere fact of its existence."[29] While conservation biologists have debated how widely to proclaim such value and how this moral commitment influences their research, no one in the field has directly contradicted Soulé's claim, so it seems that the intrinsic value of biodiversity is widely accepted among scientific activists.

This is perhaps not surprising when we remember the breadth of what biodiversity encompasses: if the concept includes the variety of all life on Earth, if it is in some sense "everything," then ascribing intrinsic value to it is a way of saying that the living Earth has value in itself. However, to claim that variety of life has value beyond human interest need not necessarily be a claim that the value of biodiversity is *independent* of human interest: as participants in life on Earth, our own value could be understood as developing out of the variety from which we come. In other words, one justification for the argument of intrinsic value is that it is difficult to distinguish human beings from the rest of life on Earth, and so in valuing biodiversity we are indirectly valuing our own lives and the context that makes life possible.

Such connections between biodiversity and humanity also help to demonstrate that appeals to intrinsic value are not solely abstract and idealistic. On the contrary, many conservationists and ecologists appeal to this kind of value with as much strategic attention to its potential influence as others bring to arguments about economic or survival value. Paul Ehrlich, for instance, argues that even if one is concerned solely with maintaining the "instrumental value" of biodiversity, a vital means of doing so is working to inspire "a quasi-religious concern for our only known living companions in the universe."[30] This use of "religious" value as a synonym for "intrinsic" is an intriguing move from the perspective of Christian ethics, but it is most important to note here that Ehrlich appeals to this "quasi-religious" concern because he sees it as something that motivates people deeply. If human beings can be convinced or taught to *believe* in the fundamental value of biodiversity, then we will do what is necessary to conserve it. Intrinsic value is not just a vague claim or an abstract belief but a strategic proposal about how to save the variety of life.

The strategic nature of some appeals to intrinsic value does not, of course, mean that they are disingenuous. Many ecologists and conservation biologists seek to protect biodiversity because they are fundamentally committed to it for its own sake, because they want biodiversity itself to thrive. That core idea of intrinsic value is at the heart of many arguments on behalf of conservation.

Why Value Matters: Applying Arguments about Biodiversity

Clearly, ecologists and conservation biologists have marshaled a substantial set of arguments that biodiversity is valuable, engaging in dialogue with philosophers, economists, and other researchers and activists to refine and publicize these arguments. Biodiversity is worth our attention and our advocacy because of its role in sustaining ecosystems and therefore human survival, its social and economic importance in helping human societies to thrive, its capacity to teach and inspire, and its intrinsic value. What's more, when these arguments are combined with the evidence already cited that biodiversity is being degraded and humanity is the cause, we are asked to feel urgency and responsibility, to change the ways we live and the decisions we make as individuals and communities in order to better live alongside the diversity of the natural world.

These arguments about the importance and urgency of biodiversity do not take place only among researchers, as the international agreement on the Convention on Biodiversity reveals. This agreement commits the nations that have signed and ratified it to conserve biodiversity, to find sustainable ways to utilize the variety of life, and to fairly and equitably share the knowledge and benefits gained from the genetic variety of the nonhuman world. The Convention created a secretariat to administer its work, coordinate and distribute information, and cooperate with the United Nations Environment Programme on biodiversity issues.[31] It is therefore an example of political conservation in action, as I discuss in chapter 6.

The Convention also serves as a reminder that biodiversity loss represents an urgent problem, all the more urgent because the commitment agreed to in Rio was to reduce the rate of loss rather than to stop it. Furthermore, a 2006 report from the secretariat suggested that even meeting that goal—the goal of losing slightly less biodiversity—would require "unprecedented additional efforts" before 2010.[32] Clearly, the threat to biodiversity remains very real and very current, so arguments about its value are deeply important.

Such arguments are especially important for those who do not yet agree that biodiversity matters enough to take significant action for its conservation. Perhaps the best example of this is my own country, the United States of America, which was one of the last to sign this Convention and has not yet ratified it. While the Convention was introduced and agreed upon at the 1992 Rio Summit, the U.S. president at the time refused to approve it. It was not signed until a new administration took office in 1993. In the following year, the agreement was debated in the Senate, but a vote was never scheduled. Despite the fact that the Convention remains the most powerful international agreement on this subject and has shaped global discussion about biodiversity, it has not been debated again in the Senate. Its official status remains "under consideration" at the time of this writing almost two decades later.

The central reasons given for not immediately signing the treaty and failing to ratify it were almost entirely concerned with its economic impact. Critics cited dangerous implications for the economic sovereignty of the United States, which they worried would no longer be able to regulate its own agriculture, industries, and intellectual property rights. Clearly opponents in this country were not convinced that the economic value of biodiversity was worth the cost of protecting it at an international level. However, it is interesting to note that these claims have never been carefully analyzed and discussed in public; this country has never had any real nationwide discussion about the economic value of biodiversity or about the many other, equally important arguments about biodiversity's intrinsic, inspirational, instructional, social, survival, or ecosystemic value. The scientists cited in this chapter seek to make this wider conversation more possible.

The fundamental assumption behind any argument about biodiversity's value is that we as human beings need to think more about the priorities we are setting as individuals, communities, nations, and a species; we need to consider how important the variety of life is and should be. Whether we emphasize that biodiversity is valuable to us, to other people, or simply to itself, the point of such an argument is to help people see that its destruction is a tragedy and requires a moral response. Scientific researchers use their data to make ethical arguments because many who study biodiversity find themselves driven to stand up on its behalf.

As E. O. Wilson puts it in his introduction to *Biodiversity*, the point of the concept is to motivate action: "In the end, I suspect it will all come down to a decision of ethics—how we value the natural worlds in which we evolved."[33] For Wilson, as for many other environmentalists, the loss of biodiversity is not merely a practical problem in need of a solution but a moral problem in which we human beings are failing to live up to our responsibilities and our potential. This moral problem is why these arguments about its value matter and why it is important for Christians to develop arguments about why it should particularly matter to those who share the Christian faith. Developing such arguments is the task to which the next chapter turns.

Notes

1. Secretariat, "Convention on Biological Diversity," preamble.

2. Darwin, *The Origin of Species*, 156.

3. See especially May, *Stability and Complexity*. Originally published in 1973.

4. Naeem et al., "Declining Biodiversity."

5. Wardle et al., "Biodiversity and Ecosystem Function." This letter was a direct response to a publication of the Ecological Society of America authored by Naeem and others: "Biodiversity and Ecosystem Functioning."

6. David A. Wardle et al., "Influence of Island Area," 1298.

7. Loreau, Naeem, and Inchausti, *Biodiversity and Ecosystem Functioning*, 242.

8. Ehrlich, "Biodiversity and Ecosystem Function?" vii. Emphasis in original.

9. The original articulation of this now-famous metaphor was in Ehrlich and Ehrlich, *Extinction*, xi–xiv. Philosopher Sahotra Sarkar critiques this as a weak analogy and therefore a weak argument, which at best only makes a case to preserve keystone species, in *Biodiversity and Environmental Philosophy*, 14–15. This seems to me to miss the point of the Ehrlich's argument, which is that, just as most of us do not understand enough about airplanes to casually remove rivets, our species does not understand ecosystems well enough to identify the keystone species that need to be conserved.

10. Tilman and Cohen, "Biosphere 2 and Biodiversity." For another account of Biosphere 2 and its lessons about the importance of conserving natural systems, see Beattie and Ehrlich, *Wild Solutions*, 48–51.

11. Takacs, *Idea of Biodiversity*, 200.

12. A list of these "ecosystem services" and a more detailed discussion is found in Kunin and Lawton, "Does Biodiversity Matter?"

13. See for instance Daily, *Nature's Services*; and Orians et al., *Biological Resources*.

14. Costanza et al., "Value," 259. The study used the 1994 value of the U.S. dollar as its baseline.

15. Sukhdev, "Economics of Ecosystems & Biodiversity," 9, 55.

16. Black, "Nature Loss 'Dwarfs Bank Crisis,'" BBC News, http://news.bbc.co.uk/2/hi/science/nature/7662565.stm.

17. Wilson, *Diversity of Life*, 289, 86. More extensive accounts of the medical benefits of biodiversity can be found in Chivian and Bernstein, *Sustaining Life*.

18. Beattie and Ehrlich, *Wild Solutions*, 204.

19. Thomas Lovejoy, testimony on the National Biological Diversity and Conservation and Environmental Research Act July 26, 1991, before the Subcommittee on Environmental Protection of the Committee on Environment and Public Works, U.S. Senate, 102nd Cong., 1st sess. Quoted in Takacs, *Idea of Biodiversity*, 197.

20. Orr, "Orr's Laws," 1459. Along similar lines biologist and philosopher Kristin Shrader-Frechette urged environmentalists to learn about their own work from the limits of scientific knowledge. See Shrader-Frechette, "Throwing out the Bathwater."

21. Wilson, *Future of Life*, 20.

22. Ibid., 131.

23. Along similar lines, philosopher Sahotra Sarkar argues that the single most compelling reason to conserve biodiversity is its "transformative value," that is, the "intellectual promise" of life's variety and the way it can change people's priorities and interests. Sarkar, *Biodiversity and Environmental Philosophy*, 82, 85.

24. Miller, "Biodiversity Conservation," 430.

25. Takacs, *Idea of Biodiversity*, 335. Emphasis in original.

26. For classic philosophical articulations of this argument, see Callicott, *Land Ethic*, and Rolston, *Environmental Ethics*. For an argument that the debate about intrinsic versus instrumental value is unnecessary because the practical results of both are the same, see Norton, *Toward Unity*. For a critique claiming that intrinsic value is an idea used "sloppily" in environmental philosophy, which in any case "has contributed little to the formulation of an adequate biodiversity conservationist ethic," see Sarkar, *Biodiversity and Environmental Philosophy*, chapter 3.

27. Redford and Richter, "Conservation of Biodiversity," 1254.

28. Philosopher Bryan Norton clarifies this difference by distinguishing between "intrinsic value," which discovers value in the natural world "independent of human values *and* human consciousness," and "inherent value," which suggests that "all value in nonhuman nature is dependent on human consciousness, but some of this value is not derivative upon human values." Both kinds of value are distinguished from "anthropocentric," instrumental values. Norton, *Toward Unity*, 235.

29. Soulé, "What Is Conservation Biology?" 731.

30. Ehrlich, "Bioethics," 1211.

31. See Secretariat of the Convention on Biological Diversity, "Convention on Biological Diversity."

32. Secretariat, "Global Biodiversity Outlook 2," 58.

33. E. O. Wilson, "Introduction," in Wilson and Peter, *Biodiversity*, 16.

Chapter 3

The Sacramental Value of the Variety of Life

In a frequently told and possibly apocryphal story, a member of the Christian clergy anxious to engage in dialogue asked the early-twentieth-century biologist John Haldane what his studies of the natural world had taught him about its creator. Haldane replied that God seems to have "an inordinate fondness for beetles," referencing the hundreds of thousands of distinct species of the insect already cataloged and the uncountable others that human beings have never seen. A noted atheist, Haldane was likely annoyed by the question and hoping his answer would shock the clergyman away from a follow-up. From my perspective as a Christian ecological ethicist, however, I am delighted by the exchange and seek in this book to imitate the questioner by expanding my theology in dialogue with scientists.

In this chapter I ask a very similar question: What can we learn about God by studying God's creation? I hope to receive a more thoughtful answer than Haldane's, but his offers a powerful starting point: What does it tell us about God's world that more than 350,000 species of beetle have evolved and now exist, and how should a fact like this change the ways we live, relate to one another, and think about God? In other words, what does it mean for Christians to understand biodiversity as part of God's creation, and what difference does the variety of life make to Christian morality? This chapter offers answers by developing a sacramental Christian ethics, an argument that we have a responsibility to the variety of life in God's world in part because we come to know God better through it. Biodiversity, I argue, is sacramental because it is a sign of and connection to the mysteries and workings of God. This calls Christians to take seriously the variety and wonder of life as well as the reality of predation and death inherent in God's world.

The argument develops straightforwardly: if we can understand God by understanding God's creation, then we should strive to understand the variety of life within that creation. If we are to understand our role in this world, then we must understand our fundamental relatedness to that variety, including our relationship to the marvels of biodiversity and to the death necessary to it. These steps are the intellectual and moral structure of a Christian argument about biodiversity's value, forming the sacramental basis of the rest of this book and beginning to offer an answer to how we should respond to God's apparently inordinate fondness for beetles, trees, owls, and human beings.

The Idea of Sacramentality

Many Christian denominations and churches have longstanding and deep sacramental traditions, ritual practices that establish a link between the world and God. While there are important arguments about the details, most Christians agree that the bread and wine of communion are sacramental, that they bear the presence of God in a meaningful way. One crucial root of this belief is biblical: as the Gospel of Matthew records, Jesus ate with his disciples, blessed bread while saying, "Take, eat, this is my body," and gave thanks for wine while saying, "Drink from it, all of you, for this is my blood" (26:26–27). This is the basis of a sacrament, a belief that the incarnate God is present in bread and wine.

Similarly, the water of baptism is widely believed to be holy, to represent the relationship between the baptized person, her community, and God. Indeed, the same gospel reports that Jesus' public ministry began only after his baptism: "just as he came up from the water, suddenly the heavens were opened to him and he saw the Spirit of God descending like a dove and alighting on him" (3:16). Here the water, like the bread and wine of communion, plays an important role: a material substance represents something important in the mediation of God and the world. Sacraments are real, material things that connect Christian communities to our creator. Sacraments are also mysteries, demonstrating the limits of our ability to fully understand God and God's working in our world. We do not and cannot fully understand baptism and communion, and so they connect us to the mysteries of the divine.

The claim of sacramentality broadens from these particular sacraments to an argument about the material world as a whole: if God can be communicated and experienced through particular materials, then it is also theologically sound to claim that God is *inherently* present in the basic elements, that God exists in some meaningful way in all wheat and grapes, all hydrogen and oxygen, and indeed throughout the world. As chemist and Anglican Archbishop John Habgood writes, "what happens to water, bread, and wine when they are used as vehicles of God's grace is no isolated miracle. All matter shares this potential."[1]

Sacramentality extends beyond particular material substances and particular rituals to emphasize that the incarnation of God on Earth in Jesus Christ signifies something about the ongoing relationship between creator and creation. God can be known through God's world because the world communicates about God, because the creator is actively present in the creation. Sacramentality is based not only on the stories of Jesus' baptism and communion but also on the basic belief expressed at the beginning of John's Gospel that God "was in the world, and the world came into being through" God, that Christ incarnate on Earth was God coming "to his own home" (1:10–11).

The environmentalist implications of such sacramentality are not difficult to anticipate: if Christian faith teaches that the world reveals God, then it clearly follows that Christians should be cautious about our impact on that world, that we should treat the natural systems around us with respect. Christian ethicist James Nash expresses this well: "Nature is sacred by association, as the bearer of the sacred. We are standing perpetually on holy ground, because God is present not only in the burning bush but in the nurturing soil and atmosphere, indeed, sharing the joys and agonies of all creatures. The sacramental presence of the Spirit endows all of creation with a sacred value and dignity."[2] The natural world is important, in part, because it provides access to the God who created it. Environmental degradation is therefore sinful because through it we abandon our place within creation and set ourselves against God's creative work. The nonhuman world should be preserved because it is a sign of God and therefore a means of moving closer to God.

A clear articulation of the environmental implications of sacramental theology came in *Renewing the Earth*, the 1991 encyclical letter from the U.S. Catholic Bishops. The bishops here lament that "as heirs and victims of the industrial revolution, students of science, and the beneficiaries of technology, urban-dwellers and jet-commuters, twentieth-century Americans have also grown estranged from the natural scale and rhythms of life on earth."[3] This disconnection from the nonhuman world is a profound theological problem, they argue, because it dims "that sense of God's presence in nature." This sacramental argument characterizes environmental degradation as the dangerous destruction of our ability to know and respond to God. Furthermore, the bishops argue, sacramentality is a way to reverse the course of environmental degradation: "Through the created gifts of nature, men and women encounter their Creator. The Christian vision of a sacramental universe—a world that discloses the Creator's presence by visible and tangible signs—can contribute to making the earth a home for the human family once again."[4] Sacramentality thus provides both a motivation to know the world better and a means by which to understand how we should care for it by feeling truly at home within it.

Interpreting the bishops' encyclical, Catholic ethicist John Hart writes that they seek to develop a "sacramental consciousness" that inspires "commitment to the well-being of Earth, the community of life generally, and people and peoples."[5] Sacramentality is not, therefore, merely an idea or a distant and abstract theological claim; it also includes an experience of God in the world. As such it can inspire people to act and structure their lives differently. Sacramentality is an attempt to change how Christians behave by changing the ways we think and feel about creation. When people gain a sacramental consciousness, they begin to understand that the degradation of the natural environment is a sin against God and a depletion of their ability to know God. This consciousness teaches that a Christian response to environmental degradation can involve appreciation of the world around us as a path to God and a teacher of our own place within God's creation. When we live out this sacramental consciousness, we gain courage and resolve to change so that we might live sustainably in this world. While such a change in consciousness is not enough by itself to save the variety of life, it is one vital aspect of a Christian ethics of biodiversity.

Sacramentality is a powerful idea and experience because it both draws on deep traditions in Christian faith and responds to the current and urgent issues of environmental degradation. Theologians and ethicists frequently stress that sacramentality is an idea with deep roots, a faithful communication of the Christian tradition that has long expressed an immanent, incarnational, and sacramental presence of God in the world. Sacramentality does not call us as believers to change the object of our worship or to reimagine God but rather to recognize the importance of the natural world in the faith we inherit.

Along these lines Larry Rasmussen is careful to distinguish nature from the divine in his discussion of sacramentality: "To identify something earthly as holy and sacred is not to say it *is* God. Rather, it is *of* God; God is present in its presence."[6] John Haught is even more careful and limited in his use of language, stressing that seeing the world as sacramental is fundamentally different from seeing it as sacred: "Nature is worth saving not because it is sacred, but because it is sacramental, capable of mediating to our religious awareness the otherwise hidden mystery of the divine."[7] While these thinkers define "sacred" in different ways, both emphasize that sacramentality is a faithful strand of Christianity, calling believers to see the natural world as a bearer of God but not as God itself. Sacramentality is about valuing, respecting, and appreciating the natural world; this is much more important, vital, and faithful to the Christian tradition than worshiping nature.

Precisely because it is a faithful inheritance of tradition, sacramentality is a powerful response to critics who argue that Christianity is too otherworldly and heaven obsessed to respond to the contemporary crisis of environmental degradation. In 1998 the biologist E. O. Wilson wrote: "The most dangerous of devotions, in my opinion, is the one endemic to Christianity: *I was not born to be of this world*."[8] This is a familiar and common critique, and one that fairly indicts some parts of the Christian tradition that are dangerously focused on ideas of heaven and the afterlife to the exclusion of this world. However, sacramentality is a deeply rooted tradition of the faith that moves in the opposite direction, emphasizing God's presence in the world and thereby demonstrating that Christianity is not exclusively about a transcendent, otherworldly God. This idea is therefore proof that otherworldliness is *not* endemic to Christianity, or at least not necessarily so.

John Hart's work is explicit about this point, highlighting the sacramental tradition as a corrective to Christianity's overemphasis "on a heavenly afterlife," an emphasis that should never take precedence over "present 'earthly' concerns, occupations, and preoccupations."[9] Ecofeminist theologian Sallie McFague embraces Christian sacramentality for the same reason, appreciative of its potential as "one of the few traditions within Christianity that . . . has included nature as a concern of God and a way to God."[10] Contemporary sacramental thinkers emphasize the presence of God on Earth and the importance of human life on Earth, a vital corrective to those who believe Christianity celebrates heaven to the exclusion of this world. Put simply, sacramentality calls us to commit to God's world rather than turning away from it.

There are of course many more examples of how sacramentality has been used by theologians and ethicists to stress the importance of the natural world and the responsibility of Christians to protect it.[11] However, the broad point remains the same in all these texts: we come to know God through the world, and so we should take care of the world and its systems as a theological and spiritual task. This basic idea is crucial for a Christian response to environmental degradation broadly and to an ethics of biodiversity in particular.

The Variety of Life as a Path to God

Christian sacramentality is a claim about the value of the world, a claim that material reality is important and should be cared for because it is the creation of God and because God created us to be a part of it. It is also a claim about the mystery of the world, a claim that this creation is beyond our ability to understand but worth seeking to understand, in part because it helps us to reflect on the great mystery of the God who created it.

If we think of biodiversity as a fundamental characteristic of this world, then the same statements can be made about it: the variety of life is a creation of God, we are meant to be a part of it, and its vast mysteriousness can teach us about its creator. Sacramentality tells us that the creatures with whom we share the world and the diverse systems they inhabit are a sign of and connection to God. This is the core of the sacramental argument on behalf of biodiversity, and it returns us to the theological definition of biodiversity: the variety of creatures in God's creation *that manifests God's glory.*

The sacramental phrase ending this definition is drawn from *Renewing the Earth*, which affirms: "The diversity of life manifests God's glory. Every creature shares a bit of the divine beauty [because] the divine goodness could not be represented by one creature alone."[12] So, we should seek to understand God's majesty, complexity, and goodness through the variety of life on God's Earth. Biodiversity manifests God's glory precisely because it is diverse, precisely because it is vast and varied beyond our ability to fully understand it.

While the concept of "biodiversity" is a new one and an explicit sacramental attention to the variety of life must be recognized as an innovation in contemporary Christian thought, there are significant precedents for this attitude in the tradition. Psalm 104 offers a clearly sacramental perspective, affirming that all creatures are enlivened by God's *ruach*, the divine breath or spirit that "renews the face of the ground" (v. 30). Psalm 148 calls all of creation to praise God, addressing the "sun and moon," "the fruit trees and all cedars," "wild animals and all cattle, creeping things and flying birds" (v. 3, 9–10).

Building on such texts, medieval theologian Thomas Aquinas argued in his *Summa Theologiae* that the vast variety of creatures on Earth is meant to reflect the goodness of God, which "could not be adequately represented by one creature alone." For Aquinas "the whole universe together participates in the divine goodness more perfectly, and represents it better than any single creature whatever."[13] Centuries later Martin Luther wrote that God's "own divine essence can be in all creatures collectively and in each one individually more profoundly, more intimately, more present than the creature is in itself. . . . It encompasses all things and dwells in all."[14] In these texts creation is not only declared to be good and not only seen to praise God. The diversity of creation is presented as a teacher, a way to understand God better, and a subject to contemplate when we want to contemplate its creator. This is the most basic sacramental claim about biodiversity: it helps us to understand God.

It would be irresponsible to suggest that the Bible or Christian theology univocally adopt a sacramental view of biodiversity. The very few examples I have just provided certainly do not encompass all the tradition has to say on this subject, and in any case one cannot anachronistically claim that any ancient text directly addresses biodiversity, a concept developed at the end of the twentieth century. What is clear is that there is precedent for a sacramental approach to the variety of life and that it is valid to argue that Christians *should* and *can* learn to see biodiversity this way.

The most basic motivation for this argument is the simple fact that biodiversity is under dire threat, a fact clearly established by the research of ecologists and conservation biologists. We live in an age of epidemic extinction and degradation, and if Christian faith is to be relevant to this time, it must respond. Sacramentality is such a response, an approach that demonstrates Christian commitment to this planet and the variety of life on it, an approach that can help to inspire the sort of commitment required to protect the variety of life. Seeing biodiversity as sacramental is a way to demonstrate the potential of a Christian ethics of biodiversity.

This is the point John Hart makes when he calls on Christians to embrace a "sacramental consciousness." Such consciousness requires attention to the variety of life, awareness of the dire threats facing it today, and willingness to admit the complicity of many human cultures in creating this degradation. When we understand biodiversity as sacramental, we will be more motivated to pay attention to the life around us, we will notice its struggles and degradation, and we will be bolstered by our faith to confess our own part in causing that degradation. In this way a sacramental Christian faith could help conserve biodiversity.

Embracing the sacramental character of biodiversity is not only expedient for conservationist reasons, however; it also enhances Christian faith. The previous chapters have made it clear that ecologists and conservation biologists do not study the variety of life merely because it is under threat but also because it is fascinating. Biodiversity is deeply complicated, reveals important information about the character of our world, and represents vast, unexplored avenues to study and ponder about the Earth. Christians should learn from ecologists that biodiversity is basic to life, it is deeply interesting, and it is mysterious. Life on Earth teaches us about God. It challenges us to consider why God made a world in which such vast diversity would evolve; it reminds us that God's presence and care for this world is not limited to human beings but extends to all creatures; and it reveals how much we do not know about both the creation and the creator.

Embracing the variety of life as a path to God is a way of taking creation seriously—of demonstrating and enacting our belief that God made this world, that this world is good, and that we are meant to be a part of it. Furthermore, a Christian faith that understands biodiversity as sacramental can take science seriously, contemplating the realities and complexities of evolution as a sign of God's work rather than competition against Christian belief.

Seeking theological insight in the findings of ecologists enhances faith through dialogue with some of the most exciting and fascinating contemporary research about the living world around us. Embracing the sacramental character of biodiversity builds upon the Christian tradition, it responds to an urgent problem in our world, and it offers insights that will enhance and enrich our faith. This is the argument for seeing biodiversity as a sign of and connection to the mysteries and workings of God.

Relating to Biodiversity

When understood as sacramental, biodiversity helps us to comprehend the importance of interrelationship in God's creation and our own place in such relationships—to accept that we are creatures of this Earth and to commit ourselves fully to it. This theological claim therefore emphasizes that God is relational and calls human beings into a relationship not only with one another and the divine but also with our living world.

Biodiversity as ecologists and conservation biologists have identified it is a way of talking about the vast and complicated interdependence of life's variety. Genes, species, and ecosystems do not and cannot exist in isolation; all depend upon one another, enhance one another, and consume one another. The reason ecologists study organisms in living and nonliving contexts is because their science assumes that such contexts are deeply important, that organisms and systems can be understood only in relationship to other organisms and systems.[15] Thus, all life involves systems of exchange, webs of relationship, and constant interaction. When applying this ecological fact to a theological project, we can conclude that God's creation is interconnected, that the variety of life as God has made it is intricate, complicated, and interdependent.

Biodiversity shows us that God did not create a world of autonomous individuals or monads, but rather of intricate, complicated, and often messy connections and relationships. If life on this Earth is about relationship and God is revealed through life on this Earth, then it is valid to say that God is also relational. The God who created a world of complex relationships should not be understood as purely outside of it but rather committed to and invested in the ways in which life relates to life and to its environments. As process theologian David Toolan puts it, "what happens in the material world happens also to God. God is unsurpassably related to all events in the cosmos and affected by them."[16]

If God is invested and interested in the fate of life on Earth, then God's creatures should be as well. This is another lesson of sacramental biodiversity: we are called to care about and commit to the variety of life. The world in which we find ourselves is made up of vast genetic diversity, millions of species mutually interacting, and countless eco-systems developing and changing throughout time. This is the world the book of Genesis declares "very good" and instructs human beings to "till and keep." Because biodiversity matters to God, it should matter to Christians.

This is not just a claim about the value of the world outside us, but also a claim about the value of human beings. When E. O. Wilson tells his readers, "You yourself are a rainforest of a kind," he offers a reminder that no study of biodiversity can ignore our own species as one part of the variety of life.[17] Human beings are interrelated with many other creatures and dependent upon healthy ecosystems for survival; a commitment to biodiversity is a commitment to the human species as well as to all the other creatures with whom humans share this world. The moral lesson we can draw from sacramentality is that we are called to participate in the world around us—to protect the variety of life upon which we depend and to play the best and most appropriate role we can as self-reflective participants in the processes of nature and biodiversity.

Sacramentality is not just a path to God. It also reveals the value of the sacrament itself. Biodiversity is not merely important because it teaches us about God; part of what it teaches us is that God cares about biodiversity for its own sake. Theologian Sallie McFague offers a helpful language for this distinction, calling for an emphasis on horizontal rather than vertical sacramentality. Vertical sacramentality teaches that nature is a way to God, valuing the world instrumentally because it helps human beings to transcend it. Horizontal sacramentality, by contrast, emphasizes the value of this world and all the creatures within it. When our focus is horizontal rather than vertical, McFague writes, we continue to "see all things in God," but our emphasis is "not on 'God in this tree,' but *this tree* in God."[18] We do not pay attention to the world and its diversity in hopes of finding God; instead we find God when we attend to the world and its diversity for their own sake. Only through such horizontal sacramentality can we truly appreciate the natural world and "tak[e] into full account the diversity, particularity, and thickness of natural forms," appreciating that our world is "a marvelously rich collection of lifeforms and things."[19]

Horizontal sacramentality is a way to recognize and appreciate the importance of biodiversity and to understand it as fundamentally relational. This way of seeing the world helps us to learn more about the variety of life, to contemplate God as the creator of that variety, and to commit to our role as participants within it.

Suffering, Creation, and the Variety of Life

Chapter 1 introduced an important and serious challenge to the claim that biodiversity is sacramental: the variety of life seems to depend upon predation, starvation, and pain. Recognizing the interrelatedness of life's variety involves recognizing the death and suffering inherent in the interactions between creatures. For example, wolves and deer are intricately interrelated in many regions of North America but their relationship is primarily based on the fact that wolves hunt and eat deer. This relationship is essential for maintaining flourishing ecosystems because unchecked deer populations inevitably overconsume plant life and degrade the health of their habitat. Healthy ecosystems therefore depend upon predatory wolves as well as herbivorous deer. Meanwhile, bacteria and other microorganisms consume the wastes and remains of deer and wolves, ultimately providing nutrients for more plants to grow. This web of relationships is not about mutual cooperation so much as it is about continual consumption and predation.

Such consumption and predation does not occur only in pastoral landscapes and among animals, either; it shapes the lives of every human being. The same evolutionary processes that produced our species produced the human immunodeficiency virus, *E. coli* bacteria, and countless other creatures that survive only by sickening and often killing their human hosts. These diseases are part of God's creation. If God loves and calls human beings to love the variety of life, then we are called to love even that life that seeks to destroy us. That is an essential part of the interrelatedness we learn from biodiversity.

Critiquing ethicists and theologians who simplistically claim that the relationships of ecological systems model harmonious coexistence, Lisa Sideris notes: "interdependence is not so much a solution to strife and suffering as it is a *source* of it."[20] Sideris's observation leads to questions that any Christian ecological ethics must address: Do we want to embrace these realities as revelatory of the character of God? Is it wise to see biodiversity as a path to God and a reality to which we are meant to relate if it inevitably includes violence and death?

These are crucial questions, in large part because their premise is utterly undeniable. Tennyson's familiar quote is always relevant: nature is "red in tooth and claw." Essayist Annie Dillard offers a similar sentiment, writing that "evolution loves death more than it loves you or me" and pointing out that the survival of any animal depends upon the destruction of another creature: "Any way you look at it, from the point of view of the whale or the seal or the crab, from the point of view of the mosquito or copperhead or frog or dragonfly or minnow or rotifer, it is chomp or fast."[21] Ethicist Roger Shinn puts this point in an even more personal way: "Out of [nature's] evolutionary processes has come human life. It sustains us, inspires us, threatens us, will kill every last one of us, and will outlast our entire species."[22]

Laced throughout Dillard and Shinn's words are Darwinian references. While Charles Darwin can hardly be credited with discovering the harsh and disturbing elements of the natural world, Darwinian biology seems to express this fact most clearly in contemporary discourse. Darwin's own scientific work was motivated by his awareness of "the universal signs of violence" all around him, and his theory of evolution was inspired in part by how disturbed he was that competition and struggle are inherent in natural processes. This view of the world is of course foundational for any attention to biodiversity, because the variety of life can be ecologically understood and studied only within the framework of evolutionary biology, an explanation of the vast array of genes, species, and ecosystems as realities that have evolved over millions of years.

Our world is diverse because of millennia of deaths as well as births, and this diversity will endure only if deaths continue to occur. Thus, if we embrace biodiversity as sacramental we are in some sense embracing evolution and the violence and predation inherent in that process.[23] Is this the right course for Christian ethics?

In part, this is the question of theodicy, of how God could possibly create and tolerate a world so dependent upon violence and pain. Perhaps the best that can be said to address this question is what Elizabeth Johnson writes: "I have thought about this all my life, and have read what many wise minds have said, and the bottom line is that nobody knows."[24] However, to concede that no one has an answer to the question of theodicy does not entirely close this issue for an ethics of biodiversity because the sacramental claim that we can learn about God and the world from biodiversity is based on the assumption that

biodiversity is good. Given that the variety of life depends upon predation and extinction, is it defensible to say that the natural world and
biodiversity within it are good?

I believe that it is not only valid but important to claim that biodiversity is good. However, this can only be done with an appreciation
for the mystery of God and God's world. We can claim that biodiversity
is good only if we acknowledge the limits of our capacity to understand
that goodness. Such an appreciation for mystery is entirely compatible with a sacramental approach to biodiversity: the more we study
the variety of life, the more we see the limits of human knowledge.
One of those limits has to do with the goodness of God's world. Real-
izing how little we understand about natural processes and how little
we can understand God helps us to humbly face the limits of human
knowledge.

The ethicist James Gustafson argues that any assertion of the goodness of God's creation must be followed by the questions "Good for
whom? and Good for what?"[25] Gustafson's own best answer to these
questions is that the natural world is good from God's perspective,
and for itself as a whole system. These answers are based on Christian
faith, based on the assumption that God's creation is good even if this
goodness is mysterious to us.

To assert that the world is good clearly does not mean that it is
always good for human beings, who suffer all too often from natural
as well as social disasters. Neither can it mean that the world is good
for any other particular creature, because all living things share our
existence and our inevitable deaths in this "chomp or fast" reality. In
short, to say that the world is good cannot mean that it is harmonious, perfect, or ideal in any way we can understand. But the goodness
of biodiversity does not depend on our understanding; rather, a faith
in the goodness of biodiversity depends on our ability to embrace a
theological mystery and the limits of our own knowledge. Asserting
the goodness of biodiversity does not mean that all creatures thrive in
a diverse world but that the world thrives when it is characterized by
diversity.

The sacramental approach to biodiversity that I am articulating
assumes that the world around us is good from God's perspective, a
claim based upon the doctrine of creation. Attention to this world offers a challenge to that assumption—God's creation is characterized
by diversity and creativity but also by violence and predation—but does

not disprove it. Indeed, this challenge is helpful insofar as it demonstrates the importance of mystery in a sacramental ethics. Christians assert that God's creation is good and therefore instructive and revelatory, but we are also reminded that we do not fully understand this creation and that we do not and *cannot* fully understand its creator.

In sum, Christians should believe that biodiversity is good for the same reason that we should believe that biodiversity is a way to better understand God: the world in which we find ourselves is a creation of God, and we are called to faith in the goodness of God even if we cannot define that goodness. If the creation is good, then biodiversity is good. If we can learn about God from what God has made, then we have much to learn from the variety of life. While the means by which this variety is created and sustained may not always seem good from our perspective, it is the reality of God's creation, the reality in which we are called to participate.

How Sacramentality Matters: A Christian Argument about Biodiversity

To argue that biodiversity is sacramental is to say that it is a sign of and connection to the mystery and workings of God. This means that we learn about God from the variety of life in God's creation and that we will learn to value this variety of life when we attend to it as instructive in theological as well as scientific terms. With careful attention to the interrelatedness of biodiversity, we see the importance of life's vast diversity for healthy functioning and recognize our own place as participants in that diversity. With careful attention to the realities of predation and death in the evolution of life, we can contemplate the mysteries of this creation and its creator.

Such sacramentality can be a foundation for a Christian ecological ethics because it provides a particularly Christian argument about the value of biodiversity. In its most basic and traditional articulation, sacramentality is an argument about the instrumental value of the created world: we need it as a means to understand and connect to God. This is a reason to value biodiversity, a reason similar to the survival and economic value described in the previous chapter. However, sacramentality as I have articulated it does not see sacraments as merely useful. Sacramentality also learns from and is inspired by them: the variety of life has instructional and inspirational value. Furthermore, when we emphasize a horizontal sacramentality along with the more traditionally vertical sacramentality, we see that the variety of life has a kind of intrinsic value, a value in and of itself, that we are called to recognize and respect and in which we are called to see ourselves as participants.

The argument of this chapter could therefore be summarized by saying that biodiversity has intrinsic, inspirational, instructional, survival, and economic value. However, the Christian tradition of sacramentality helps to articulate these claims in a particular way designed to resonate with those who believe that this world is God's creation. In some ways this is a limitation—atheists and agnostics may not be swayed by explicit appeals to God, and many will reject the characterization of the world as God's good creation; many people of other faiths will be unmoved by the explicit appeal to biblical and Christian traditions; and some Christians may feel that a sacramental approach is distant from their own interpretation of the faith. However, the power of a sacramental claim is that those who are prepared to hear it will be far more moved by it than by abstract arguments about value.

Those who believe in God as creator will relate to biodiversity differently when it is explicitly presented as part of God's creation. Those who embrace the goodness of creation and creator will need to ponder the mystery of suffering and predation in this world and the necessity of those realities for the variety of life. Those for whom ritual sacraments are a meaningful sign of and connection to ultimate reality will need to think carefully about what it means to see all the living creatures of this Earth as sacramental. The argument that biodiversity is sacramental is meant to stir Christians to think deeply about the variety of life, its current degradation, and our call to act quickly and decisively. Today, this connection to God's mysterious workings is being degraded carelessly, drastically, and irreversibly. We are driving species and populations and ecosystems to extinction without working to understand them or their role in God's world, and this is a sinful betrayal of sacramental biodiversity. In light of these facts, sacramentality is a call to action.

It might be possible to justify some reduction in biodiversity. Given that predation and death are fundamental characteristics of God's living creation, one cannot say that all extinction is morally wrong, or even that all degradation of the variety of life caused by human beings is wrong. Death, destruction, and extinction are a natural part of life's processes, and we are called to participate in those processes. Consumption is a necessary part of our lives, and no human being can survive without causing death in some other creatures. While we may be called to recognize that diseases are a part of God's creation, this does not mean we should not follow our instincts and use our best tools to fight against them. Thus, the moral call of a Christian ethics of biodiversity is not to end the destruction of all life. That would be impossible, impractical, and in some way unnatural.

However, the problem with our current behavior is that populations are being decimated, species are going extinct, and ecosystems are being destroyed carelessly. We are causing these changes at an unprecedented rate without fully understanding the consequences of our actions. As industrialized peoples, we are destroying systems and creatures we don't understand, and so losing all that they could teach us along with the chance to grasp and be transformed by our relationship to them. We privileged human beings in the twenty-first century are not simply participating in the processes of biodiversity and nature; rather, we are changing and degrading without care or attention. That is not a sacramental approach, it does not respect biodiversity as a sign of and connection to God, and it does not recognize the importance of modesty and self-limitation in response to God and God's world.

The moral call of sacramentality is to humility, to appreciate the fundamental mystery of this creation and the God who created it, and to be cautious and careful because of that humility. The only way to respect biodiversity is to know it as well and as completely as we can, and we are currently destroying it without such knowledge. That is the key moral lesson of sacramentality and a basic claim for a Christian ethics of biodiversity. If we value biodiversity because of its sacramentality or because of its economic, survival, instructive, inspirational, or intrinsic value, then we must do something about its rapid and careless destruction in our world. In other words, we must act to conserve biodiversity.

Notes

1. John Habgood, "A Sacramental Approach," 48.
2. Nash, *Loving Nature*, 115.

3. United States Conference of Catholic Bishops, *Renewing the Earth*.

4. Ibid.

5. Hart, *Sacramental Commons*, 62.

6. Rasmussen, *Earth Community, Earth Ethics*, 239.

7. Haught, *Promise of Nature*, 78.

8. Wilson, *Consilience*, 245. It is important to note that in his more recent work Wilson is less dismissive of Christianity. Indeed, he has written an entire book devoted to the project of convincing a hypothetical evangelical Christian to see biodiversity conservation as important work: Wilson, *The Creation*.

9. Hart, *Sacramental Commons*, 34.

10. McFague, *The Body of God*, 184.

11. See for instance Chryssavgis, *Beyond the Shattered Image*; Irwin, "Sacramentality of Creation"; and Ruether, "Theological Resources for Earth Healing."

12. United States Conference of Catholic Bishops, *Renewing the Earth*.

13. Aquinas, *Summa Theologiae*, 36 (47.1.ans).

14. Quoted in Santmire, *The Travail of Nature*, 130.

15. It is important to note, however, that the *purpose* of ecology as a science is not to establish the interconnectedness of natural systems. That interconnectedness is a foundation of the enterprise, but as one theoretical analysis of the science puts it, "the whole reason for doing ecological research is to find which connections are stronger and more significant than others. We do not wish to show that everything is connected, but rather to show which minimal number of connections that we can measure may be used as a surrogate for the whole system in a predictive model. That is the strategy of the basic scientist in ecology." Allen and Hoekstra, *Toward a Unified Ecology*, 284.

16. Toolan, *At Home in the Cosmos*, 148. Toolan opposes this view to "classical theism," which emphasizes the perfection of a transcendent God.

17. Wilson, *Future of Life*, 20.

18. McFague, *Super, Natural Christians*, 172. Emphasis in original.

19. Ibid., 173. McFague is building in this text on the sacramental claim she developed in her previous book, which argued that Christians in our time should learn to see the Earth as the body of God. See McFague, *Body of God*.

20. Sideris, *Environmental Ethics*, 221. Emphasis in original.

21. Dillard, *Pilgrim at Tinker Creek*, 178, 240. Of course, Dillard's point does not strictly speaking apply to all "creatures" since it indicts only animals, not inanimate creation or the plants that autotrophically synthesize their nutrition and growth from inanimate matter and sunlight. For philosophical reflection on whether a living world made up solely of autotrophs might be morally superior to ours, see Attfield, "Evolution, Theodicy, and Value."

22. Shinn, "Mystery of the Self," 98. Shinn goes on to ask why cosmologists formulate an anthropic principle to explain the conditions that make

human life possible but not "a viral principle" to explain the fact that "nature supports viruses that combat human life and health, forces that by all signs have a far greater staying power than we," 100.

23. For a broader and more detailed discussion of this problem and the ways many theologians and ethicists have failed to deal with it, see Sideris, *Environmental Ethics.*

24. Johnson, *Women, Earth, and Creator Spirit*, 58.

25. Gustafson, *Theocentric Perspective*, 95.

Part III

The Levels of Biodiversity

Chapter 4

Scaling Conservation

An Inconvenient Truth, the book released alongside former Vice President Al Gore's celebrated presentation and film about global climate change, begins with two pictures of the Earth from space, one of which Gore credited with changing the consciousness of humanity and helping to spark the environmental movement, another of which he identified as "the most commonly published photograph in all of history." Gore uses these pictures—just as he used one in his earlier book, *Earth in the Balance*—to call for a global attention, an awareness and concern for the entire planet, and a moral affirmation that all lives on Earth are connected.[1] Gore's work is a call to "think globally," a familiar rallying cry for environmentalists. This is, as I will argue in this chapter and the next, an argument about scale: about the time and space of our moral attention, which is vital to the conservation of biodiversity.

However, the call for global thinking is not the only scalar perspective available. Aldo Leopold, an early-twentieth-century forester whose writings have shaped the environmental movement and the science of ecology, famously encouraged his readers to "think like a mountain," to expand moral attention beyond ourselves in order to understand the systems and communities around us. Leopold's moral call is for an "expansion of ethics" so that we human beings can learn to care for— and recognize our own fate as dependent upon—the nonhuman systems of which we are a part. He believed that because we had learned to care for other human beings, we could also learn to extend our care outward to the other species with whom we share our habitats and ecosystems. In light of environmental degradation, Leopold argues, this moral vision that encompasses other species and ecosystems must be embraced as "an evolutionary possibility and an ecological necessity."[2] Like the picture of the Earth from space, this is a call to expand our moral attention. However, Leopold's expansion of ethics is not as broad as Gore's call; rather than attending to the entire Earth, Leopold calls for attention to the ecosystem of a particular mountain.

Still a third scalar view of environmental ethics is apparent in the work of the conservationist economist E. F. Schumacher. In *Small Is Beautiful*, another classic environmentalist text, Schumacher argues that human beings in contemporary cultures have become distracted and ungrounded by life in a global economy, and as a result we have great difficulty acknowledging the particulars of our own communities. Schumacher therefore calls for an ethics focused on a more sensible, local scale rather than on sweeping universal claims. Arguing that our culture suffers "from an almost universal idolatry of giantism," Schumacher's thesis is that the most vital contemporary ethical project is "to insist on the virtues of smallness." He argues that global ideas and systems are too complicated and too grand for real people ever to understand or relate to them meaningfully. As an alternative, he calls for technologies and political policies designed and enacted on a more local, familiar, "human scale."[3]

Although they are obviously making different arguments, Schumacher, Leopold, and Gore have in common the insight that ecological ethics must incorporate a careful and rigorous attention to the scale of human morality. For each, the question of how human beings should relate to the natural world is in large part a question of the scope of our awareness. The fundamental moral question common to all three might be characterized as: How encompassing should our moral attention be?

That question is crucial for any effort to conserve biodiversity. Gore's perspective calls for a global response to global biodiversity destruction, a united human effort in the face of a challenge all humans share. Schumacher's perspective calls for attention to our local human communities, and our immediately local flora and fauna, asking for a deep commitment to a particular habitat rather than a broad responsibility to the biodiversity of ecosystems or of the entire planet. Leopold's argument calls for an intermediate level of thinking, attention to the life and land of our ecosystems and regions as well as to the fellow human beings in our societies.

Such perspectives about the scale of conservation must be analyzed both scientifically and morally. To make such thinking more possible, this chapter offers tools from scientific ecology, hierarchy theory, and environmental philosophy with which to recognize the scalar choices inherent in the project of conservation. The scientists and thinkers cited here show that even when we agree on a goal such as the conservation of biodiversity, we must still think carefully and closely about what we seek to conserve, how our conservation will develop, and how much we hope to accomplish with it.

Ecological Tools for Scalar Choices

Scientific ecologists provide an important set of tools with which to think about what is at stake in decisions about the scale of our attention. Ecologist Simon Levin writes that scale is "the fundamental conceptual problem in ecology, if not in all of science."[4] In this context, scale refers to the choices researchers make about how to measure and establish boundaries around their subject matter. Calling this a "problem" means that it is the source of myriad fascinating and pivotal questions with which, Levin argues, ecologists must deal throughout their work.

The most common ecological measurements of scale involve the physical size of a subject and its variability over time. To simplify discussions of these observational perspectives, ecologists frequently identify the scales of their attention by naming the "resolution" and "extent" of their data. Resolution clarifies the unit of measurement that has been attended to, referencing "the smallest temporal or spatial intervals in an observation set." Extent, on the other hand, shows how broad a scale has been accounted for, referring to "the total area or length of time over which observations of a particular [resolution] are made."[5] This distinction is perhaps most readily understandable with a comparison to photography: The resolution of a picture refers to how much detail has been captured, and the extent tells us the size of what has been photographed. Similarly a researcher studying an ecological system must identify a resolution—how carefully and how narrowly will it be examined?—and an extent—how large an area will be studied?—of attention.

Such measurements are important to ecologists because the phenomena they study vary vastly in the resolution and extent required to understand them. A scientist who wants to understand how an organism participates in an ecosystem will make very different choices about the resolution and extent of her attention based on whether she is studying an elephant or a bacterium. In other words, scale is important because the spatial and temporal measurements with which a system or organism is observed determine what an ecologist will observe and what she will miss.[6] Furthermore, ecologists attempting to understand a complicated ecosystem—in which elephants, bacteria, and countless other species and processes interact—must find ways to combine measurements at such divergent scales into a coherent data set, a process called "scaling."

Perhaps the most important claim ecologists make about scale is that researchers must be deliberate and open about the resolution and extent of their observations: ecological work must reflect an awareness of scale and carefully explain which scales have been chosen. Such deliberation is especially important because it is all too easy to view the world at the scales that come most naturally and thereby miss a great deal of what is going on. As the theoretical ecologists Thomas Hoekstra and Timothy Allen observed, "Most animals experience their environment at scales different from the field biologist. . . . Even reasonable attention to scaling can be misplaced because the animals lie in a space defined by criteria independent of human perceptual categories."[7] The more aware and explicit a researcher can be about the scale of her own attention, the thinking goes, the more aware she and her readers can be about what is understood and what might have been missed.[8]

Of course the choices researchers make about scale are much broader than the differences between tiny and large organisms because most ecologists also study the much more complicated ecosystems in which organisms live. To differentiate, monitor, and disclose all the various scales of attention necessary to this work, ecologists have developed a common set of hierarchical levels of attention, nested within one another. For instance, the organism articulates a level of attention to individual creatures, whether they are bacteria or elephants. This is one level of attention, nested within ecosystems, which are made up of multiple organisms and their immediate environments. Ecosystems are, in turn, nested within landscapes, which are made up of multiple ecosystems and encompass a larger area. Landscapes are nested within biomes, which are nested within the planetary system. Each of these is a category of organization, a way of mapping the natural world and conceptualizing its variety into a helpful guide for researchers.[9]

Such hierarchical thinking reminds ecologists to pay attention to the ways structured bodies such as ecosystems or complex organisms are made up of substructures, and no structure can be understood without paying attention to its interaction with others. Furthermore, any part of a system likely plays multiple roles within it. For example, an elephant represents a subsystem nested within a larger structure (such as a forest ecosystem), but it is also itself made up of subsystems (including organs and cells). The living world in this view is a set of boundaried entities that contain and are contained within entities at other levels of scale. Ecology is therefore not the study of organisms and environments connected in simple, linear ways; rather, it assumes that organisms and environments encompass and make up one another and thus must be studied at a wide range of scales and levels of attention.

Understanding life in this hierarchical manner helps build scalar awareness. In general an ecologist studying organisms should work at a smaller extent and higher resolution than one attempting to understand an entire landscape because organisms are physically smaller and tend to change more quickly. At the same time, an ecologist making a claim about the planetary system as a whole will of necessity be speaking at an incredibly broad scale and so will not be able to study high-resolution details, particularities, or short-term dynamics.

With their scalar awareness and hierarchical levels, ecologists remind us that scientific descriptions of the world are always and inevitably descriptions of parts of the world. The attention required to understand a particular ecosystem has a certain resolution and extent, so details will be missed, as will the broad phenomena of which this system is just one small part. A coherent and useful explanation of that system will of necessity elide what is happening in the landscape of which it is a part and the organisms nested inside it. This not only calls ecologists to work at multiple scales and levels of attention but also to recognize that there are inevitable trade-offs—that in studying certain scales, they must choose not to study others.[10]

Again, the parallel to photography is helpful: to see the details of a bee's pollen-soaked legs and the flower on which it rests, a photographer takes a narrowly focused picture centered exclusively on that subject, accepting that her photograph will not record the vast world surrounding the insect and the plant. On the contrary, when the same photographer wants to capture the majesty of a mountain range, she accepts that the details of each leaf and life on the mountainside will not be visible in her picture. When astronauts photograph the Earth from space, they know that the broad extent of their picture will prevent the capture of high-resolution details of particular mountain peaks or flowers. It is possible to take all three kinds of pictures, but not at the same time. This is a scalar trade-off, and ecologists help to remind us that such trade-offs are inevitable whenever we pay attention to the natural world.

The Scales of Ecological Ethics

When studying biodiversity, ecologists mark scalar differences by distinguishing the variety of life with three familiar categories: genetic, species, and ecosystemic diversity. These are hierarchical levels, and they offer a set of lenses from which ecologists must choose when focusing their attention on biodiversity. A researcher focusing on genetic diversity will pay attention to individual organisms and will likely be concerned with a shorter time span and physical area than one who is interested in studying a species as a whole. An even larger scale of attention is required to learn about the diversity within and between ecosystems. Like any ecological work, research on biodiversity involves choices about resolution and extent, and these choices must be explicit and carefully made.

Awareness of scalar choices not only helps us to understand ecological research, but it also begins to develop a *moral* question about how we should pay attention, because concerns about level and scale apply to how we live in the world just as much as to how we describe it. Conservationists and ethicists, too, must decide about the scales of our attention and advocacy. While virtually all agree that biodiversity is a multiscalar concept, there are differences about how fully multiscalar conservation efforts should be. With full awareness of the importance of biodiversity across a wide range of scales and levels, we must seek the optimal level on which to focus conservation efforts.

Philosopher Bryan Norton offers a helpful vocabulary for this task. Even if we can assume that there is broad consensus that biodiversity should be conserved, he writes, "the meaning of that consensus, especially its meaning for preservation priorities, has not been worked out. Should our goal be to protect genes? Individuals? Populations? Species? Communities? Ecosystems? All of the above? None of the above?"[11] We must distinguish and choose among various levels of attention. Informed by ecological science and hierarchy theory, Norton has developed a set of three hierarchical levels of morality for just this purpose.

The first and narrowest level of moral attention is the local, an ethics that focuses on individuals, their contexts, and their immediate needs. A local ethics asks what will serve a particular entity or particular place in the near future. The next level up is what Norton calls "community-oriented," including a system of individuals organized into social and ecological structures, with temporal concern extending across a full century. Thinking on the community level, an ethicist asks what will be good for a society or species for the next century. The third and final level is "global," attending to the entire planetary community over an indefinite time. Ethical questions raised at this level concern the good of Earth and all life thereon for the foreseeable future and beyond.[12]

Articulating these hierarchical levels allows Norton to argue that "environmental problems are, most basically, problems of scale"[13] and to thereby help conservationists and ethicists pay attention to the choices we make about the scales and levels of our attention. Using this language, it is easier to understand the differences between the three perspectives introduced at the beginning of this chapter: E. F. Schumacher worries that human beings lose our balance when we try to think at the global scale and manage the whole planet. He therefore calls his readers to become comfortable with the "human" scale at the first level of moral attention, arguing that "small is beautiful" precisely to encourage a more focused attention on our immediate environments and time scales. Aldo Leopold, in contrast, calls for an expansive ethics that would encompass other species and entire ecosystems. His is a morality extending outward from the first level to the second, learning to see ourselves as a part of a broader community that includes the land and other species as well as ourselves. Al Gore offers still another view, suggesting that the crisis of environmental degradation is so encompassing that it can only be addressed at the third, planetary scale. His is a global morality, stressing the common identity of all creatures on Earth and developing an incredibly broad moral attention.

Norton's typology of local, community, and global thinking is a tool with which to recognize the scalar and hierarchical choices we are making. It makes a difference whether we focus on our own individual relationships to a particular place, on the relationship of our society to the land and systems on which it depends, or on the relationship of the human species as a whole to all the Earth's natural systems.

The scale of attention we use defines the extent of our moral attention and thereby determines the degree of resolution we can have.

To think about the entire Earth on an indefinite time scale is an impressively expansive vision, but doing so makes it difficult to focus on the particularities of individual lives and individual needs. To focus on the particular needs of particular creatures in a particular place allows such high-resolution attention, but it requires a relatively narrow scope of attention. These choices, with an awareness of the trade-offs inherent in them, are vital for any ethics that takes ecology seriously.

Norton emphasizes the middle scale as the most practical and ethical, a position he credits to Leopold. Indeed, Norton labels Leopold's call to think like a mountain "the single most dramatic, creative, and productive idea in the history of environmentalism."[14] But the power of Leopold's image is not just its call to thinking on the community level; it also concisely communicates the importance of thinking across scales, calling human individuals to learn to recognize the levels of our attention. Thus, the central idea Norton draws from Leopold—consistent with the work of Schumacher and Gore—is not about which scale is primary but about the importance of paying attention to scale.

Norton offers a multiscalar tool for ecological ethics, suggesting that each environmental problem will have different scalar attributes and should be approached on different levels. He does not suggest that we should choose among the three available levels of moral thinking once and for all but rather that we should draw upon the appropriate level depending on the kind of problem we are addressing. This begs the question of what kind of problem biodiversity loss might be, a question about which conservation biologists have thought extensively.

Scaling the Conservation of Biodiversity

Based on both ecological science and environmental philosophy, it is clear that the conservation of biodiversity must be attentive to issues of scale, carefully considering the proper "place" from which to work. Is biodiversity loss so pervasive and singular that we must think about it as a single, global problem? Or is it best understood at the level of communities and ecosystems, focusing on assemblies of species and processes? Alternatively, might biodiversity be best preserved if we concentrate our attention locally, emphasizing a particular population or species familiar to individuals and asking them to conserve it?

The narrowest level of attention, local and high resolution, is best represented in conservation biology by those who focus on particular species as the object of conservation. Even if biodiversity should be understood as a broad and multiscalar concept, many argue that the most effective and practical policies of conservation will come from a clear and consistent attention to particular species. So Thomas Brooks and his colleagues argue in *Conservation Biology* that species data should be central in determining the focus of conservation efforts: "Species are essential in conservation planning and cannot be disregarded or replaced by broad-scale surrogates." They support this argument with the observation that "although the variety of life ranges from single genes to the entire biosphere, many argue that the species is the fundamental unit of biodiversity."[15]

Brooks and his colleagues reference E. O. Wilson, who has frequently identified species as "the fundamental unit" of measurement and is without doubt the most public advocate of a species-focused conservation strategy. Indeed, Wilson argues that while genes and ecosystems are important, "the real units that can be seen and counted as corporeal objects are the species."[16] Following logically from this claim that species are the most recognizable component of biodiversity is the idea that diversity measured at the species level will be the easiest to monitor, to conserve, and to convince society to support. Wilson's argument also demonstrates a strategic ethical motivation behind the focus on species: because they are the "fundamental unit" of the natural world, humanity has evolved with an awareness of species and thus has a natural predilection to treat them with moral consideration.

However, some conservation biologists find this focus on species problematic, limiting the public's perception of what biodiversity really is and what true conservation requires. Instead, they argue, conservation should take place on the second level—a broader emphasis on communities over a longer time. These conservationists frequently focus on ecosystems, working to save species, populations, and genetic diversity indirectly by conserving the habitats upon which they depend. Insect ecologist Terry Erwin puts this starkly: "I'm not interested in species at all. I'm interested in ecosystems, and habitats, and microhabitats."[17] Frequently, ecologists who think this way call for aggressive strategies of land conservation, attempting to restrict human expansion into certain types of ecosystems. In other words, they seek to create protected areas for the sake of the systems rather than particular species within them. Such "site-based biodiversity conservation" ensures the conservation of ecosystems and can even extend to those that do not happen to contain endangered species.[18]

By focusing on the ecosystem level rather than species, these ecologists claim, they are able to identify areas more representative of biodiversity as a whole and to offer a more wide-ranging and consistent strategy of conservation. Like most scalar arguments, this is partly about moral attention: the assumption in this camp is that we human beings must become concerned with more than other species, that we must also learn to pay attention to the systems that make life possible. Frequently this is expressed in terms of respect for "ecosystem integrity," which many conservation biologists see as a fundamental moral principle. This is clearly revealed in David Takacs's interviews with conservation biologists. For instance, David Ehrenfeld told Takacs: "I think that the highest priority for conservation ought to be relatively intact ecosystems," and Ke Chung Kim said: "The ultimate goal in my mind is basically the biodiversity or preservation of ecological systems."[19]

Just as the ecosystem focus argues that a broader level than species is necessary, a group of ecologists who emphasize the third scale of moral attention argue that even the ecosystem might be too narrow. These thinkers believe that conservation strategies must not be limited by national borders in determining which species and systems are in need of conservation. Instead, strategies should be developed in the context of the planetary biosphere as a whole, creating a truly global strategy for conservation. If the loss of life's variety is a global problem, these thinkers argue, then it must be understood in the widest context possible. As conservation biologist Reed Noss puts it, when it comes to conservation, "the defensibility of thinking small has vanished with increasing ecological understanding. . . . A major lesson is to consider each phenomenon in a broader, ultimately global, context; that is, to 'think big.' "[20]

Drawing on this broadest approach to the conservation of Earth's biodiversity, Carl Folke and his coauthors argue that conservation is shortsighted if it works only to create secluded areas protected from development. Given that humanity already dominates the vast majority of Earth's ecosystems, they argue that conserving particular communities will not be a sufficient strategy: "Whether we like it or not the growing human impact on the planet is a fact. 'Keeping humans out of nature' through a protected-area strategy may buy time, but it does not address the factors in society driving the loss of biodiversity."[21]

To conserve particular ecosystems is not enough, they argue, because it remains in some sense a local rather than a global effort, not changing human behavior as a whole, just restricting where human beings can act. The answer, instead, is to change the ways human beings act so that people can be parts of systems in which biodiversity thrives. They continue: "Most reserves cannot alone deal with ecological attributes that cover large scales. . . . The goal of a conservation strategy should be to protect not all biodiversity in some areas, but biodiversity thresholds in all areas."[22] This is thinking at the third level, an encompassing attention that calls us to see biodiversity in a global context first and foremost.

Triage, Hot Spots, and Thinking Big

Clearly there are important arguments in conservation biology for attention and action on each of these three scales. In part the debate over which level of conservation should be primary is a debate about how much biodiversity *can* be conserved. Advocates for global conservation tend to emphasize that the problem of degradation is too large, too sweeping, and too deep to be solved by anything but a global and totalizing effort. Advocates for local and community conservation tend to stress that their goals are more realistic and attainable, that a more narrow focus is the best way to conserve *some* biodiversity in the face of inevitable loss.

As an example of this practical advocacy for focused attention, one book on biodiversity concludes by noting: "The world is destined to lose some species. There is no other possible outcome, given an expanding human population, and expanding consumption." In light of this, the authors argue, societies must make decisions "about managing and preserving regional diversity," must develop priorities about which species and which areas to fight to conserve.[23] This is a call for what many call "conservation triage," developing clear priorities and accepting the inevitably tragic consequences of that strategy for some species and ecosystems.[24]

Perhaps the most developed approach to setting such priorities is the notion of biodiversity hot spots. Identifying such hot spots involves tracking regions of the world with particularly large numbers of species that are under particular threat of destruction. According to Norman Myers, a chief advocate for the idea: "As much as 20% of species of plants and a still higher proportion of species of animals are confined to 0.5% of Earth's land surface. These species are endemic to their areas, so if the local habitats are eliminated, these species will suffer extinction. The areas in question are indeed threatened with imminent habitat destruction."[25]

Given these facts, Myers suggests, the bulk of conservation resources should be focused on that 0.5 percent of land area. Such prioritizing means devoting fewer resources to other areas of the world, but identifying and focusing on these hot spots is the way to "protect the most species per dollar invested."[26] This is a deliberate focus on the first and second level of attention, an acceptance that global biodiversity cannot be saved as a whole and an attempt to instead focus attention on particular ecosystems and species.

Advocates of global conservation refuse to accept the premise that some biodiversity must be sacrificed. David Falk, for instance, takes a firm stance: "You cannot persuade me that we are in a triage situation with respect to the resources to save life on earth. I do not accept it. I think it's a completely fallacious argument. Just as medicine tries to save every patient they can, that has absolutely got to be our mission."[27] The mission of ecologists and environmentalists, in this view, is to fight for all biodiversity and not to accept any partial solutions. Behind such a claim is the assumption that human societies are capable of vastly more conservation than has so far been attempted or even imagined, and that to accept the limitations of current methods and commitments is to refuse to push for better means and more resources. Reed Noss, who has called on conservationists to "think big," and therefore advocates the conservation of global biodiversity, develops the argument this way with coauthor Allen Cooperrider: "We must also think big in terms of ambition and try to do more with conservation than we ever thought possible. . . . To think only in terms of what is politically reasonable, practical, or financially profitable is shortsighted. At worst, a lack of ambition and acceptance of the status quo is an invitation to mass extinction."[28] These ecologists refuse to focus on particular ecosystems or species because they believe that a call for expansive conservation can inspire the public to commit to a diverse world. This approach is very different from triage and hot spots, and the difference is primarily about the level of attention.

It is important to emphasize that all the conservation biologists cited here agree that biodiversity is valuable and that it should be conserved. They also agree that biodiversity is a multiscalar concept, a complicated reality that exists at more than one level. The challenge of conserving biodiversity becomes clear when we recognize that agreement about its importance and its complexity is only the beginning of a conversation; we must also decide about *how* we should conserve it, on which level we should focus our attention, and what scale of biodiversity we should emphasize in rallying the public around it. It is common to hear arguments that the variety of life should be protected at the species, ecosystem, and global levels, and all these are admirable goals. But given the limited time and resources of the conservation movement, which level is most important and which should receive the most attention?

The Necessity of Scalar Choices

The work of ecological scientists, the debates of conservation biologists, the categories of Bryan Norton, and the differences between the three environmentalists cited at the beginning of this chapter all help to establish the same basic idea: we must make choices about the scales of our attention when we think about any environmental issue, including biodiversity. While there are good reasons to pay attention to both local species loss and global biodiversity degradation, these are different kinds of attention, and we must consider the possibility that it is not always realistic to address both simultaneously. Even when we agree that biodiversity should be conserved, there are important debates to have about the scale of its conservation.

The basic core of the scalar analysis articulated here comes from ecological science. In that context, despite the fact that consideration of these issues has been an extensive project in that science for at least the last thirty years, there remain vast areas of disagreement and countless unanswered questions about what scales and levels should be of primary importance. To pay attention to scale in ecology is a complicated and challenging enterprise. This will be just as true for the attempt to scale our attention in ecological ethics.

Such complexity and the inevitability of scalar trade-offs set the context for the next chapter, which will offer an argument that a Christian

ethics of biodiversity must consider all three levels of attention as partners in conservation. Christians should, in my view, agree with E. F.
Schumacher about the importance of thinking locally, and with Aldo
Leopold about the importance of thinking like a mountain, and with
Al Gore about the importance of thinking globally. This does not mean
that we can avoid trade-offs between different scales of attention—this
chapter has made clear that such trade-offs are inevitable—but rather
that we must constantly and continually make scalar choices, shift-
ing between different levels of attention to develop a truly multiscalar
ethics.

Notes

1. See Gore, *An Inconvenient Truth*, 15. See also Gore, *Earth in the Balance*.

2. See "The Land Ethic" and "Thinking Like a Mountain" in Leopold.

3. Schumacher, *Small Is Beautiful*, 66.

4. Levin, "Pattern and Scale," 1944.

5. R. V. O'Neill and A. W. King, "Homage to St. Michael; or, Why Are There
So Many Books on Scale?" in Peterson and Parker, *Ecological Scale*, 7. They use
the word "grain" rather than "resolution," which is common in ecological literature. I have chosen to use "resolution" because I believe it is a more acces-
sible concept to nonscientists and because in my understanding the two terms
are synonymous.

6. Levin, "Pattern and Scale," 1954.

7. Allen and Hoekstra, *Toward a Unified Ecology*, 155.

8. See especially Gardner et al., *Scaling Relations in Experimental Ecology*.

9. Ecologists draw this attention to "nested hierarchies" from the broader
findings of "hierarchy theory," a study of "how a system of discrete functional
elements or units linked at two or more scales operates." See Forman, *Land
Mosaics*, 9. Theorist Timothy Allen reminds his colleagues that hierarchies
should not be seen as straightforward representations of the world, but rather
as a heuristic model: "the philosophically sophisticated scientist is not interested in the model being correct but is keenly interested in where and the
extent to which the model maps to the material system." T. F. H. Allen, "The
Landscape 'Level' Is Dead: Persuading the Family to Take It Off the Respirator"
in Peterson and Parker, *Ecological Scale*, 47.

10. Levin writes: "The existence of these tradeoffs makes clear that there is
no natural level of description: The problem is not to choose the correct scale
of description, but rather to recognize that change is taking place on many
scales at the same time, and that it is the interaction among phenomena on

different scales that must occupy our attention." Levin, "Pattern and Scale," 1947.

11. Norton, *Searching for Sustainability*, 376.

12. Ibid., 67–72. See also Norton, *Sustainability*, 230–31. Norton refers to these three categories as "scales," but based on the terms I have adopted from ecological theory, I identify them as "levels" because they concern the categories of observation that govern our attention rather than the particular measurements.

13. Norton, *Searching*, 311.

14. Norton, *Sustainability*, 455.

15. Brooks, Rodrigues, and da Fonseca, "Protected Areas and Species," 617.

16. Wilson, *The Future of Life*, 13–14.

17. Quoted in Takacs, *Idea of Biodiversity*, 70.

18. See Redford and Richter, "Conservation of Biodiversity."

19. Takacs, *Idea of Biodiversity*, 69–75.

20. Reed Noss, "Issues of Scale in Conservation Biology," in Fiedler and Jain, *Conservation Biology*, 248. In the same context, Noss argues that conservationists should extend the temporal scale at which they work in order to think truly long-term, moving from the goal of "sustaining viable populations of existing species" to creating the conditions for "future evolutionary diversification" (245).

21. Folke, Holling, and Perrings, "Biological Diversity," 1019. In part this is an argument about the relationship of human societies to biodiversity conservation, asserting that if biological diversity and human society at its contemporary scale are both to be conserved, it will be together rather than apart.

22. Ibid., 1021–22.

23. "Conclusion" in Kinzig, Pacala, and Tilman, *Functional Consequences of Biodiversity*, 329.

24. Ecologist Brian Walker states this perspective starkly: "Ecologically, all species are not created equally," and so some must be allowed to die off so that the limited resources of conservation can be dedicated to saving the others that scientists deem to be most vital to healthy functioning more broadly. Walker, "Biodiversity and Ecological Redundancy," 20.

25. Myers, "The Rich Diversity of Biodiversity Issues" in Reaka-Kudla, Wilson, and Wilson, eds., *Biodiversity II*, 125.

26. Myers et al., "Biodiversity Hotspots," 853.

27. Quoted in Takacs, *Idea of Biodiversity*, 60.

28. Noss and Cooperrider, *Saving Nature's Legacy*, 94.

Chapter 5

Multiscalar Christian Ecological Ethics

The scientists and thinkers cited in chapter 4 demonstrate that an ethics of biodiversity should be multiscalar, attending to multiple levels of attention and learning from ecological theory about how to identify and distinguish those levels. Conservationists must be aware of the scales of our attention, recognize the trade-offs inherent in scalar choices, and struggle to nurture a flexible, multiscalar approach to our work. This chapter brings Christian ethics into the conversation about multiscalar morality in order to develop a set of tools with which to address this question: How should Christians make choices between the conservation of the biodiversity immediately around us, the biodiversity of a broader regional context, and global biodiversity?

A nuanced answer to this question requires two steps. First, we must recognize that Christians have resources within our traditions by which to develop a faithful multiscalar ethics. Drawing particularly on the Catholic ideas of subsidiarity and socialization, a theologically informed language of Christian attention to scalar issues will take shape. This language then helps in the second step, which shows how three Christian ethicists concerned about the environment have already begun developing multiscalar ethics and applying them to biodiversity. The works of Larry Rasmussen, John Hart, and Michael Northcott reveal that while naming ethics as multiscalar might be new, the careful and deliberate attention to scalar issues it signifies is not. The language of socialization and subsidiarity and the work of these three ethicists offer the insights needed to answer the question of scale for a Christian ethics of biodiversity, advocating a multiscalar attention that remains aware of the trade-offs and risks inherent at each scale of thinking.

Resources for Multiscalar Theology:
Subsidiarity and Socialization

Perhaps the most useful Christian resources in the development of a multiscalar ethics are the Catholic principles of socialization and subsidiarity. Socialization affirms that individuals exist in and can only be understood within their social context: the communities, organizations, and nations of which we are a part inevitably shape our lives in significant ways. The complementary principle of subsidiarity asserts that the global systems of nation–states and global communities, while important, should be in service to rather than dominant over the more local and individual expressions of human life. In these two principles, we find a Christian attention to multiple levels of attention and a clear expression of multiscalar ethics. Neither has been formally developed in the context of ecological ethics or conservation, but close study reveals that they have much to offer this work.

Subsidiarity, an idea often traced back to the twelfth-century theologian Thomas Aquinas, is widely influential today, frequently discussed by political scientists and government officials, and explicitly included in the constitution of the European Union. Within theological circles, its contemporary influence began with Pope Pius XI's 1931 encyclical *Quadragesimo anno*. Written in response to the rapid expansion of economic powers and the increasingly interdependent nature of political life at the beginning of the twentieth century, this letter is in part an argument that theological morality is essential to modern political and economic life. In this context Pius asserts the principle of subsidiarity to affirm the continued importance of individuals and the local communities that shape them as moral beings. He admits that, given the growth of industrial technologies and the increasingly global scope of human influence, "much that was formerly done by small bodies can nowadays be accomplished by large organizations" and thereby justifies the existence of large and powerful nation–states. But Pius sees these states as "overwhelmed and submerged by endless affairs and responsibilities," increasingly expected not only to manage national affairs but also to offer the moral formation and community that can be provided only by smaller-scale organizations. According to Pius, "true and genuine social order" depends upon a commitment to the common good, a commitment that takes shape only in more personal groups where members can be empowered and supported as individuals.[1] The trend toward increasingly large-scale activities and governance cannot be sustained unless human individuals and their local communities continue to thrive.

This situation justifies the principle of subsidiarity, which acknowledges that large social structures should see themselves primarily as in service to individuals and small communities. Pius writes:

> One should not withdraw from individuals and commit to the community what they can accomplish by their own enterprise and industry. So, too, it is an injustice and at the same time a grave evil and a disturbance of right order to transfer to the larger and higher collectivity functions which can be performed and provided for by lesser and subordinate bodies. Inasmuch as every social activity should, by its very nature, prove a help to members of the body social, it should never destroy or absorb them.[2]

The emphasis here is on human beings and their immediate communities, which should not be dismissed as "subordinate" in our ever-expanding, globalizing world. As a corrective to this trend, Pius's principle argues that large structures and institutions should see themselves as subsidiary to the individuals and local communities that make them up, and any problem that can be solved at the local or individual level should be.

Of course, despite the clear emphasis on human personhood in the principle of subsidiarity, it is based on the assumption that humans are social beings, dependent upon and necessarily participants in communities and institutional structures. Pius's hope for "true and genuine social order" and his reference to "the body social" make this clear. In other words, subsidiarity does not advocate individualism by claiming that human beings should be treated as distinct and independent bodies but rather assumes that every person exists in a network of social relationships. It calls people to accept and embrace those relationships, balancing their individuality and local communities with their membership in national and global systems.

Thirty-four years after Pope Pius XI's encyclical, the Second Vatican Council emphasized this balance, with the document *Gaudium et spes* instructing that the people served by large organizations and institutions must, in turn, devote themselves to "the advancement of the common good," attending "to the welfare of the whole human family, which is tied together by the manifold bonds linking races, peoples, and nations."[3] This is the principle of socialization, which calls attention to the responsibility human beings have to the broader systems of which they are a part. While subsidiarity responds to the dangers of growing systems that consign individuals to insignificant anonymity, socialization responds to the dangers of an individualistic culture in which people too often think only of themselves and their own well-being.

As social structures have continued to develop and change over the last fifty years, the need for both principles has become clear: human beings in the contemporary world have reason to be cautious about both the dangers of individualism and the dangers of treating people as if they did not matter. So Catholic social teaching calls for both subsidiarity and socialization, for a morality that treats human beings with appropriate dignity and value while also attending to and serving the entirety of the human family. The common good is best achieved when individuals accept their role in society and society respects the integrity of individuals and local communities.

Although they have frequently been interpreted as guidelines for political and economic systems, subsidiarity and socialization are also guidelines about how we human beings should think about our place in the world. *Quadragesimo anno* is explicitly concerned with "moral discipline," and *Gaudium et spes* calls for a shift in attitudes, cautioning against a simplistic trust in and acceptance of any single social structure or level of societal order. Although this language is not used, the principles implicitly make scale a moral issue. Subsidiarity and socialization guide us not only in the distribution of power but also in the multiscalar ways we should think about morality.

Understood this way, the principles of subsidiarity and socialization offer a resource for multiscalar ecological ethics, although it is important to emphasize a point that was not explicit in twentieth-century Catholic social teaching: human systems are always and inevitably in relationship to natural systems. The structured levels of human societies cannot exist without the biological, ecological, and planetary structures that created us and support our continued life. The human and social systems that have traditionally been considered in discussions of subsidiarity and socialization must now be understood as subsystems within the broader structures of creation as a whole; our nations, our communities, our economies, and our selves are all parts of ecosystems, landscapes, and biomes. When socialization calls for attention to "the common good," we should understand this even more broadly than the "human family," extending outward to a family encompassing all of God's creatures. Similarly, while subsidiarity has emphasized the importance of human personhood, it is important to consider the possibility that we should also put our social structures and institutions in service to the other beings with whom we share the planet.[4]

When adapted in this way these principles are clearly relevant to the development of a multiscalar Christian ecological ethics, and they will help us to understand the work of three ethicists, each of which has contributed to the project of developing multiscalar Christian responses to biodiversity loss.

The Global Variety of Life: Larry Rasmussen's Earth Community

Larry Rasmussen is a Lutheran ethicist with a longstanding commitment to nurturing a faithful Christian response to environmental degradation. Rasmussen's most developed consideration of scalar issues comes in *Earth Community, Earth Ethics*, a book written in response to contemporary environmental crises that argues that, given the seriousness of the problems facing humanity, "our most basic impulses and activities must now be measured by one stringent criterion—their contribution to an earth ethic and their advocacy of sustainable earth community."[5] Rasmussen bases his central idea of an "earth community" in large part on scientific ecology—from which he learned that "nature is a community"—and he argues that we must learn to take this fact seriously as a *moral* directive: "All that exists, coexists. Community rests at the heart of things." Thus, "all creatures great and small, and inorganic matter as well, have worth that rests proximately in their membership in the Community of Life."[6] Recognition of the "earth community" is a necessity for Rasmussen because it is the only way we will recognize that we are part of the world we are degrading, that we depend in a fundamental way upon and are fully interconnected with the structures and networks of this planet.[7]

The opposite of such global attention and consideration in Rasmussen's view is "apartheid thinking," which dismisses the interconnections and interdependence between human communities and between the human species and the rest of the world. Such thinking, which pulls things apart rather than linking them, "will never resolve earth's distress. It will only exacerbate it."[8] We must instead think as part of the Earth in recognition of the complexity and vitality of our connections to the entirety of its systems.

While Rasmussen does not use the word, his central argument is an ecologically informed version of socialization, calling readers to pay attention to the larger systems of which they are a part, to commit themselves to the common good of the entire planet. He worries that just as our habits of thinking in the modern world can be too individualistic, they can also be too anthropocentric, focusing provincially on our species while ignoring the grand and inspiring world in which our species participates. This argument emphasizes the importance of scaling our attention outward, embracing Norton's third level by attending to global issues and encompassing as much of the creation in our moral consideration as possible. Such broad-scale thinking is clearly evident throughout Rasmussen's Earth ethics, which calls for an "ecumenical" response to environmental degradation and critiques economic globalization for the fact that it is not "truly global," leaving behind poor people and the nonhuman creation.[9]

Rasmussen advocates expansive thinking, a perspective emerging from the picture of Earth in space.[10] However, his insight into the multiscalar dimensions of ethics is evident in the fact that he balances the call to scale up with explicit attention to the necessity of small-scale thinking. Indeed, he explicitly calls on the principle of subsidiarity as one of his "norms of sustainability."[11] Thus, while the primary emphasis of *Earth Community, Earth Ethics* may be a call for global thinking, Rasmussen attends carefully to the necessity of the smaller and more personal scales that contribute to planetary attention. He recognizes that a healthy Earth community depends upon healthy neighborhoods, ecosystems, nations, and biomes. The key to Earth ethics, he concludes, "is *appropriate* scale and action" solving problems that are truly global on a global scale while allowing local communities to address the problems that are manageable on that scale.[12]

To emphasize this point Rasmussen explicitly appeals to the variety of life as a model, arguing that an Earth community constructed of numerous and diverse healthy subcommunities will be resilient, just as a variety of genes, species, and ecosystems makes natural systems resilient: "The practices of economy and society ought to be ordered in such a way as to be able to shift and adapt, like nature, to changing conditions. In nature, biodiversity is the mechanism by which adaptation to demanding changes occurs, the means by which nature is resilient in the face of often traumatic changes. As such, it is the basic source of all future wealth and well-being."[13] Biodiversity thus relates to Rasmussen's caution against "apartheid thinking," helping him to emphasize that diversity should be embraced as a vital characteristic of natural systems, including human communities. Earth ethics must not ignore the differences and distinctions inherent within Earth's systems.

This attention to diversity reveals Rasmussen's awareness that global thinking is not enough on its own, that such a large-scale attention should not blind us to the importance of the particularities and differences within Earth's systems and human communities. He makes this explicit by noting that it is too sweeping and too simplistic to say that "'we humans' are presently degrading 'nature,'" because both humanity and the natural world are diverse systems in which different parts participate in and respond to environmental degradation in different ways.[14] A key example comes from the reality of environmental injustice, the fact that people who are poor and marginalized—who frequently consume less and therefore cause less degradation—bear a disproportionate burden of the scarcities, pollution, and dangers caused by environmental degradation. Rasmussen therefore learned from the environmental justice movement that "not all are being poisoned equally, or even breathing the same air. . . . Environmental problems typically shake out much the way others do: the population that derives the benefits is not the same population that suffers the loss."[15] To make this vital point requires *multiscalar* thinking, attending to the distinctions and differences within human and natural communities while simultaneously calling for acceptance of a singular Earth community.

Rasmussen's argument for an Earth ethics is about nurturing a global awareness, an incredibly broad extent of attention, but he insightfully insists that we must maintain a fine enough resolution of attention to recognize the crucial differences between human communities. The ideal of an Earth community emphasizes the connections and relationships between diverse human and nonhuman communities but nevertheless recognizes this diversity. This is, therefore, one example of a multiscalar Christian ethics of biodiversity.

Biodiversity and Community: John Hart's Sacramental Commons

Another example comes from John Hart, the Catholic ethicist mentioned in chapter 3 as one of the foremost contemporary thinkers about sacramentality and its importance for contemporary environmental thinking. Embracing what he calls a "sacramental consciousness," Hart asserts: "The universe as a whole and in its parts reveals the presence of its Creator," and this attention to both the "whole" of the cosmos and the distinct "parts" that make it up demonstrate a multiscalar attention to morality.[16] Hart draws upon the work of Augustine, Aquinas, and many other luminaries in the Christian tradition to develop his sacramental perspective, but his primary source is contemporary Catholic Social Teaching, particularly the U.S. Catholic Bishops' letter *Renewing the Earth* and its discussion of a "sacramental universe."

Hart's book *Sacramental Commons* expands upon the bishops' sacramentality by offering an extended reflection of what they mean by "sacramental universe" and then working to localize it. While emphasizing the presence and revelation of the creator throughout the entirety of the creation is important, the complementary notion of a "sacramental commons" focuses upon "a moment and locus of human participation in the interactive presence and caring compassion of the Spirit who is immanent and participates in a complex cosmic dance of energies, elements, entities and events."[17] The commons exists on a smaller scale, implying that God is revealed and present in *this* community at *this* time. While the "sacramental universe" makes a claim about the eternal nature of creation, a sacramental commons refers to a more particular or personal experience. It attends to more particular spaces and times with more careful detail. Hart explains that the sacramental commons is an important localization of the sacramental universe because people can often recognize God's presence and mystery in the world when their attention shifts "from the macro to the micro, from the cosmos to the commons."[18]

Hart's argument is that we Christians must learn to pay attention to the ecosystems and regions in which we live. By emphasizing that sacramentality is a reality of *the commons*, of the localities and times familiar to our experience, Hart develops an intermediate-level sacramentality, appealing primarily to intraspecies communities across a region. Drawing upon this understanding he argues that a sacramental consciousness nurtures a commitment to "the common good," which he defines in two distinct ways: "First, it describes the collective well-being of a community, whether solely human in constitution or including the biotic community as a whole." In addition to this more focused claim, however, the common good also signifies "an Earth benefit" that encompasses "all of biokind."[19] These two definitions reveal Hart's multiscalar thinking and demonstrate his emphasis on balance: he calls Christians to devote themselves to the common good of all creatures but notes that the community of the more localized "commons" is also crucial. He simultaneously embraces socialization and subsidiarity.

This balanced, midscale attention is well reflected in Hart's discussion of biodiversity. His focus is not on a global phenomenon but rather on a bioregion and a species, with extensive analysis of the endangered salmon of the Columbia–Snake river system in the northwestern United States. Labeling the decline of salmon populations a tragic loss and a clear sign of disharmony between the salmon, the rivers, and the indigenous peoples of the region, Hart advocates change among the Euro-Americans who have fundamentally disrupted the system in the last centuries. To emphasize the agency and balance of power in this region, Hart chooses to write not that salmon are "going extinct" but rather that "salmon are being extincted" by the "hydroelectric dams and aluminum plants along the rivers, and overfishing by fish factory ships in the Pacific Ocean at locations of salmon fisheries and along salmon migratory paths."[20] In other words, it is the industrialized system of the European-influence culture that is causing salmon extinction, destroying the balance of this community of humans, fish, and ecosystems.

Learning particularly from the Wanapum, a native community that has fished the Columbia River for millennia, Hart argues that the traditions and attitudes of First Peoples model a more sustainable life in harmony with the salmon and the river. The dominant culture refuses to learn this lesson, he writes, because it lacks the commitment to sacramentality and justice that would be required. A consciousness that embraces the relationships between human cultures and the nonhuman world would stop extincting salmon and destroying their habitat, and it would commit to treating the indigenous peoples of the Columbia–Snake river system with justice and honesty. To view this bioregion as a sacramental commons would transform all the relationships within it, reshaping human lives even as it ensured a thriving salmon population. Such community-oriented attention to extinction and its remedy is balanced by a multiscalar attention to the broader implications of such thinking, as is clear in the argument that salmon should be seen as "a representative species [capable of] stimulating human consciousness of the intrinsic value of all species and abiotic nature, and catalyzing human conscience to translate that into committed efforts to benefit Earth and biokind."[21]

Unlike Rasmussen's Earth ethics, Hart's sacramental commons primarily emphasizes the importance of moral attention on the middle scale of bioregions, on particular communities rather than on a singular Earth community. However, like Rasmussen, Hart's scalar focus comes in the context of a multiscalar awareness, recognizing the continued importance of more global and more localized attention. He may devote much of his moral attention to the Columbia–Snake river system, but he also attends to the lives of particular people within it and to the broader, global implications of what he learned there. Hart's sacramental commons therefore provides another, vital example of a multiscalar Christian ethics of biodiversity.

Local Biodiversity: Michael Northcott's Ecology of the Parish

A final example comes from the work of Michael Northcott, an Anglican ethicist who wrote one of the most comprehensive and systematic accounts of how Christian theology and morality can respond to environmental degradation: *The Environment and Christian Ethics.* Like Hart and Rasmussen, Northcott is aware of the importance of scalar attention as an element in Christian ethics, but unlike them he is deeply suspicious of calls for global and broad moral attention. He instead develops a locally focused ethic seeking to conserve biodiversity by emphasizing the importance of local ecosystems to particular peoples in local communities.

In all his work Northcott emphasizes that ecological and environmental issues must be understood in the context of the political and economic structures that condition human lives and relationships to the creation. In part this grows out of his commitment to social justice, and his work emphasizes that environmental issues are most immediate and urgent for those who are poor and marginalized. While degraded land and scarce resources may currently inconvenience the wealthy of the world, they are life threatening for oppressed peoples: "For the peasant farmer or the landless rural labourer in drought-ridden Africa the state of the environment is a matter of basic survival."[22] According to Northcott, social injustice is caused by the same forces that cause environmental degradation: global capitalism, its incumbent industrial technologies, and the utilitarian philosophy that justifies both.

Northcott also connects capitalism, industrialism, and utilitarianism through their common attempt to assert universal authority over the world, noting that all are dangerously expansive: "The international economic system is too global, too vast and anonymous." The alternative to such global forces is to empower local communities "to find new ways of expressing democratic control over economic and technological processes, and of controlling their impacts on human and nonhuman goods in particular regions and habitats."[23]

Northcott's environmentalist vision primarily celebrates local communities and emphasizes the need to scale downward rather than upward. Environmentalists should not celebrate the rapid transportation of food and other commodities across the planet but should instead resist the careless linkages between all of industrialized humanity seamlessly in economic and political interdependence. Such globalism, he argues, "undermines the self-sufficiency and economic stability of local communities while generating other social and environmental costs in terms of noise and inconvenience for people living near main roads and airports, increases in the cost of food and increased energy costs in food production which impact negatively on human welfare and the environment."[24] Like E. F. Schumacher, therefore, Northcott seeks a human scale of life, a system that emphasizes local community, local food production, local resource usage, and local conservation.

Along these lines, Northcott questions the prevalence of the famous pictures of the whole Earth from space in environmentalist rhetoric, calling such pictures "full of ambiguity" because of the enormous cost required to take such photographs through the space program and "because of the distance it sets between the observer and the observed." Instead of presenting Earth as "a unitary sphere which is amenable to unitary management," he argues, environmentalist arguments should be multiple and diverse, adapted to the "particular places or communities of species which we inhabit."[25] Northcott names this an "ecology of the parish" based on his understanding of the traditional parish as "a uniquely local institution . . . defined by its proximity to land," which can inspire and organize resistance to environmental degradation in particular places rather than vague and abstract global protests.[26]

However, Northcott did not completely dismiss all global and large-scale thinking. His book ends by urging readers to recognize "that the world is also a parish," and so we must continue to also think globally, reform national and global structures, and care for people across the world. However, to see the world as a parish is to give primacy to the local scale, to trust that people first learn how to care for a place and others in small, intimate communities and that these must be the basis and foundation of ecological ethics.[27] Familiar Christian calls to treat people across the world as "neighbors" have the same emphasis: if I do not know and care for the people who live near me, then it is meaningless to see the poor and starving on a distant continent as neighbors I am called to love. In Northcott's view the local scale is primary, even if the regional and global scales remain important.

Clearly Northcott's vision of Christian ethics is one that heavily emphasizes subsidiarity. While he does not reject socialization entirely, he does argue that people will not recognize or value themselves if they are only members of global or even regional communities. Instead, he advocates attention to the common good on a local scale, at the parish level where people can encounter others face-to-face and develop long-term relationships with one another and the natural systems in which they live. For Northcott the pursuit of the common good must have "a presumption in favour of the exercise and sharing of social power by local human communities, rather than the concentration of sovereign power in centralised states or transnational corporations."[28]

Northcott applies this locally focused "ecology of the parish" to biodiversity by emphasizing that people will care for the diversity of ecosystems and creatures only when they understand them, live with them, and consider them part of their own habitat. We must, in other words, learn to relate to variety of life locally. This stance is related to but slightly different from the conservation biologists who call for small-scale thinking by focusing on species or populations because Northcott advocates a focus on what is actually nearby, what is necessary to the land on which and with which one lives. True conservationist energy and attention comes from "community land ownership," which Northcott identifies as the opposite of industrial agriculture and urban life. "The local welfare of local people interacts much more transparently with the local environmental goods than the welfare of the nation state or the profits of the corporation," and so it is local communities that can understand and care for the variety of life.[29]

According to Northcott, the way to ensure "the independent flourishing of wildlife in all its natural diversity" is to empower local communities. This is not only a pragmatic solution to contemporary degradation, but also a faithful translation of Christian heritage, because such local communities are consistent with "the Hebrew land ethic," which emphasized "food quality and animal welfare and a greater attempt to conserve the biodiversity of the countryside instead of treating it simply as a spare resource for industrial farming."[30] This appeal to the Hebrew tradition also allows Northcott to emphasize again the link between social injustice and environmental degradation, as the Hebrew prophets frequently observed a connection between oppressive political structures and ravaged land. Inspired by such prophecy, he urges readers to repair the structures that shape our relationships to both the diversity of human communities and the variety of nonhuman life.[31]

The local communities Northcott advocates are inclusive in the sense that they embrace the prophetic Hebrew commitment to the poorest and least fortunate among us, including marginalized human beings, marginalized species, and marginalized land. They are also multiscalar, in the sense that they are intended to serve as models for better relationships to global and national communities. However, Northcott's text is clear that the most effective and faithfully Christian way to oppose the forces of destructive expansion is to base our ecological work and the conservation of biodiversity on robust, local parish communities.

The Common Ground and Difficult Choices of a Multiscalar Ethics of Biodiversity

Northcott, Hart, and Rasmussen clearly demonstrate that multiscalar attention is familiar in the work of Christian ecological ethics and that both socialization and subsidiarity have a place in the conservation of biodiversity. Thus, there is an important agreement represented in this chapter: Christian ethics can and should be multiscalar by analyzing the levels of attention available when we recognize a moral problem and the inevitable scalar trade-offs we face in responding to it.

Taking seriously both socialization and subsidiarity, and learning from Rasmussen, Hart, and Northcott, it is clear that Christians should take all three levels of moral attention seriously. Biodiversity is not a problem that exists on any one scale, and so it is not a problem that can or should be solved with only one level of attention. This answer must be balanced, however, by the primary lesson from the ecologists discussed in the previous chapter: scalar attention requires trade-offs. While Christians should absolutely be willing to move flexibly between local, regional, and global conservation, we must not ever assume that this means we have seen and understood every relevant aspect of a system or a problem. Even the choice to think about biodiversity in a multiscalar way causes us to miss some aspects of it because devoted attention to local or global biodiversity would no doubt offer lessons and opportunities that a divided attention cannot.

The three ethicists discussed in this chapter help us to recognize that even within multiscalar ethics, we must make choices about the emphases of our attention, choices that should arise from an assessment of which scales of attention are most neglected and which require the most rigorous attention. Northcott emphasizes the "ecology of the parish" because he worries about the global market economy and the dangers of big thinking; he hopes to empower people to live in and devote themselves to particular places. Hart emphasizes a regional sacramental commons because he is concerned that global experiences and associations are too abstract to be powerfully motivating but nevertheless hopes to call people to a more encompassing attention. Rasmussen emphasizes an Earth community because he fears any exclusion or separation in our thinking; he hopes to inspire a sense of interrelatedness that extends to the entirety of the planet.

These are disagreements in emphasis rather than starkly different views of Christian ethics. Rasmussen would certainly agree with Northcott that global political and economic structures are dangerous, and Northcott would certainly agree with Rasmussen that we must learn to recognize the interconnections between all of Earth's human and nonhuman systems. But the two nevertheless chose to make different arguments. John Hart, for his part, attempts to strike a balance by introducing the notion of a "commons" at a middle level. These differences in emphasis within a multiscalar ethics are deeply important. They represent choices that must be made by Christians committed to the conservation of biodiversity.

A multiscalar ethics is the only way to respond to the reality of life's variety and to think carefully about the challenges of conserving the variety of life. However, which levels of attention to emphasize *within* a multiscalar ethics is a more controversial and difficult question. If the greatest danger to which Christian ethics responds is an overly individualistic, self-centered, anthropocentric view that refuses to extend moral concern outward to other creatures, then our primary emphasis should be socialization, scaling outward. If the greatest danger to which Christian ethics responds is an overly general, globalizing economic and political structure, then our primary emphasis should be subsidiarity, localizing our attention. If we see these as equivalent dangers, then our emphasis should be on striking a balance between the two.

My own preference is for the middle level of attention represented here by John Hart because I believe that thinking at this scale allows for the most flexibility. Emphasizing the importance of a regional community allows conservationists to be engaged as individuals while calling them to belong to something beyond their familiarity. This level of attention can balance the equally vital goals of socialization and subsidiarity by working against both unhealthy individualism and unhealthy expansionism. However, my primary intention in this chapter has not been to advocate my own preference but rather to note how seriously we must take each of these levels of attention.

A flexible, multiscalar Christian ecological ethics should recognize the need for more global, communal, and local thinking. The multiscalar reality of biodiversity will be conserved only if we learn to think in such multiscalar ways and to be honest about the limits of our attention. This will not be an easy task, as the differences between these ethicists and the decades of work by ecologists attest, but it is an essential task if Christians are to help to conserve the variety of life of which we are, ourselves, a part.

Notes

1. Pope Pius XI, *Quadragesimo anno*, §§ 79, 78, 84 in O'Brien and Shannon, *Catholic Social Thought*.

2. Ibid., § 79.

3. Second Vatican Council, *Gaudium et spes: Pastoral Constitution on the Church in the Modern World*, § 75 in O'Brien and Shannon, *Catholic Social Thought*.

4. For a compatible suggestion about adapting subsidiarity as an environmentalist principle, see Daly and Cobb, *For the Common Good*, 17–18. I know of no explicit discussion of the environmentalist implications of socialization.

5. Rasmussen, *Earth Community, Earth Ethics*, xii.

6. Ibid., 324, 345.

7. Ibid., xii and 7. Rasmussen identifies his work as *"earth* ethics" rather than *environmental* ethics precisely because of the concern that it is too easy to feel distinct and separate from "the environment," while Earth is an inclusive term.

8. Ibid., 39.

9. Ibid., 271, 349.

10. This picture occupies the cover of *Earth Community, Earth Ethics*. Rasmussen has elsewhere written about the moral power of that image, in language similar to Al Gore's. See Rasmussen, "Drilling in the Cathedral," 202.

11. Rasmussen, *Earth Community, Earth Ethics*, 336.

12. Ibid., 337. Emphasis in original.

13. Ibid., 339.

14. Ibid., 39.

15. Rasmussen, "Environmental Racism," 8.

16. Hart, *Sacramental Commons*, 4.

17. Ibid., xviii.

18. Ibid., 61.

19. Ibid., 147.

20. Ibid., 108.

21. Ibid., 113.

22. Northcott, *Environment and Christian Ethics*, 28.

23. Ibid., 298, 310.

24. Ibid., 68.

25. Northcott, "From Environmental U-Topianism to Parochial Ecology," 76–77.

26. Northcott, *Environment and Christian Ethics*, 323.

27. Ibid., 327.

28. Ibid., 310.

29. Ibid., 291.

30. Ibid., 294.

31. Ibid. See especially chap. 5.

Part IV

Political and Morally Formative Conservation

Chapter 6

Regulating Biodiversity: The Endangered Species Act and Political Conservation

Responding to a French naturalist who had dismissed the new world as impoverished and capable of sustaining only "cold men and feeble animals," Thomas Jefferson wrote a long tribute to the North American mammoth in his *Notes on the State of Virginia*. He knew this animal only from reports of its fossilized bones but found clear evidence therein of its greatness and therefore of the greatness of his continent. The bones were "tusks and skeletons [that] are much larger than those of the elephant, and the grinders many times greater than those of the hippopotamus." This suggested without a doubt that North America had produced "the largest of all terrestrial beings," a claim Jefferson believed resoundingly refuted the libelous dismissal of his home country.[1]

Perhaps the most interesting aspect of this exchange is an offhand remark Jefferson makes to explain why he includes the mammoth in a list of living North American species: "It may be asked, why I insert the Mammoth, as if it still existed? I ask in return, why I should omit it, as if it did not exist? Such is the oeconomy of nature, that no instance can be produced of her having permitted any one race of her animals to become extinct; of her having formed any link in her great work so weak as to be broken."[2] Jefferson did not believe in the possibility of extinction, and so mammoth bones not only proved that these creatures had once existed but also that they must still be thriving somewhere on the continent. His trust in the order of nature was such that he could not imagine a species would die off or that the world's carefully balanced systems could be maintained if such an unthinkable event were to occur. He therefore expressed confidence that further exploration of his continent would lead to sightings of living mammoths.[3]

Centuries later it is beyond controversy to observe that species do in fact die off. We know that mammoths no longer survive anywhere, and we have incontrovertible evidence that polar bears, spotted owls, and monarch butterflies are in danger of following them into extinction. However, given the fact that dismissing this possibility was a reasonable prospect at the founding of our nation, it becomes a bit more understandable that we as a society are still struggling to decide what to do about extinction. Even knowing that contemporary activity by industrialized human societies is vastly accelerating the rate at which extinctions take place, and that this unprecedented anthropogenic mass extinction will have unpredictable results on what Jefferson called the "oeconomy of nature," we find ourselves largely unprepared to think about the extinction of species or to change our behavior in response.[4]

This chapter begins with one of the founders and most famous political leaders of this nation because its primary subject is the United States' most wide-ranging and influential political response to extinction: the Endangered Species Act (ESA). As previous chapters have shown, ecologists and conservation biologists seek to change the ways people think and feel about biodiversity—encouraging us to value it and to pay attention to the scales at which we relate to it. However, scientists also devote considerable time to advocating laws that force us to act differently toward the variety of life, laws that make conservation political, creating enforceable rules that must be respected regardless of our beliefs or feelings. The ESA is the centerpiece of such efforts, and the political work to create, sustain, and resist it has profoundly influenced the ways citizens of this country relate to biodiversity.

The U.S. Endangered Species Act

The current Endangered Species Act was passed in 1973, and it greatly increased the federal government's authority over how citizens relate to the nation's nonhuman species and the habitats upon which they depend.[5] The act was passed with widespread public support and no significant opposition in either the House or the Senate, a particularly astonishing fact given how sweeping and comprehensive its requirements are.

The opening clauses of the law, which summarize its expansive justifications and purposes, are worth quoting at length:

The Congress finds and declares that—

(1) various species of fish, wildlife, and plants in the United States have been rendered extinct as a consequence of economic growth and development untempered by adequate concern and conservation;

(2) other species of fish, wildlife, and plants have been so depleted in numbers that they are in danger of or threatened with extinction;

(3) these species of fish, wildlife, and plants are of esthetic, ecological, educational, historical, recreational, and scientific value to the Nation and its people;

[Therefore, the] purposes of this Act are to provide a means whereby the ecosystems upon which endangered species and threatened species depend may be conserved, to provide a program for the conservation of such endangered species and threatened species.[6]

This is clearly a law intended to have substantial impact, recognizing extinction and the threat thereof as deeply serious problems and committing the entire country to the conservation of every species that can possibly be saved.

The executive branch of government is responsible for enforcement of the ESA, and the law is administered under the authority of the secretary of the Department of the Interior, primarily through the Fish and Wildlife Service, which accepts and evaluates citizen petitions to list species as endangered or threatened with endangerment. The National Oceanic and Atmospheric Administration within the Commerce Department oversees marine species and some other fish, but for sake of simplicity I will follow the act itself by referring to the responsible government agency simply as "the Secretary."

Virtually any species can be listed, as can distinct geographic populations of vertebrate animal species.[7] Once a species is listed, it becomes illegal to "take" any member of that species, with "taking" defined in the law as "to harass, harm, pursue, hunt, shoot, wound, kill, trap, capture, or collect." Trade in such species, land developments that destroy their habitat, and any substantial changes to their environments are also stipulated as examples of taking.[8]

In addition, the Secretary defines a "critical habitat" necessary for each listed species to recover and survive, and all federal agencies are then required to ensure that their work will not jeopardize that habitat. The act also instructs the Secretary to develop a recovery plan for every listed species and to report to Congress on the progress of each one. Decisions about listing must be made "solely on the basis of the best scientific and commercial data available," and the act offers similarly clear guidelines about the importance of science to critical habitat and recovery plans.[9]

In 1982 Congress amended the ESA to introduce some flexibility in its enforcement: small-scale takings became permitted if they are scientifically conducted for the ultimate benefit of the species, the incidental result of a lawful activity, and/or intended to mitigate a short-term hardship created by a recently listed species. These exceptions were intended to soften the act somewhat, but the core of the legislation remains, as becomes clear when the amendment notes that the Secretary may grant these exemptions only if they "will not operate to the disadvantage of such endangered species." So, for example, the most widely utilized aspect of this amendment has been the application for permits to "incidentally take" species, a process allowed only after the submission of a comprehensive and careful Habitat Conservation Plan that demonstrates the impact of the taking and the ways the responsible party will offset this impact to ensure that the endangered or threatened species is not harmed overall.[10] Takings can now be allowed in special circumstances, but they are legal only if it is demonstrated that they do not stand in the way of listed species recovery. The deeply conservationist emphasis of the act remains.[11]

As of this writing 1,320 domestic species are listed under the act. Of these, 1,011 are classified as endangered and 309 are threatened with endangerment; 573 are animal species, 747 are plants; and 1,135 have recovery plans on file.[12] However, almost 300 additional species are candidates waiting to be assessed by the office of the Secretary, which does not have a sufficient budget to process these claims. In recent years, two-thirds of the Fish and Wildlife Service's listing budget has been spent dealing with legal challenges. In September 2005 the service was engaged in sixty-one lawsuits regarding its listing decisions and was dealing with court orders from fifty-one other suits.[13]

As these statistics suggest, the ESA is both an extensively used and a very controversial law. The number of species listed and proposed shows that environmentalists have widely and enthusiastically embraced the act, finding in it a tool to save not only species but also their habitats, and even to oppose developments considered harmful or problematic for a host of other environmentalist reasons. In 1992

Donald Barry of the World Wildlife Fund summed up the virtues of the law from his perspective: "The Endangered Species Act is the pit bull of environmental laws. It's short, compact, and has a hell of a set of teeth. Because of its teeth, the act can force people to make the kind of tough political decisions they wouldn't normally make."[14] This is the conventional wisdom about the ESA among environmentalists: it is an effective tool to create social change by giving legal standing to the non-human world and the environments upon which all species depend.

The Endangered Species Act is the most important law protecting the variety of life in the United States. Written almost four decades ago, the act does not include the words "biological diversity" or "biodiversity," but it is nevertheless very much a law for the conservation of the variety of life. The act explicitly seeks "to provide a means whereby the ecosystems upon which endangered species and threatened species depend may be conserved," a goal that contributes greatly to the conservation of biodiversity, even though it attends primarily to the particular level of species.[15] Because it is a law with such a powerful "set of teeth," and because it is so relevant to biodiversity, most ecologists and conservation biologists consider it the most relevant law in service to the cause of conservation, and so they are vocal and active supporters of the act, defending it against critiques and seeking to strengthen and expand it.

Recognizing the importance of the act, E. O. Wilson goes so far as to call it "a rudimentary bill of rights for biodiversity."[16] Striking a similar note, the Union of Concerned Scientists sent a letter signed by "5,738 scientific experts" to Congress in support of the act, urging legislators to "take into account scientific principles that are crucial to species conservation" and then immediately noting that "biological diversity provides food, fiber, medicines, clean water, and myriad other ecosystem products and services on which we depend every day."[17] These scientists see the ESA as a concrete, political expression of what their research reveals: human beings in industrial societies must carefully reevaluate their relationships to the variety of life and strictly enforce the rules that limit their impact upon it. In short, the Endangered Species Act is the best legal means currently available to conserve biodiversity, offering the most binding and expansive rules about how citizens of this country must relate to the variety of life.

However, the ESA's "teeth" have created widespread and powerful objections among numerous detractors. The most common objection is that the act's modest successes cannot justify its considerable economic costs. Inspired by such criticisms, the House of Representatives passed a bill authored by California Representative Richard Pombo in 2005 proposing major amendments that would have weakened the ESA substantially. The Senate never discussed or passed a companion bill, so these amendments are not part of the law. Three years later another attempt was made to weaken the act, this time by changing its enforcement. The secretary of the interior proposed a rule that would allow federal agencies to monitor their own compliance with the act when undertaking construction projects rather than requiring an independent review by the Fish and Wildlife Service or the National Marine Fisheries Service.[18] This change was reversed by a new administration in the next year, but attempts to reduce the scope and effectiveness of the law nevertheless continue, serving as reminders that the Endangered Species Act is far more controversial now than it was when it was written and passed.

The "Incalculable" Value of Species

To explain the extent of the Endangered Species Act's authority and the reason it is so strongly opposed, it is worth recounting one of the most famous cases ever litigated about it. The Tellico Dam and Reservoir Project was begun by the Tennessee Valley Authority in 1967, part of a regional redevelopment scheme funded by the U.S. Congress. The dam, on the Little Tennessee River to the south of Knoxville, creates a reservoir thirty-three miles long, covering 15,560 acres. Construction was begun the first year the project was funded but not completed until 1979. The delay is blamed on a variety of citizen and legal protests, but by far the most remembered is the proposal to halt construction entirely through the Endangered Species Act.

In 1973, the same year the act was passed, ichthyologist David Etnier discovered a new species of fish, the snail darter, living in the Little Tennessee River and apparently dependent upon that shallow river habitat for its survival. The Secretary listed the snail darter as an endangered species in 1975 and declared parts of the river its critical habitat. Under section 7 of the act, this meant that all government projects were required to ensure that they did not interfere with the area. Despite this decision, however, Congress continued to fund the Tellico Dam, and the construction continued. The subsequent legal battle, *Tennessee Valley Authority v. Hill,* reached all the way to the Supreme Court, which was asked to decide whether the ESA required abandoning a multimillion-dollar project to ensure the continued existence of a small fish.

The Court's opinion, written by Chief Justice Warren Burger, has defined the scope and power of the Endangered Species Act ever since. It insists that "examination of the language, history, and structure of the legislation under review here indicates beyond doubt that Congress intended endangered species to be afforded the highest of priorities." Burger continues: "Congress viewed the value of endangered species as 'incalculable,'" and the Court therefore concluded that the snail darter had the right to continued existence despite the fact that $100 million had been appropriated for the building project.[19] Here, the highest court in the land affirms the strongest interpretation of the act, upholding the importance of species above and beyond all economic calculations.

One account suggests that Chief Justice Burger originally disagreed with this decision but "switched his vote to join the majority so he could write an opinion that would spur Congress to change the law."[20] Whether this is true or not, it is clear from the opinion that Burger did not personally agree with the law he was interpreting. He refers to the snail darter population as "a relatively small number of three-inch fish among all the countless millions of species extant" and comments on its discovery in a way that deemphasizes its importance: "Until recently the finding of a new species of animal life would hardly generate a cause celebre. This is particularly so in the case of darters, of which there are approximately 130 known species."[21] Burger's summation leaves little doubt that he finds the ESA ill advised:

> Congress has spoken in the plainest of words, making it abundantly clear that the balance has been struck in favor of affording endangered species the highest of priorities, thereby adopting a policy that it described as 'institutionalized caution.' Our individual appraisal of the wisdom or unwisdom of a particular course consciously selected by the Congress is to be put aside in the process of interpreting a statute. . . . We do not sit as a committee of review, nor are we vested with the power of veto.[22]

Chief Justice Burger was not the only one to regret the act's preference for the snail darter over the dam, so the Court's finding was not the end of the story. Soon after the judgment was handed down, Congress passed an amendment to the act making exemptions possible and naming an Endangered Species Committee responsible for them. The committee, whose power over life and death quickly led to the nickname "the God Squad," met in 1979 and almost immediately decided not to grant an exemption in the Tellico dam case. Later that year Congress passed a more specific exemption for this particular project as part of a Water Appropriations Act. The dam was completed and put into operation. The snail darter's critical habitat was destroyed, and the species was believed to have been extincted. However, other populations of snail darters were soon discovered in nearby tributaries, and the status of the species has since been changed to threatened.[23]

Opponents of the Endangered Species Act argue that the extreme measures required to build the Tellico Dam were ridiculous, seeing it as a worthwhile project that is now an important source of power and a contributor to the local economy. Furthermore, they note, the fact that the snail darter survived despite the exemption is clear evidence that the ESA is too demanding and too rigid even for the purpose of conservation. Their arguments generally center on a basic affirmation of economic freedom: the federal government should not tell property owners what they can do with their land and their resources; to do so interferes with economic development and prosperity.

One response to this argument can be found in the act itself, which argues that human development should continue only when it does not threaten other species. As the opening clauses of the law make clear, it is designed as a corrective to "economic growth and development untempered by adequate concern and conservation"; it seeks to act as a cautionary check to economic activity by assigning rare species a value that Chief Justice Burger insightfully called "incalculable" because it is not to be measured against economic costs but enforced despite them.[24]

This characteristic of the act is the one most praised by conservationists, who see such a challenge to "untempered" economic growth as a great success. As Kathryn Kohm puts it, the Endangered Species Act is valuable because it "requires us to look beyond our day-to-day business of building dams, harvesting timber, or improving crop yields and learn to live in a way that is compatible with our fellow species."[25] However, Kohm is also quick to point out that the act's discussion of tempering economic interests is not an attempt to curb *human* well-being. Instead, the basic assumption behind the law seems to be that what is best for this country and for human beings is to prevent the extinction of species, whatever the economic cost. As philosopher Holmes Rolston writes: "The act claims that what is good for the fauna and flora is good for the people. Anyone who thinks the contrary has the burden of proof."[26] To temper growth and development with a concern for endangered species is not to oppose humanity but to see the health of our species as aligned more fundamentally to the health of the world around us than to our current economic structures.

The Endangered Species Act uses the legal system to create absolute duties for citizens and establish a right to survival for other species. Contrasting the act with the Convention on Biological Diversity reveals the forceful and uncompromising nature of U.S. law: the Convention commits only to "significantly reduce the rate of biodiversity loss" and articulates actions that signing parties should take "as far as possible and as appropriate." In the international agreement the conservation of biodiversity is affirmed as a common goal, but this is clearly one goal among many and there is no absolute duty to which signatories are held accountable.[27] The ESA is something very different: it affirms that all species have a basic right to exist and requires the citizens of this country to rethink any and all activities that make this impossible. It is therefore somewhat ironic that the United States has failed to ratify the Convention but continues to uphold a law that is much more restrictive and effective at conserving the variety of life.

Scaling Political Conservation

While those seeking to conserve biodiversity praise the act for its strength and draw on it frequently in courtrooms to further their cause, they also point to important limitations. Ecologists and conservation biologists frequently critique the act because of the scale of attention it requires and accentuates. The Endangered Species Act focuses the attention of both government and citizens on species, thus isolating one level of the variety of life and deemphasizing the importance of broader-scale thinking and action to conserve biodiversity.

One example of the potential and limits of such thinking is found in the case of the northern spotted owl. Attention to these owls began in 1984 when a group of ornithologists formed a symposium to study the status and health of the subspecies. This inspired the first signs of the controversy to come: representatives from the timber industry immediately and publicly opposed the symposium, arguing that thousands of jobs were dependent upon the continued harvest of valuable old-growth wood in the Pacific Northwest and that any attempt to save owls would endanger these jobs. At the end of 1987, likely in response to such arguments, the Secretary announced that the northern spotted owl would not be listed under the Endangered Species Act.

This spurred an immediate backlash from scientists and environmentalist groups, twenty-three of which joined to file a lawsuit against the Secretary. The core of their critique was that the decision not to list the owl was based on economic rather than scientific interests, thus defying the act's commitment to "incalculable value" and "the best scientific data available." The Ninth U.S. District Court agreed and found in *Northern Spotted Owl v. Hodel* that the decision not to list was "arbitrary and capricious," noting that the only scientific opinion sought had been entirely in favor of listing and had predicted a likely "extinction of the subspecies in the foreseeable future" if no protection were offered.[28] Following the court's order, the Secretary began the listing process, and the northern spotted owl was declared a threatened subspecies in 1990.

However, the Secretary declared shortly after the listing that there was insufficient scientific data with which to define the owl's critical habitat and announced that there would be no such habitat established. Again, environmentalist groups sued, and again the Ninth District Court found in their favor. In *Northern Spotted Owl v. Lujan*, the court mandated a critical habitat designation, and so in 1992, 6.9 million acres of old-growth forest were designated and logging on them was forbidden.[29]

Within a year of that decision the federal government applied for an exemption from the act in order to sell forty-four tracts of old-growth forest within the owl's habitat to timber companies. This application went before the Endangered Species Committee, called together for the first time since it had decided against the Tellico Dam.[30] The committee met in 1992 and, in an intricate compromise, authorized the sale of thirteen tracts while forbidding the other thirty-one from being sold. However, even these thirteen plots of land were never sold because as soon as a new presidential administration entered office in

1993, the new secretary of the interior withdrew the exemption application and adopted a different approach to forest management.[31]

Most discussions of the spotted owl controversy emphasize the same tensions around economic interests evident in the story of the snail darter. The opposition to listing the owl, and then the impetus to seek an exemption, came largely from the logging industry, which sponsored numerous rallies and public relations campaigns designed to stress an inevitable choice between saving the species and conserving the economic health of the region, at one point predicting that the listing could cause the loss of 290,000 jobs.[32] The supporters of the act, on the other hand, emphasized that the law guarantees uncompromising protection for the northern spotted owl, demanding enforcement for the sake of both the human and nonhuman populations of the region.

Interestingly, however, ecologists and conservation biologists rarely talk at length about the value or scientific importance of the owls themselves. At best, the owl is an indicator species, signaling the health of the old-growth forest of which it is a part. It is the forest as a whole that most conservationists are truly interested in protecting. This is made explicit by Jack Ward Thomas, the wildlife biologist commissioned to write the first government report on the topic, who told journalist William Dietrich that "this issue was never just about a bird. . . . The owl was a surrogate" for the forest ecosystem.[33] Those who sought to save northern spotted owls were not working to protect a single subspecies but rather the old-growth forests of the Pacific Northwest.

In this respect the virtues of the spotted owl are its dependence upon old-growth forest, the many detailed studies that have been conducted on it, and its requirement of a vast habitat for survival. It is therefore no surprise that environmentalists did not stop when the owl was listed as a threatened species but kept agitating and advocating until *Northern Spotted Owl v. Lujan* required a protected habitat. For most environmentalists and scientists the conservation of the owl itself was secondary to the critical habitat protected from logging and development.

In other words, the scale of these advocates' attention is not on the subspecies, but on the vast forest ecosystem upon which it depends. The ESA is useful because it contains provisions to defend habitat and because its "teeth" are the most powerful tool available to protect that habitat. Peter Brussard's comment to David Takacs expresses this clearly:

Well, the battle over the spotted owl is not really whether we need a spotted owl. It's whether we're going to preserve some tiny remnant of old-growth forest. And I think there are lots and lots of sound arguments for preserving old-growth forest. But unfortunately we don't have an Endangered Old Growth Act; we have an Endangered Species Act. So that's why we're fighting over the spotted owl. Frankly, if the spotted owl were to vanish the day after tomorrow, I doubt there would be the slightest ripple in the ecology of the forest in the big sense.[34]

Brussard's attention is on the vast forests in which the owl lives. In this case, therefore, a particular population of a single species was used as the means to protect an entire ecosystem.

The desire to protect biodiversity at scales other than the species has led many conservationists to call for a more comprehensive policy explicitly designed to protect biodiversity, a "Conservation of Biodiversity Act" or an "Endangered Ecosystem Act." Such proposals suggest a much longer-term, more encompassing legislation for the conservation of biodiversity broadly construed.[35] As one legal scholar puts it, "The question now is whether we can eliminate the middlemen of endangered species and get to the business of protecting their landscapes in a more straightforward fashion."[36] Such a broader-scale attention would also look beyond the borders of the United States in a more rigorous way, calling for ratification of the Convention on Biological Diversity and likely also advocating another, stronger international agreement.

A more comprehensive policy would not only work at a larger level of attention than just species but also incorporate a broader time scale. By offering legal protection only after species are endangered or threatened, the Endangered Species Act comes into play only when there are few spotted owls or snail darters left to be found and saved. Many conservationists feel that their work would be more effective if the law took effect earlier, attending to species that are not yet threatened but may be by development or other changes in ecosystems.[37] Extinction and the degradation of biodiversity are incredibly long-term changes that human beings are causing in ecosystems, and so ecologists argue that our attention to these changes must match this reality with a political system that can think about the far-distant consequences across a broad area.

Despite advocating such expansions beyond the Endangered Species Act, ecologists and conservation biologists continue to overwhelmingly support the law in its current form, calling for more funding and energy for the identification, listing, and protection of threatened species. Although the act may not be multiscalar enough, and may not have a broad-enough level of attention to match the problem of biodiversity degradation, it is a means of extending human moral attention to a far broader scale than is now common, extending the sphere of legal rights beyond human economic interests and pushing attention outward to species at risk and the habitats upon which they depend.

The Importance and Limits of Political Conservation

To summarize: the Endangered Species Act of 1973 is one of the most sweeping legislative achievements of the conservation movement, explicitly aiming to temper economic development for the sake of nonhuman species and establishing legal protection for at least some aspects of biodiversity. The act establishes a basic right of existence for all species and requires this nation and its citizens to ensure their survival. The most common environmentalist position on the act is that it is an impressive accomplishment whose continued existence is vital, but it is not enough. For many environmentalists the limitation of the act is the scale of its influence: it is a wonderful way to protect species, some habitats, and a few populations, but a more comprehensive legal recognition of biodiversity is required.

I want to suggest that an equally important limitation of the Endangered Species Act is not something that can be solved by another law. Without careful attention to the ways people think and feel about other species and about biodiversity more broadly, no policy will be sufficient to conserve the variety of life in this nation or in the world.

Created and supported by political coalitions rather than any single movement, the ESA lacks a clear and consistent moral argument on behalf of endangered species and biodiversity. The opening clauses note that the endangered species are "of esthetic, ecological, educational, historical, recreational, and scientific value to the Nation and its people," but this is a vague and unspecific list.[38] Indeed, as Bryan Norton observes, the act's list is in virtually alphabetical order, which implies a desire to avoid any argument or prioritization in the justifications of the law.[39]

There are many similarities between this list and the list of values leading into the Convention on Biological Diversity, and this is no coincidence. Sweeping political legislation seeking wide support is most successful when it is not aligned to a single moral argument but instead attempts to synthesize the interests of a variety of citizens and constituencies into a single policy. This is exemplified in the act and the Convention not only by a word order that refuses to prioritize justifications but also in the fact that these are vague and relatively uncontroversial justifications. Few will explicitly object to the ecological, educational, or scientific value of species, even if many might not be clear about what exactly these terms represent in this context. The Endangered Species Act therefore asserts a bold and controversial argument—that nonhuman species have a right to survive superseding our economic interests—with a vague and unexplored set of justifications. Indeed, the vagueness of justification in the act seems to be a strategic choice that allowed the law to be passed and to maintain support throughout its history.

The real power of political conservation is its widespread and enforceable influence on the ways people act. As "the pit bull of environmental laws," the Endangered Species Act is remarkably influential, and it must be enforced even in the face of considerable disagreements. Some advocates of the ESA seek to save species for the sake of the animals themselves, others value species primarily as indicators of the health of a broader ecosystem, and still others protect species for the benefits they currently or may someday provide to human beings. Others fundamentally disagree with the act for a variety of reasons. But despite this range of moral views, the act is enforced throughout the country: as long as it is law, it pertains to all people regardless of their feelings or attitudes toward endangered species. This political response to biodiversity is therefore capable of organizing divergent perspectives and constituencies to create strong and enforceable rules.

However, this strength also suggests a limitation of the law: its continued existence depends entirely upon the consensus of a coalition, and if the act were to be repealed or weakened, much of the good it has done in protecting species and habitats could be quickly undone. Furthermore, the characteristics that so many environmentalists celebrate about the ESA—its pervasive authority, its explicit challenge to untempered economic growth, and its broad application beyond solely human interests and rights—make it deeply controversial and dangerous in the minds of its opponents. Again the controversy over the spotted owl is an example: this was not just a political conflict, it was a clashing of very different worldviews where many people believed that their fundamental way of life was being attacked by advocates who cared more about owls than human beings. Among the logging community, slogans such as "I Love Spotted Owls—Fried" and "Save a Logger— Eat an Owl" became popular, reflecting that the law and its enforcement actually nurtured animosity against an endangered animal, an animosity that also extended to the environmental community and the federal government.[40] Thus, the act itself has inspired many campaigns to repeal or restrict its policies, which is a familiar response to a powerful law in a divisive political environment. If such campaigns gain traction, or if political leaders unsympathetic to the act gain power in other ways, its legal protections could cease to exist entirely.[41]

Any political approach to the conservation of biodiversity depends upon continued public support, and when a law creates major changes or harsh penalties, its enforcement can reduce such support. No matter how strong and sweeping a policy is, it can work in a diverse, democratic society only if multiple vocal and influential constituencies of citizens agree that it is worth its costs. This means that a political approach to saving species depends on a public that wants to save species. Any political campaign to conserve biodiversity will require a widespread belief in the value and importance of the variety of life, a willingness to make changes, perhaps even sacrifices, in our lives to conserve it. Creating such attitudes is the work of moral formation rather than policy, and so calls for a different kind of conservation.

With its strength and scope the Endangered Species Act reveals the potential of political approaches to conserving biodiversity. However, in its divisiveness and tentative legal standing it also reveals the limits of such an approach and the importance of moral formation. If we are to be a nation that values biological diversity, we need policies such as the Endangered Species Act, but we also need new ways of thinking as moral beings about the natural world and our own places within it.

Notes

1. Jefferson, *Notes*, 45–47. The words of the Comte de Buffon's *History of Earth and Animated Nature* are quoted in Martin, *Thomas Jefferson: Scientist*, 156.

2. Jefferson, *Notes*, 55.

3. It is likely that the bones Jefferson described belonged to the American Mastodon, which paleontologists today believe to have been extinct for approximately ten thousand years, due to either climactic change or human hunting.

4. Of course, while he himself denied the possibility, Jefferson nevertheless suggests an important argument that we should take action to prevent such extinctions: he affirms the value of this nation by celebrating the majesty of its wildlife and in so doing implies that the health of a human population is linked to the health of the nonhuman world. A response to extinction must therefore emerge not only from the startling realization that it is possible for entire species to die out but also the certain knowledge that the viability of human communities is not separable from that of other species.

5. Previous endangered species acts, with significant authority but much less sweeping mandates than the 1973 law, were passed in 1966 and 1969. For a careful history of the act in the context of this previous legislation, other environmental politics, and particularly the Convention on International Trade in Endangered Species, see Dunlap, *Saving America's Wildlife*.

6. U.S. Congress, Endangered Species Act of 1973, § 2.a.1–3, 2.b.

7. Ibid., § 3.16. This allows, for instance, the grizzly bear to be listed as a threatened species in the lower forty-eight states despite the fact that the population in Alaska is not at substantial risk.

8. Ibid., § 3.19. The only exception to this rule in the original act was for Alaskan natives, who are allowed to take listed species for subsistence purposes and to sell nonedible by-products of the animals they catch. However, the Secretary is given the right to restrict even these native rights if necessary for the good of a species.

9. Ibid., §§ 7, 4, 4.b.1.a. In context, "the reference to 'commercial' data does not soften the best science mandate [but instead] refers to data concerning the impact of commercial trade on listed species." Doremus, "Purposes, Effects, and Future of the Endangered Species Act," 8, n. 46.

10. U.S. Congress, Endangered Species Act of 1973, § 10.

11. Other amendments, passed in 1978 and 1988, were less sweeping and, again, did not fundamentally change the act.

12. U.S. Fish and Wildlife Service, "Summary of Listed Species." Also listed are 573 additional species that do not occur in the United States, making it illegal for citizens to trade them internationally and calling upon the Secretary to encourage their conservation in other nations.

13. Stokstad, "What's Wrong?" 2151.

14. Quoted in Egan, "Strongest U.S. Environment Law May Become Endangered Species," A11.

15. U.S. Congress, Endangered Species Act of 1973, § 2.b.

16. Wilson, *The Future of Life*, 186.

17. Union of Concerned Scientists, "A Letter from Biologists," www .ucsusa.org/scientific_integrity/restoring/biologists-letter-on.html.

18. Eilperin, "Endangered Species Act."

19. *Tennessee Valley Authority v. Hill*. "Incalculable" is in quotes in the opinion, but the source of the quotation is unclear. The act itself does not include the word.

20. Patrick A. Parenteau, "The Exemption Process and the 'God Squad,'" in Baur and Irvin, *The Endangered Species Act*, 132.

21. Ibid.

22. *TVA v. Hill*.

23. For accounts of this long and complicated legal saga, see especially Petersen, *Acting for Endangered Species*; and Bean et al., *Evolution of National Wildlife Law*.

24. It is possible that many members of Congress who voted for the act did not intend to pass such a sweeping law with such substantial economic implications. Lynn Greenwalt, the director of the Fish and Wildlife Service when the act was passed, writes that many legislators claimed after the episode of the snail darter that they had not understood the implications of the law: "They thought they were voting for legislation to protect eagles, bears, and whooping cranes. They professed not to understand at the time of passage that this law might raise questions about irrigation projects, timber harvests, the dredging of ports, or the generation of electricity." Lynn Greenwalt, "The Power and Potential of the Act," in Kohm, *Balancing on the Brink*, 31.

25. Kohm, *Balancing on the Brink*, 3.

26. Holmes Rolston III, "Life in Jeopardy on Private Property," in Kohm, *Balancing on the Brink*, 46.

27. Secretariat, "Convention on Biological Diversity."

28. *Northern Spotted Owl v. Hodel*.

29. *Northern Spotted Owl v. Lujan*.

30. This committee has been convened only a few times, and this ruling is the only case in which it has loosened the strictures of the act at all.

31. See Parenteau, 147–51. Instead, President Clinton convened a team of experts called the Forest Ecosystem Management Assessment Team, which developed the Pacific Northwest Forest Management Plan, a plan that attempted to give decision-making power to professional resource managers rather than the courts and federal government. The spotted owl faded from national attention but has remained controversial in the region.

32. Petersen, *Acting for Endangered Species*, 90. Petersen also reports that the president of Summit Timber declared the event of the owl's listing "a dark day in the history of the Northwest," 95.

33. Dietrich, *The Final Forest*, 231.

34. Takacs, *Idea of Biodiversity*, 69.

35. Such proposals are found in Burgess, *Fate of the Wild*; and Bouma-Prediger and Vroblesky, *Assessing the Ark*.

36. Houck, "On the Law," 872.

37. See Carroll et al., "Strengthening the Use of Science."

38. U.S. Congress, Endangered Species Act of 1973, § 2.a.3.

39. Norton, *Why Preserve Natural Variety?* 4. Of course, the first term, "esthetic" is out of order. I take this to be an anomaly rather than a contradiction to Norton's point and would posit that perhaps the word was spelled "aesthetic" in a previous draft.

40. For an extensive account of the resistance among logging communities, see Dietrich, *Final Forest*.

41. For this reason, even some ardent supporters of the Endangered Species Act have suggested that it could be softened, proposing economic incentives for compliance and reimbursement for lost profits, because it is difficult "to determine how much regulation that causes a loss of economic value will be tolerated before compensation would be mandated by the Court," weakening the act from the outside. Dwyer, Murphy, and Ehrlich, "Property Rights Case Law," 737. Inherent in such a suggestion is the awareness that the act has been in some ways a divisive presence in our society, and this endangers the legislation's own future as well as the future of other environmentalist causes.

Chapter 7

Christian Care for Biodiversity:
Moral Formation as Conservation

Scholarly discussions of the relationship between Christianity and environmentalism invariably engage Lynn White Jr.'s famous essay, "The Historical Roots of Our Ecologic Crisis," and this book is no exception. White's essay has served as a source and foil for theologians and ethicists ever since it was published in *Science* in 1967 because it provocatively claims that Christianity is "the most anthropocentric religion the world has ever seen" and, as such, is a prominent foundation of environmentally destructive social structures. The prevailing Christian mentality, White writes, is this: "Despite Darwin, we are *not*, in our hearts, part of the natural process. We are superior to nature, contemptuous of it, willing to use it for our slightest whim." White presents this as the fundamental belief system of Western culture, a belief system that has trained us to separate ourselves from our environments and therefore "bears a huge burden of guilt" for environmental degradation. He suggests that the best way to overcome this guilt-inducing Christian doctrine, and thereby to reverse environmental degradation, would be to recover more nature-friendly traditions within Christianity itself. White concludes by proposing St. Francis as "the patron saint of ecologists."[1]

Many thinkers and scholars have accepted White's basic argument and used it to call for a fundamental restructuring and rethinking among Christians, an "ecological reformation" toward a faith that will remind us in a new way that we belong on Earth and are a part of its systems.[2] Others have worked to refute, or at least to complicate, White's argument and therefore to demonstrate that Christian tradition has long been far more environmentalist and far less guilty than he suggested.[3] While I am not as interested in assigning exclusive "guilt" to the Christian tradition, my own approach in this book has been similar to, and inspired by, White's: I believe that the Christian tradition is complicit in environmental degradation, and I seek hitherto unrecognized traditions within Christian history in order to nurture a new attitude toward creation that will inspire believers to protect and recognize themselves as part of the variety of life.

Perhaps even more important than this argument, however, is the foundational assumption of White's article and those who have argued with it. "The Historical Roots of Our Ecologic Crisis" is based upon the idea that religious beliefs and ideas heavily influence how human beings relate to the world, so much so that the "roots" it identifies are habits and attitudes of thought. A historian, White discusses industrialization and technological innovation as causes of environmental degradation, but he argues that the most basic foundation of these trends was a belief system: "What people do about their ecology depends on what they think about themselves in relation to things around them. Human ecology is deeply conditioned by beliefs about our nature and destiny—that is, by religion."[4]

White therefore suggests that the solution to environmental degradation is a new kind of faith: "Since the roots of our trouble are so largely religious, the remedy must also be essentially religious."[5] The assumption behind this claim—that the ways people think, believe, and feel about the world shape their treatment of it—suggests the importance of moral formation. Conservation is not, therefore, merely a political or practical process but must also address the ideas and attitudes of human beings.[6] This means that an essential part of any response to environmental degradation must be the ethical and theological process of examining and reforming the ways people think and feel.

Applying this to the work of an ethics of biodiversity, White's essay seems to suggest that to protect the variety of life, Christians need new belief systems that address and change the ways we feel and think about biodiversity. This chapter builds on that claim and seeks to flesh it out, calling for moral formation in our attitudes about biodiversity: revisioning, reprioritizing, and recognizing the power inherent in the ways we understand the degradation of biodiversity.

The Call for Moral Formation

Moral formation first calls people to see differently, to understand existing challenges in a new way and to notice moral problems where they have been ignored in the past. It then asks people to evaluate their priorities, to feel urgency about new challenges and to deemphasize less immediate, less important, or less relevant issues. Finally, moral formation calls for recognition of the power and agency of human beings and human cultures: when people see new challenges and prioritize the work of meeting them, they must also accept their own capacity to make a difference.

Morally formative conservation seeks to change the ways people think about the variety of life. It presents those who do not understand the moral challenge of biodiversity loss with a new perspective, it offers those who do not believe biodiversity loss is a serious and urgent problem a new way of ordering their concerns, and it invites those who do not believe that they can prevent the destruction of biodiversity to recognize their own power and agency. While political conservation forces people to behave differently, moral formation encourages them to want to behave differently and to understand the changes required to reshape human relationships with the variety of life.

Although they do not use this ethical terminology, calls for moral formation are common in the writings of ecologists and conservation biologists. These scientists frequently call for an additional and different approach, a change in the moral attitudes of individuals and communities so that we will treat biodiversity with respect, demand better laws and enforcement from our leaders, and teach future generations to work toward a world where humanity recognizes its place within the variety of life. They call, in other words, for moral formation. For instance, Paul and Anne Ehrlich write that, given the drastic rate of biodiversity destruction and the current direction of human societies: "Nothing less is needed than a rapid ethical evolution toward readjusting our relationship with nature so that the preservation of biodiversity becomes akin to a religious duty."[7] Along similar lines, conservation biologist Michael Soulé told David Takacs that "only a new religion of nature . . . can create the political momentum to overcome greed that gives rise to discord and strife and the anthropocentrism that underlies the intentional abuse of nature."[8]

Perhaps the most extensive example of such religious appeals from a scientist is E. O. Wilson's book *The Creation*, an extended argument directed specifically at evangelical Christians. Wilson writes that religion and science "are the two most powerful forces in the world today, including especially the United States," and he predicts that if they "could be united on the common ground of biological conservation, the problem would soon be solved."[9] While not all ecologists share Wilson's optimism or his particular focus on Christian religion, many agree that the project of conservation will be improved by a better understanding of and engagement with religious ethics. David Takacs summarizes such views: "If the value of biodiversity were felt not merely in the pocket or in the brain but in the *soul*, then the most effective, permanent conservation ethic imaginable might result."[10]

Scientists clearly do not think that they are equipped to manage the work of moral formation on their own, and in their calls for partnerships with religious communities, people of faith should hear an invitation to think alongside scientists about conservation. Moral formation matters deeply to the cause of conservation, and religion is one of the primary sources of moral formation in our world.

It is beyond the scope of this chapter—or, indeed, of any single book—to offer a comprehensive plan for morally formative conservation. Instead, I focus on three examples of moral formation within Christian communities and traditions—ritual blessings of animals, scriptural interpretation of Noah's ark and the rainbow covenant, and a theological analysis of the idea of dominion. Each of these is an attempt to influence the morality of Christians, and each helps to offer a perspective on the importance and limits of moral formation more broadly.

Blessing the Animals: Seeing Biodiversity in Christian Rituals

Lynn White Jr. suggested that St. Francis be recognized as the "patron saint of ecologists" because Francis famously prayed to the creator in thanks for the kinship of humanity with the world around us: brother sun, sister moon, brother fire, sister Earth. Francis is also an environmentalist hero because the hagiographies about him include numerous examples of worship that blurs the boundaries between human beings and other creatures: negotiating with wolves, preaching to birds, and embracing life in the wilderness.[11]

Many contemporary Christian communities commemorate Francis's connection with the nonhuman world by holding a special service on his traditional feast day, inviting congregants to bring their pets and ritually blessing them and all animals. The most famous such service in the United States takes place at the Cathedral of St. John the Divine in New York City, where an incredibly diverse parade of creatures marches down the center aisle of the church. Attendees have included not just cats, dogs, and birds but also tortoises, sheep, chickens, snakes, llamas, a camel, and an elephant. After the service, clergy—frequently with pets alongside—bless each animal. People flock to this service both to have their pets blessed and to appreciate the diversity of nonhuman life with which they share their city.

Perhaps the most powerful lesson taught by such a ceremony is the visual and experiential sign that the church sanctuary, the ritual space in which tradition teaches that Christians meet God, is not just for human beings but for all creatures. Inviting animals into a Christian sanctuary validates the love people feel for their pets and animal companions, demonstrating that there is a theological justification for such love. This is moral formation, teaching believers a lesson by modeling an interspecies community in church.

Homilists and preachers at such services frequently emphasize this moral formation in their spoken messages, and they often continue Francis's tradition of speaking directly to the nonhuman animals present, hoping that the human beings overhearing their words will learn from them about the integrity and beauty of God's creation. For example, at a St. Francis Day celebration at the Lutheran School of Theology at Chicago, biblical scholar David Rhoads assured the animals present that "God loves you for your own sake and not because of what you can do for humans," and he offered an apology for the ways humans have failed and continue to fail to learn from this divine love. He called on the human beings present to remember not just the pets and animals who share their lives but also distant animals who lack human protection, particularly those "threatened with extinction: snow leopards and timber wolves and green sea turtles and condors and paddlefish and fin whales among so many others."[12]

The blessing of animals on St. Francis Day could be a straightforward celebration of the connection between people and their pets, but preachers like David Rhoads insist that there are wider lessons to be learned about the importance of nonhuman animals and the variety of life. Attendants at such a ceremony are taught to scale their attention outward, to consider not just the animals immediately around them but also biodiversity around the world. The pets people bring are a sign of the vast variety of life outside the church walls, also beloved by and created by God. Another approach to a St. Francis Day sermon might also scale downward, reminding congregants that each of us is a vast rain forest of microorganisms, and each of us brings countless nonhuman creatures with us to church and everywhere else we go. Attention to the microscopic life with which we live each day is yet another reminder that we depend upon biodiversity and are, ourselves, a part of life's variety.

Ceremonial blessings offer an experiential and pedagogical opportunity to demonstrate a sacramental appreciation of biodiversity. In these services nonhuman animals teach a theological lesson to human congregants, a lesson about the love of God and the importance of loving all God's creatures. However, these animals are not simply there to serve the needs of human beings—that would be a solely vertical sacramentality. Instead, the animals themselves are addressed and blessed, their connection with God is intrinsic to their created nature, and so believers are taught to respect and love them for their own sake as well as for the sake of better knowing God.

These ceremonies are, generally, small affairs. Even the famous celebration at the Cathedral of St. John the Divine includes only a few thousand human beings and a smaller number of other pets, which does not represent a significant percentage of the population of Manhattan. Relatively few other communities celebrate the feast of St. Francis in this way, and even those that do bless animals only once in a long liturgical year. But these rituals nevertheless serve as a sign of how Christian churches can shape the moral vision of believers. The practices and rituals in our churches are the tools that form and develop our faith and belief. The ways we worship profoundly influence the ways we think about the world around us, particularly when they are repeated regularly and examined by thoughtful communities of faith. As liturgical theologian Troy Messenger writes, "What we believe is being created week after week as the assembled reenact the sacred stories of God's action in the world. These actions testify to a theology that is being molded into our very selves."[13]

Thus, if Christian communities seek to respond to the degradation of biodiversity with a theological argument about the sacramental value of God's creation, we will need ritual practices to convey this message. The blessing of the animals is one such practice, a practice that explicitly brings the variety of life into the sanctuary, demonstrates that the Gospel is intended for all of creation, and calls upon human beings to learn about God by paying attention to what God has made. It might also serve as the model for other practices. Churches could bless plants and remember the endangered flora of the world. Congregations could work to ritually recognize the bioregion in which they exist and bless their local ecosystem, native species, and populations. Ministers and priests could hold services of confession and contrition in which they and their communities could repent for the roles they have played in destroying local and global biodiversity. Such rituals would help to morally form Christians into human beings who value and appreciate the variety of life in God's creation.

Emphasizing the Urgency of Conservation: Noah's Ark and the Variety of Life

Another tool for moral formation in the Christian tradition is scriptural interpretation, imaginatively applying ancient, sacred texts to contemporary issues to help believers recognize our moral responsibilities and assess our moral priorities. The narratives and parables of the Bible, when read critically and carefully, provide inspiration and motivation to think deeply about contemporary moral challenges. Previous chapters have noted many scriptural passages that can be interpreted as relevant to the loss of biodiversity, but no story is more often applied to this issue than that of Noah's ark and the rainbow covenant.

The narrative, told in Genesis, chapters 6–9, is familiar to many: grieved by their wickedness, God decides to "blot out from the earth the human beings I have created" (6:7) with a torrential, destructive flood. However, God instructs one righteous man, the patriarch Noah, to build an ark in preparation, explicitly specifying that Noah should save his own family and at least two of "every living thing" in order to "keep them alive with you" (6:19).[14] Following each of God's commands, Noah builds an ark that successfully saves his family and representatives of all other species from the mighty flood while "all flesh died that moved on the earth, birds, domestic animals, wild animals, all swarming creatures that swarm on the earth, and all human beings; everything on dry land in whose nostrils was the breath of life died" (7:21–22). After the return of dry land, God offers a covenant to Noah, his descendants, "and with every living creature that is with you, the birds, the domestic animals, and every animal of the earth with you"

(9:10), promising never again to destroy the Earth through flood and that "as long as the earth endures, seedtime and harvest, cold and heat, summer and winter, day and night, shall not cease" (8.22). God places a bow in the sky as a reminder of this covenant, and Noah's family and the animals they had saved repopulated the planet.

The textual history of this narrative, its role in the self-identity of the community that wrote the book of Genesis, and its possible roots in historic Middle Eastern floods are all important topics of study, but the most central question for the work of moral formation in Christian ecological ethics is how this text can be interpreted and communicated to contemporary people of faith. Ethicists frequently relate this story to current conservation efforts, with the philosopher Holmes Rolston labeling the ark "the first Endangered Species Project."[15] Along the same lines, in 2005 a group of evangelical Christians named themselves the Noah Alliance when they banded together to advocate the protection and expansion of the U.S. Endangered Species Act, which they labeled "our national ark."[16]

Perhaps the best starting place for an interpretation of this biblical narrative is its conclusion: God's rainbow covenant is with all creatures, a covenant of peace that signifies not only God's unwillingness to destroy life in this way again but also the commonality between all the animals that have survived the flood. God speaks in one voice, offering a single message to all creatures that came off the ark. As theologian Steven Bouma-Prediger has noted, this covenant is incredibly inclusive: just as human beings were saved alongside all others, so God makes a promise to "the earth and its plethora of creatures."[17] Just as most human beings died alongside most creatures in the flood, those who are saved receive God's promise together. Earlier in the story God's command that Noah respect other species and "keep them alive with you" is an expression of the same interconnected thinking reflected in the covenant: we are graced by God alongside other creatures, and we will survive only alongside other creatures. James Nash identifies this as an "ecological covenant" because it "implicitly recognizes the interdependent relationships of all creatures in their ecosystems."[18]

While this story offers a promise that God will not destroy the world again by flood, it also serves as a parable for the environmental degradation that can be wrought by human activity. While the story suggests the theological mystery of why God would so angrily punish the entire world, it is unequivocally clear that the root cause of the flood was human wickedness. This is a story about the reality that all creatures suffer the consequences of bad decisions on the part of one species. Noah's ark is the story of a natural disaster brought about by human sin. While the story tells us that a small remnant of each species was saved, we should not forget that every other terrestrial animal suffers and perishes: "all flesh died that moved on the earth."

A conservationist interpretation of Noah's ark can therefore also help us to represent the contemporary reality of environmental degradation with a familiar story, to show that the scriptures carry a lesson about the ways our mistakes have impacts not only on our communities but also on the nonhuman world around us. Ultimately, the "ecological" worldview James Nash finds in this story emphasizes that the fate of human beings and that of the rest of Earth's species are inseparable: when human carelessness causes an environmental catastrophe, other creatures suffer alongside us. If we are to prevent such catastrophe or to survive inevitable degradation, we must envision solutions as big as the ark, with space to save not only human beings but also the other species with whom we share the planet. This interpretation of Noah's ark clearly shows that the Bible speaks about what we now call biodiversity, calling us to think and feel differently about the variety of life so that we can learn to act differently toward it and keep biodiversity alive with us.

This brief analysis demonstrates how the interpretation of scripture can contribute to moral formation, helping Christians to think about our ethical attitudes and what we must do. By reminding us of God's merciful covenant not to destroy creation, this interpretation teaches that the loss of species and the reduction of life's variety go against God's will. By comparing the loss of biodiversity to the impending flood Noah faced, this interpretation emphasizes that we face an urgent and immediate task, that God calls us to act boldly to save other creatures.

Virtually no one is opposed to the conservation of biodiversity, but very few people cite this task as a high priority for society or devote much of their own energy to it. The story of Noah's ark and the rainbow covenant is one way to argue that Christians should not only care for biodiversity but should also make that care a priority for their governments, their churches, and their own lives. Just as Noah was called to devote himself to a grand and bold project to save his family and other creatures in the biblical story, we are called to work hard to build a world where human beings recognize the value of other creatures and seek to keep them alive with us, where human wickedness no longer causes catastrophe and careless destruction. Reading the Bible in this way and allowing its narratives and parables to shape our morality is a vital part of Christianity's contribution to conservation.

Recognizing Our Power: Questioning and Accepting the Theology of Dominion

While God's covenant at the end of Noah's story is with the whole of the Earth, it differentiates humans from all other creatures at one point, promising our species that "the fear and dread of you shall rest on every animal of the earth, and on every bird of the air, on everything that creeps on the ground, and on all the fish of the sea; into your hand they are delivered" (9:2). This text is a troubling reminder of the power humans have and the damage that human wickedness can cause to other creatures. In the context of the Hebrew Bible, it is a return to a familiar Christian claim that God has given human beings dominion over the rest of the planet.

The most famous claim along these lines comes earlier in the book of Genesis, when God tells the newly created human species to "be fruitful and multiply, and fill the earth and subdue it; and have dominion over the fish of the sea and over the birds of the air and over every living thing that moves upon the earth" (1:28). This is an important part of the self-identity that Christians have been taught: human beings play a special role in God's creation, overseeing all other beings for God's sake. Any moral formation of Christian conservationists must involve a careful theological analysis of this idea.

Dominion has caused a great deal of controversy among environmentalist Christians, some of whom have worked to supplant the idea with a more harmonious and environmentally friendly theology. This was part of the reason Lynn White lifted up St. Francis as a model for ecological thought, noting that Francis "tried to substitute the idea of the equality of all creatures, including man, for the idea of man's limitless rule of creation."[19] White proposed a refutation and alternative to dominion.

Interestingly, most Christian theologians have not followed White along this track, more often reinterpreting and supplementing the idea of dominion without dismissing it. H. Paul Santmire offered one such reinterpretation, stressing that the biblical command to "subdue the earth" affirms human connection to the rest of creation rather than emphasizing our distinction. He writes that this divine command must be understood "in the context of that all-pervading, harmonious world of *Shalom* that Genesis 1 presupposes a world where humans and animals enjoy a marked commonality and where the Creator clearly has purposes for all of creation that transcend instrumental human needs." The biblical discussion of dominion is therefore "an ecological construct" that "refers to humans assuming their divinely given niche in the earth alongside other creatures" rather than the permission for unchecked authority that has often been read into it.[20] Many theologians argue that, given this context, the best way of expressing dominion in our day is stewardship over creation: human beings do not own the planet but are called to care for God's earth responsibly.[21]

The ideal of stewardship does not reject the basic premise of dominion: human beings have power over other species. As theologian Jay McDaniel explains, "'dominion' names a historical fact," the fact that our species has become the dominant one on the planet, with the most influence and a decisive power over others. Furthermore, given the quantity of resources it takes to support current human population levels, abdicating our authority over the rest of creation in the short term is not a viable suggestion: we currently require agricultural and technological dominion over much of the rest of the planet in order to keep ourselves alive. Thus, McDaniel wrote: "In the best of scenarios, we are doomed to dominion." We must accept this and discern "an image of what might be called *right dominion*" or "dominion-as-stewardship."[22]

McDaniel's point is consistent with contemporary scientific discussions of conservation. When Peter Vitousek and his colleagues wrote about "Human Domination of Earth's Ecosystems," they chose the word "domination" advisedly, concluding that the human species "cannot escape responsibility for managing the planet." Indeed, the conservation of biodiversity depends upon a willingness of human beings to accept that we are responsible for species and ecosystems: "There is no clearer illustration of the extent of human dominance of Earth than the fact that maintaining the diversity of 'wild' species and the functioning of 'wild' ecosystems will require increasing human involvement."[23]

Dominion is, at present, a reality. It is possible to lament this fact. Christians or human beings more broadly might decide that they do not want to be the dominant species on Earth with this much power over other creatures. However, it is not realistically possible to quickly abdicate this role because the continued health of both human and nonhuman species is now up to human beings, and to decide not to manage either would be to decide to let many creatures, ecosystems, and persons suffer and die. The fate of the variety of life is now in human hands, and we must decide what to do with it. A theology that takes science seriously must affirm human dominion, and we must do our best to live out that dominion as faithful stewards. The choices we make will shape the world for our species and all others, and will determine the future of the planet's ecosystems.[24]

This assertion is a vital part of Christian moral formation because we cannot act morally and develop our priorities carefully unless we honestly face contemporary reality, recognizing who and where we are. Human beings are the dominant species on the planet, in a position to make decisions that will save or destroy the variety of life. This reality demands that we recognize our power and therefore our responsibility. We cannot throw up our hands and despair about the degradation of biodiversity because we are in control of the processes that degrade it, and we have the power to change them.

To accept the reality of our dominion over the planet and to strive to be responsible stewards who use that dominion well is to theologically accept the power of humanity. As members of the planet's dominant species, we must recognize that we have enormous influence over the fate of the variety of life. Of course, it is also vital to note that "we" as human beings do not share in this dominant role equally. We Christians in the United States, who tend to have vastly more resources and freedom than most of the planet's human population, must particularly accept that we have the capacity to make significant changes in the lives of other people and other creatures. The ways such privileged peoples live, spend money, and influence the government have enormous impacts on the world. Theology should remind us of these truths and call attention to our power as it asks us to use that power responsibly. To be morally formed for conservation, we must recognize not only that biodiversity is all around us and that its loss is an urgent moral problem but also that we can make decisions that will conserve the variety of life and change the social structures that are destroying it.

The Importance and Limits of Moral Formation

These three approaches to biodiversity within Christian community—rituals that help us to see the variety of life as beloved by God, interpretations that help us to work for conservation in the face of biodiversity loss, and theology that helps us to accept our power and responsibility—are examples of moral formation. These examples offer a sense of how and why Christian attitudes can revise the ways we understand biodiversity, reprioritize our feelings about its degradation, and learn to recognize our own power to change.

Such moral formation is an essential aspect of any comprehensive effort at conservation because it alters the place of biodiversity in the hearts and minds of Christians. To see biodiversity in our rituals, to find biblical analogues for our current challenge, and to accept the reality of dominion is to approach the variety of life in God's creation in a new way, to grasp and accept the importance of conservation for Christian communities and the societies of which we are a part.

Moral formation is important because it shapes believers' core values and attitudes. It accomplishes what David Takacs describes as making biodiversity's importance something we feel "not merely in the pocket or in the brain but in the *soul*," a move that, he claims, is required for "the most effective, permanent conservation ethic." To form Christian morality is to work toward a pervasive and abiding ethic, to nurture responsibility and care alongside a renewed awareness of our participation in the variety of life.

This is far deeper and longer term than the political approach exemplified by the Endangered Species Act. The act is based upon multiple, ambiguous moral foundations in order to appeal to a wide coalition, and so it does not call for changed attitudes about the variety of life. Indeed, because its enforcement is so strong, the ESA creates resentment against such species as the spotted owl as often as it calls citizens to appreciate and value nonhuman life. Furthermore, because it is sustained by a coalition of interests, the Endangered Species Act could be repealed at any time, causing all its authority and influence to disappear. In contrast, a believer who recognizes biodiversity as a crucial moral issue over which she has power will remain committed to conservation regardless of changing leadership and legal structures.

This contrast with political conservation reveals another strength of moral formation: its flexibility in the face of changing knowledge and conditions. The Endangered Species Act was written in 1973 and, because of the risks and difficulty of amending it, has remained relatively unchanged since then. Thus, despite the fact that it is the country's most powerful political protection of biodiversity, the act makes no explicit reference to the concept and defends the multiscalar variety of life only indirectly. Rituals, interpretations, and theologies of moral formation are far more flexible. They are not rigidly tied to a certain set of written rules or goals but instead offer a broad set of beliefs about the world and our place in it, beliefs that can evolve and grow along with a changing awareness of biodiversity and what is needed to conserve it. Because moral formation occurs primarily inside the minds and hearts of believers and in their communal conversations, it can adapt and change along with our understanding of the phenomena it is designed to protect. When our knowledge about biodiversity and the threats to it change—as they inevitably will—our rituals, interpretation, and theology can change as well.

However, the flexibility and depth of moral formation are matched by inevitable limitations. A convincing and substantive claim about biodiversity's importance cannot be effectively made in vague and unspecific terms but must instead appeal to particular people and their particular belief systems. This chapter demonstrates moral formation with very specifically Christian examples, examples that would mean little or nothing to people of other faiths or of no faith at all. Appealing to and reshaping core beliefs requires that we work within particular contexts. So, any attempt at moral formation will inevitably be focused on a certain audience. Furthermore, while revisioning, reprioritizing, and recognizing our power over biodiversity is a pervasive change for those who believe it, it has no direct effect on those who do not.

Again, a contrast with a political approach is informative: while the Endangered Species Act was built on a consensus between diverse groups and passed into law despite a lack of clarity about its justification, moral formation about the importance and threats to the variety of life instead appeals to a narrow group of people who can agree on which rituals, sacred texts, and theological ideas should shape their attitudes. Moral formation does not have the same teeth as the Endangered Species Act, and this is its central limitation. Its impact on societies is likely to be more incremental and limited than the political approach.

Just as political approaches require moral formation to inspire and sustain support for their continued influence in a democratic society, morally formative approaches require political efforts to protect the variety of life in an immediate sense and create the regulations and practical gains that can sustain a movement. Political advocacy works through legal and institutional structures, is universally applied within them, and can be overturned relatively quickly. Moral formation, on the other hand, works through the more abstract and diffuse ideas and feelings of human beings, is shaped by and shapes the values of particular communities, and is incremental but persistent. The attempt to form people so that we care for biodiversity is necessarily only a partial effort, just like political efforts to establish and enforce limits on our treatment of other species. Both are important, and both are limited.

The Conservation of Polar Bears: An Example of Politics and Moral Formation

In 2005 a coalition of environmentalist organizations filed suit to demand the listing of polar bears under the Endangered Species Act. These bears, which have been hunted and poached for centuries and have also been threatened by the pollution of the marine life they eat, have now become a symbol for the threat of climate change. Weather patterns influenced by human industry have warmed their habitat, reduced the ice from which they hunt, and are therefore threatening the survival of the species.

The Center for Biological Diversity, one organization leading the charge for listing the polar bears, made it clear that the power of the act and its capacity to enforce decisions across multiple scales motivated this listing request. The center sought not only to protect the polar bear but also to address the wide-ranging systemic causes of their decline. The organization's website on the campaign makes this clear: "We're at the forefront of the fight to protect polar bears and their habitat from the direst threat to their continued existence: global warming. As greenhouse gas emissions drive global warming at unprecedented rates, Arctic sea ice—critical to nearly every aspect of polar bear survival—melts earlier and more extensively each decade. The rate of summer sea-ice decline is so dramatic that leading researchers believe the Arctic could be completely devoid of ice in the summer as early as 2030."[25] Polar bears, like spotted owls, are not merely an endangered species but also a wedge with which to address the problems causing their extinction: in this case, the emission of greenhouse gases. The political effort to list the polar bear made sense not only for this particular species but also for the broader goals of the environmentalist movement.

However, the response of the Interior Department to this listing request also reveals the limitations of a political conservation strategy. In May 2008 Secretary of the Interior Dirk Kempthorne announced that the polar bear would be listed as a threatened species and noted that this makes hunting the bears or trading in their pelts illegal. However, he also emphasized the limits of this decision: "While the legal standards under the ESA compel me to list the polar bear as threatened, I want to make clear that this listing will not stop global climate change or prevent any sea ice from melting." Thus, Kempthorne inserted a rare exception into the listing that protected the right of oil and gas companies to explore and extract in polar bear habitat. The department's press release on the topic emphasizes this with its subtitle, "Rule will allow continuation of vital energy production in Alaska."[26] Kempthorne explicitly limited the scale of the Endangered Species Act's implications, basing his controversial decision on the claim that this law was not intended to shape climate change policy when it was written.

The listing of the polar bear is an important accomplishment for the environmental movement, and debates about the legal implications of that listing continue as of this writing. Such debates are inevitable because the Endangered Species Act depends on the enforcement of political leaders with different views about the variety of life. This is why politics alone is not a sufficient response to environmental problems. If polar bears and other arctic species are to be saved, people will need to think, feel, and act differently enough that democratically elected leaders will be forced to change national and international policies.

Moral formation calls for a campaign of education about polar bears—how and where they live and the many ways our choices throughout the rest of the world affect their habitats. It requires that those of us who consume substantial amounts of fossil fuel and contribute to other climate-changing processes contemplate the impacts of our actions on other species both near and far, and it requires that we make it a priority to change our destructive behaviors. It necessitates agitation for a new political structure: national and international laws that connect the decline in species in many parts of the world to the polluting technologies of industrialized human societies. This will happen only when people learn to think differently and demand laws that force us to act differently.

Such new thinking is very difficult, and it is hard to imagine it happening in the abstract, with arguments that can simultaneously appeal to many different people with many different views of the world. Thus, changing minds is perhaps best understood as a focused and localized process, and particular efforts must be undertaken to convince particular peoples to take the plight of polar bears seriously. The arguments of this chapter suggest that Christians should be concerned with these bears: we must recognize ourselves as their stewards, hear God's command to keep them alive with us, and find ways to ritually remember our relationship to them.

Moral formation requires political expression, and politics requires a moral public. Neither approach to conservation is enough on its own. The work of conservation must therefore resist the temptations to indulge only in theoretical and attitudinal changes or to pursue only practical and immediate results that do not shape the attitudes of citizens and peoples of faith. An ethics of polar bears and of biodiversity must therefore seek both the widespread change that laws can require and the deep, abiding shifts that moral formation can inspire.

Notes

1. White, "Historical Roots," 25, 28, 27, 30. White is very clear that the "we" referred to here is not just practicing Christians but also "those who fondly regard themselves as post-Christians" who are, he assumes, still deeply informed by the Christian worldview. He does not discuss non-Western peoples or traditions at all, except to say that Zen Buddhism, for all the environmental potential it may have, "is as deeply conditioned by Asian history as Christianity is by the experience of the West, and I am dubious of its viability among us," 27–28.

2. See for instance McFague, *Life Abundant*, chap. 3.

3. See for instance Northcott, *Environment and Christian Ethics*, chap. 2.

4. White, "Historical Roots," 24.

5. Ibid., 30.

6. Laurel Kearns notes that in this way White's argument mirrors that of Max Weber in *The Protestant Ethic and the Spirit of Capitalism*, using this similarity to argue that White is too focused on ideas as opposed to practices and institutional structures: "As in Weber's case, the link between a certain ethic and the development of a complex social structure such as capitalism, or in White's instance, the scientific-technological complex, is complicated." Kearns, "Saving the Creation," 40. While I agree that White's emphasis on the importance of religious ideas is simplistic, and attempt to balance it with the more practical concerns of public policy, I find his emphasis on the ways religious ideas have societal and material implications an important contribution to a more nuanced understanding of conservation.

7. Ehrlich and Ehrlich, *One with Nineveh*, 270.

8. Takacs, *Idea of Biodiversity*, 254.

9. Wilson, *Creation*, 5.

10. Takacs, *Idea of Biodiversity*, 256. Emphasis in original.

11. For theological analysis of Francis's life and its implications for ecological ethics, see Boff, *Saint Francis*; and Hart, *Sacramental Commons*, chap. 2.

12. David Rhoads, "Blessing the Animals," in Rhoads, *Earth and Word*, 239–40.

13. Troy Messenger, "These Stones Shall be God's House: Tools for Earth Liturgy," in Hessel and Rasmussen, eds., *Earth Habitat*, 174.

14. The text of the Hebrew scriptures has different accounts of *how many* of each creature was saved, at one point recounting that Noah saved "two of every kind" (Gen. 6:19), but then later listing "seven pairs of all clean animals. . . and a pair of the animals that are not clean" (7:2).

15. Holmes Rolston III, "God and Endangered Species," in Hamilton, Takeuchi, and East-West Center, *Ethics, Religion and Biodiversity*, 43.

16. See Noah Alliance, http://noahalliance.org/.

17. Bouma-Prediger, *For the Beauty of the Earth*, 99.

18. Nash, *Loving Nature*, 101.

19. White, "Historical Roots," 29.

20. H. Paul Santmire, "Genesis Creation Narratives Revisited," 374–75.

21. See for instance DeWitt et al., *Caring for Creation*.

22. Jay B. McDaniel, "The Garden of Eden, the Fall, and Life in Christ," in Tucker and Grim, *Worldviews and Ecology*, 74–75. Emphasis in original.

23. Vitousek et al., "Human Domination of Earth's Ecosystems," 499. Ecologists Reed Noss and Alan Cooperrider make the same point, noting that even a decision to fence an area and leave it alone as a reserve is a managerial decision, particularly because virtually anywhere in the world such an action requires considerable enforcement and monitoring to sustain. "Letting things be" is simply not an option. Noss and Cooperrider, *Saving Nature's Legacy*, 24–25.

24. For further exploration of this perspective, see Kevin J. O'Brien, "Toward an Ethics of Biodiversity: Science and Theology in Environmentalist Dialogue" in Kearns and Catherine Keller, *Ecospirit*.

25. Center for Biological Diversity, "Saving the Polar Bear: Background," www.biologicaldiversity.org/species/mammals/polar_bear/background.html.

26. U.S. Department of the Interior, "Secretary Kempthorne Announces Decision to Protect Polar Bears," http://www.doi.gov/news/o8_News_Releases/o80514a.html. A year later Kempthorne's successor affirmed his decision, continuing protection of the bears under the act but also explicitly noting that "the Endangered Species Act is not the proper mechanism for controlling our nation's carbon emissions." U.S. Department of the Interior, "Salazar Retains Conservation Rule for Polar Bears," www.doi.gov/news/o9_News_Releases/o50809b.html.

Part V

Social Justice and the
Conservation of Biodiversity

Chapter 8

Biological and Cultural Diversity

In 1983 Dwight Dion Sr. was arrested for hunting and killing four bald eagles in South Dakota. At the time eagles were a severely threatened species, protected not only by the Endangered Species Act but also by the Bald Eagle Protection Act, passed by Congress in 1940. The earlier act, designed to protect the nation's symbolic animal long before the extinction of other species was a widespread concern, makes it illegal to take "any bald eagle . . . or any part, nest, or egg thereof."[1] The protection of eagles is therefore one of the longest-standing conservation commitments in the United States.

However, Dwight Dion argued that the Endangered Species Act and the Bald Eagle Protection Act did not apply to him. A Yankton Sioux, Dion was hunting on his tribe's reservation, an area declared sovereign at its establishment in an 1858 treaty with the U.S. government. In that treaty the Sioux were explicitly guaranteed the right to hunt on their land undisturbed. Dion did not dispute that he had taken eagles in violation of the law; instead, he claimed that these laws did not bind him. The case eventually made its way to the Supreme Court, which finally upheld Dion's conviction. The justices determined based on a close reading of the Eagle Protection Act that the 1940 legislation "abrogated the rights of members of the Yankton Sioux Tribe under the 1858 treaty."[2]

At issue in Dion's case was not just the conservation of a species but also the sovereignty of minority communities in the face of federal conservation laws. In 1996 representatives from tribes and tribal organizations across the country gathered in Seattle to discuss this broader issue, focusing particularly on the implications of the Endangered Species Act for their sovereignty. They forcefully argued that this law "does not and should not apply to Indian Tribes," asserting that "tribal rights to manage their resources in accordance with their own beliefs and values must be protected."[3] While this group did not dispute the goal of conservation, they did object to the U.S. government's claim that it can enforce conservation on Indian lands. Indeed, many tribal participants were committed to going further than the ESA requires, and another consensus at the Seattle meeting was that traditional practices would conserve biodiversity at a broader and better scale of attention: "the ESA is too narrow; its emphasis on single-species management fares poorly in comparison with the tribes' holistic management approach."[4]

The case of Dwight Dion and the issue of tribal sovereignty are complicated because they represent an encounter between two vital and important moral interests. On the one hand, the people of the United States and our federal government have a legitimate interest in protecting endangered species and so must enforce conservation laws. On the other hand, native communities in this country have a legitimate claim to sovereignty on their lands and good reasons not to trust the federal government to manage their lives or their relationship to the natural world. This is an issue where conservation meets another valid moral interest, where an ethics of biodiversity must recognize the problems it causes and the possibility that it should be limited in the face of other moral concerns.

The work of this book so far has been to make an ethics of biodiversity more possible: to offer definitions of the idea and explanations of its value, introduce the importance of scale in our approaches to it, and advocate both political and morally formative approaches to its conservation. The work remaining is somewhat different because this chapter and the next seek to make an ethics of biodiversity more complicated, to bring it into dialogue with an ethics of cultural diversity and then analyze the issues of social justice raised by and relevant to conservation efforts.

This chapter expands the conversation outward from the conservation of biodiversity to a related but nevertheless distinct contemporary problem: the degradation of cultural diversity. The destruction of Native American communities is one important example of this degradation, as it is increasingly difficult for these communities to preserve their languages, practices, and traditions. However, the problem also extends globally because many traditional and indigenous cultures are threatened by homogenization from the overpowering influence of dominant, industrialized cultures.

To analyze this broad and important problem, it is necessary to move beyond the ecologists and conservation biologists who have served as primary discussion partners thus far and turn to the work of anthropologists, activists, and philosophers who discuss the threats to human diversity in our world and the importance of preserving the differences between us. After evaluating both the ways this problem has been linked to biodiversity and the arguments cautioning against such links, I will argue that the conservation of biodiversity and cultural diversity must be seen as related but distinct activities and offer some suggestions about how this approach might help to relate an ethics of biodiversity to other moral challenges.

The Degradation of Cultural Diversity

"Culture" is of course a concept at least as complicated and broad as "nature" or "biodiversity," and a full account of the ethical implications of "cultural diversity" would require a book of its own. Culture, most broadly, is the way we human beings organize our relationships to one another and to our environments, the ideas and systems we pass on to the next generation. Culture, like all of life, is constantly evolving in response to the world around it. As with biodiversity, it is therefore possible to witness new cultural innovations in our own time: the information revolution makes contact between distinct peoples possible and creates the potential for global cultural exchange; new forms of artistic and linguistic expression develop and thrive throughout the world, expanding and changing the cultures from which they emerge.

However, the prevailing trend most observers of cultural diversity find in the twenty-first century is degradation, a loss of cultural variety and distinction in the face of a few dominant ways of living. A small number of globalizing cultures have overwhelmed the myriad ways of life that evolved among diverse peoples for thousands of years. One of the clearest and most direct accounts of cultural diversity's degradation comes in *Light at the Edge of the World*, a book by the ethnobotanist Wade Davis that focuses on "the demise of cultural diversity, the erosion of what might be termed the ethnosphere, the full complexity and complement of human potential as brought into being by culture and adaptation since the dawn of consciousness."[5]

The primary cause of this erosion, Davis argues, is not the natural decline of certain cultures as others take their place but rather the imperialism of Western, globalizing, industrial forces that drive traditional peoples off of their lands and away from one another:

> Traditional cultures have survived precisely because of their ability to cope with change, the one constant in history. People disappear only when they are overwhelmed by external forces, when drastic conditions imposed on them from the outside render them incapable of adapting to new possibilities for life. . . . It is not change that threatens the integrity of the ethnosphere, it is power, the crude face of domination.[6]

Davis's is just one voice in a movement that seeks to call attention to and stop the degradation of cultural diversity. The argument of this movement can be understood in three steps: (1) cultural diversity is threatened, (2) the source of the threat is the domination of globalizing cultures, and (3) members of those globalizing cultures must make changes to ensure that the variety of human cultures survives.

The first step of this argument is the claim that cultural diversity is threatened, which is difficult to prove conclusively only because "culture" is such a broad and vague term. So, many advocates for cultural diversity turn to a synecdoche by counting the number of languages spoken on Earth, and they find in this metric strong evidence of drastic loss. Some languages that exist today are spoken by only one or two elderly people, making their demise in the near future virtually inevitabile. Hundreds of other languages have only a handful of speakers and will not be taught to the next generation, making their death increasingly likely. Thousands more are dwindling and will soon be in the same situation. When these languages die, advocates assume, they will take with them the richness and diversity of their peoples' cultures.

In the year 2000 linguist David Crystal estimated that roughly six thousand distinct languages were spoken on Earth. He further estimated that during the twenty-first century three thousand of these languages would cease to be actively spoken, that "at least one language must die, on average, every two weeks or so."[7] These numbers are important, Crystal argues, because "language lies at the heart of what it means to be human. If the development of multiple cultures is so important, then the role of languages becomes critical, for cultures are chiefly transmitted through spoken and written languages."[8] In other words, threats to linguistic diversity are threats to cultural diversity, urgent threats that demand attention.

Language provides a clear measure for the drastic threats to cultural diversity, but it does not explain these threats. For that, many activists turn to the complex dynamic of trends labeled "globalization," the expansion of economic and cultural forces that has simplified exchanges across borders and made the world a smaller place for industrialized societies. For many advocates of cultural diversity, globalization is a dangerous trend all too often accompanied by domination. Along these lines researcher and activist David Harmon argues that cultural diversity is being destroyed by the expansion of global capitalism and the attitudes that fuel it: "We seem bent on reducing civilization to a single type, that of Western (largely U.S.) post-industrial society—a kind of Global America."[9] Harmon believes that minority cultures and traditional ways of life simply cannot compete with this Global America or the economic, political, and military powers that back it. Behind this argument are critiques of cultural globalization—worries about the "McDonaldization" of global society, about homogenous television and movie entertainment that reduce the differences between peoples and places. Harmon suggests that the root of this monolithic culture is a "particular worldview," a belief that "diversity produces discord, and uniformity is the only road to unity."[10] Thus, the globalization of Western, industrialized culture is identified as the root of the degradation of so many other cultures throughout the world.

The final step in the case for cultural diversity is an argument that the destruction of other cultures should matter to people in the industrialized world, to members of the dominant, globalizing culture. Davis makes such a case in *Light at the Edge of the World*, a plea for moral formation and a call for us as citizens of the dominant culture to recognize the value of the threatened traditions and peoples throughout the world so that we will work to help them survive and make room for them alongside our own cultures. In part this argument appeals to our survival instinct, arguing that the preservation of other cultures and other ways of seeing and living in the world can be useful when and if our own approach fails. Davis notes, for instance, that our own culture has few tools for sustainable life within the limits of natural systems. He proposes that we need to draw on other traditions to become "a conscious species aware of our place on the planet and fully capable not only of doing no harm but of ensuring that all creatures in every garden find a way to flourish."[11] Davis's primary plea, however, is for respect and awe in the face of difference, for an appreciation of the intrinsic value of other cultures precisely because they are different from our own. He hopes his readers will believe along with him that it is a tragedy when a culture is destroyed because every culture is valuable and interesting in its own right: "Every view of the world that fades away, every culture that disappears, diminishes a possibility of life and reduces the human repertoire of adaptive responses to the common problems that confront us all."[12] When languages die off and cultures fade away, we are all impoverished.

Of course, there are many perspectives on what cultural diversity is, what threatens it, and why we should save it, but it is enough for now to note these broad arguments that cultures and their languages are threatened by dominant cultures and should be protected.[13] Understanding the degradation of cultural diversity, even at this basic a level, raises the question of how this issue might relate to the distinct but related problem of biodiversity loss.

Linking Cultural Diversity to Biodiversity

Perhaps it is not surprising that activists advocating the protection of cultural diversity frequently draw parallels to biological diversity, arguing that people should care about the decline in cultural variety in the same ways that we care about the declines in ecological variety. For instance, according to David Crystal, "the arguments which support the need for biological diversity also apply to language."[14] Wade Davis applies the same logic to cultural diversity as a whole: "Even as we lament the collapse of biological diversity, we pay too little heed to a parallel process of loss, the demise of cultural diversity."[15] David Harmon works for a nongovernmental organization called Terralingua, the mission of which is to protect what members have labeled "biocultural" diversity, a concept that includes the linguistic, cultural, and biological variety of the world.[16]

The linkage between biological and cultural diversity is generally explained and defended first based on the rhetorical similarities between them. The work of defending cultural diversity is related to the conservation of biodiversity because both depend on the moral value associated with diversity itself. The calls to stand up for cultural and biological diversity both assume that variety matters, that diversity is good. This can be at least partly explained by the fact that both causes became prominent in the United States at the end of the twentieth century, a time when it was becoming popular to believe that differences are important and valuable, when diversity was developing into an ideal against which natural and human communities would be measured.[17] This shared context creates a vital common ground and common interest between the movements seeking to save cultural and biological diversity. Activists who care about one form of diversity have a vested interest in fighting for the other because the more the broad idea of diversity gains credibility, the more both biological and cultural diversity will thrive.

An even more basic defense of the link between cultural and biological diversity emerges from the fact that the human beings who shape and are shaped by cultures are biological creatures, evolved from the same processes as all others. Thus, the intraspecies differences between us are themselves an expression of the variety of life. Anthropologists and biologists consider the social and genetic differences between apes to be an expression of biodiversity, so it only makes sense to consider the social and genetic differences between our own primate species the same way. In this sense cultural diversity is an expression of biodiversity, a subset of it. Along these lines Harmon argues that the object of activists' protection should be biocultural diversity, "the evolutionary process through which the vitality of *all* life has come down to us through the ages."[18] Harmon goes on to argue that languages are comparable to species and should be protected by the same sorts of methods that have developed in the conservation movement.[19] From this perspective the differences between humanity and other species are much less important than the commonalities, so the diversity of cultures is best understood as an expression of biology.

A third argument linking biological and cultural diversity notes that the highest concentrations of each tend to be grouped together, so there is a pragmatic reason to see their protection as a cooperation rather than competition. For example, the anthropologist Darrell Posey finds an "inextricable link" between biological and cultural diversity because of the simple fact that "many of the areas of highest biological diversity on the planet are inhabited by Indigenous peoples" whose cultures are threatened.[20] Endangered languages and societies tend to coexist with endangered species and ecosystems, so the protection of these cultural and biological hotspots should be seen as a single project.

The most frequent proposal along these lines is for industrialized societies to give up control of threatened areas, returning the land to indigenous peoples and marginalized communities precisely because their societies have a proven ability to coexist in harmony with healthy ecosystems. This was the fundamental argument made at the 1996 Seattle meeting of tribal leaders, who argued that they would not be bound by the Endangered Species Act in part because their traditional practices were better conservationist tools. Supporting such thinking, conservation biologist Gary Paul Nabhan proposed that endangered territories should be entrusted to "cultures of habitat," communities that have proven their ability to live stably with their environments across many generations.[21]

Perhaps the most prominent advocate of the link between cultural and biological diversity is Vandana Shiva, an Indian physicist and activist who teaches, speaks, and organizes to oppose destructive domination, advocating the protection of both threatened creatures and threatened ways of life. For Shiva diversity is about alternatives, about cultivating multiple options and the capacities by which to select between them, offering a variety of ways to think about the natural world and our cultural relationship to it.

Shiva characterizes the importance of diversity primarily by contrasting it with its opposite, monoculture. The current trends of globalization, she argues, are the result of a "monoculture of the mind," which produces uniform systems of control, farms that grow only one crop over thousands of acres, and societies that encourage only one approach to thinking and living over thousands of communities. Diversity is here understood as a problem, or it is ignored entirely: "Monocultures of the mind make diversity disappear from perception, and consequently from the world."[22] Opposing this perspective, Shiva embraces the alternative "logic of diversity," which recognizes the intrinsic value of nature, acknowledges the importance of multiple perspectives on any problem, and pays particular attention to the voices of minorities and marginalized groups in human communities.[23]

Diversity matters, Shiva argues, because it is the driving force of both biological and cultural evolution. Ecosystems, species, societies, and communities develop and succeed only when they accept and embrace variety and the flexibility that comes from it: "Diversity is the characteristic of nature and the basis of ecological stability. Diverse ecosystems give rise to diverse life forms, and to diverse cultures. The co-evolution of cultures, life forms and habitats has conserved the biological diversity on this planet. Cultural diversity and biological diversity go hand in hand."[24] Evolution is the foundation of both types of diversity, and the root of the connection between them.

To Shiva the monocultures of globalization seem to desire only to limit, control, and own all of Earth's systems, and this explains their denial of the evolutionary link between humanity and the nonhuman world. A prime example of this attitude is demonstrated by biotechnology, which involves patenting species and natural processes for human profit, claiming ownership over what has evolved naturally and assuming that human markets can determine the value of a genetic tendency that occurred without human input or was bred over generations of nurturing by a nonindustrial society. This approach to the world "makes biology stand on its head. Complex organisms which have evolved over millennia in nature, and through the contributions of Third World peasants, tribals and healers are reduced to their parts, and treated as mere inputs into genetic engineering."[25] In Shiva's view the conservation of biodiversity cannot be well managed through the free markets of globalization; rather, it requires the opposite logic of diversity, which allows marginalized cultures and organisms to thrive on their own terms.

Like many advocates of the link between cultural and biological diversity, Shiva argues that indigenous peoples should be given the authority to control their own lives and the lands on which they have traditionally lived. This is the best way to ensure both healthy human communities and healthy habitats: "stable communities, in harmony with their ecosystems, always protect biodiversity."[26] She writes:

> Biodiversity is therefore not just an indicator of sustainability, it is also an indicator of justice. Compassion for other species translates into compassion for our fellow humans. If we can protect the earthworm, the butterfly and the bee, we will also protect our small farmers, because the same technological and trade structures that push butterflies and bees to extinction are pushing small farmers everywhere to extinction.[27]

Shiva offers a helpful example of the intersection between cultural variety and biodiversity from her native India, where forty thousand children go blind each year from vitamin A deficiencies. The solution of industrialized, globalized society is to spend millions of dollars on research, supplements, treatment, and genetic engineering; one such project is "golden rice," a genetically modified grain that includes the necessary vitamin. Shiva identifies a far safer and less expensive solution in traditional practices: Indians used to grow a leafy green vegetable called bathua, rich in vitamin A among other nutrients, alongside their grains, cultivating both in the same field and consuming the greens along with wheat and rice. Bathua is currently eradicated as a weed in cash-crop fields, but if it were grown and eaten again, it could address a key health problem while also encouraging traditional agriculture that is friendlier to local biodiversity. A mind-set capable of valuing diversity could see that this a truly integrative solution, healing the people and feeding them at the same time, even if it reduces the cash value of their exports.[28]

Shiva scales upward from this example to make a global claim: the industrialized world must preserve, respect, and learn from more traditional cultures if we are to protect the diversity of life on Earth. So, the work of conservation goes hand-in-hand with the work of saving cultural diversity. If diversity matters, if we pay attention to evolution and our place within it, and if we attend to the twin threats of social and environmental degradation, we will see cultural and biological diversity as fundamentally linked.

Distinctions between Biology and Culture

However, there are also strong arguments that caution activists not to take this link too far, emphasizing important distinctions between cultural and biological diversity. These arguments make the case that an encompassing idea of diversity is too vague to inspire concrete and practical actions, that human cultures are different from other species in important ways, and that it is unfair and unjust to make generalizations about "traditional" peoples and their ecosystems.

Perhaps the most straightforward argument against identifying cultural diversity too closely with biodiversity is that such a move will distract from the more focused effort of protecting just one or the other. This argument is well demonstrated by the conservation biologists Reed Noss and Alan Cooperrider, who do not doubt that human cultures evolved from natural systems but nevertheless question whether it is advisable to stress this connection. They ask: "What would be the practical effect of including the diversity of human languages, religious beliefs, behaviors, land management practices, etc., in a biodiversity definition and striving to promote this diversity in conservation strategy? We believe the effect would be to trivialize the concept and make it unworkable, even dangerous."[29] As advocates for the conservation of biodiversity, Noss and Cooperrider are cautious of anything that might dilute or distract from their primary goal, and cultural diversity appears to be such a distraction.

Conserving biodiversity is already a complicated goal. It is already difficult to convince the general public about threats to the variety of life and the sacrifices required to conserve it. Why, Noss and Cooperrider ask, should that goal be made more complicated by adding another dimension to that diversity? A more straightforward approach, focusing clearly on nonhuman biological diversity, seems much more manageable. So they identify their primary interest in human systems as "how culture might adapt to nature. We want to conserve all cultural approaches that are compatible with conserving biodiversity."[30] It is not difficult to imagine the same sort of argument from an advocate of cultural diversity, who might argue that conservation is a distraction from the project of protecting the diversities of human life. Such an advocate of cultural diversity might suggest that attention should be focused only on those biological systems that are compatible with the varieties of human culture in our world.

Alongside this strategic argument about separating the two forms of diversity, a more abstract argument suggests that cultural and biological variety really are different and must be distinguished if we are to understand them properly. This case is made well by the philosopher Jürgen Habermas, who asserts, "The ecological perspective on species conservation cannot be transferred to cultures." He explains: "Cultural heritages and the forms of life articulated in them normally reproduce themselves by convincing those whose personality structures they shape, that is, by motivating them to appropriate productively and continue the traditions."[31] In other words, cultures should continue to exist only when the people within them *agree* that they should continue to exist: each person and each generation should decide whether or not to continue the traditions, practices, and beliefs they inherit.

The same is not true, Habermas assumes, for a nonhuman ecosystem, which may change over evolutionary time but does not have a recognizable agency of its own.[32] Thus, our responsibility to other species and ecosystems is to guarantee their survival, to manage them in a way that conserves them. We should not take that approach to human systems; instead we must allow human beings to make their own decisions whenever possible. Cultures may be understood to evolve, but this evolution takes place through the voluntary choices of human beings. This means that the approach to cultural diversity should not be conservation in the same sense that we would conserve an ecosystem. Instead, it is important to honor the possibility that some peoples will not want to keep all aspects of the culture they have inherited. Indeed, Habermas writes, a human culture is only authentic if its members choose to sustain it. So "to guarantee survival would necessarily rob the members of the very freedom to say yes or no that is necessary if they are to appropriate and preserve their cultural heritage."[33] According to this argument, it is inappropriate and unfair to conserve a culture from the outside; cultural diversity is different from biodiversity because only the latter should be externally protected.

Another version of the same argument could draw on the claim of the previous chapter that human beings are stewards over other species. Such stewardship may be necessary and appropriate as a response to biodiversity degradation: the management of ecosystems and species is an inevitable responsibility our species must accept given contemporary realities. However, stewardship and management are not adequate or accurate expressions of how threats to cultural diversity should be handled. Privileged people in dominant cultures should not take on a role of stewardship over other human beings and should not claim the responsibility of managing other cultures. Instead, we should work to ensure that those peoples are able to manage and steward themselves, preserving tradition or changing it as they choose.

This emphasis on the importance of agency, of allowing human beings to make choices, leads to a third and final argument against linking cultural and biological diversity too closely, an argument that it is politically problematic to assume that traditional or indigenous cultures will necessarily make choices compatible with the conservation of biodiversity. Advocates for the connection frequently find hope in the idea that the cultures marginalized by industrialized global dominance—the groups Nabhan calls "cultures of habitat" and Shiva refers to as "Third World peasants, tribals and healers"—will manage their lands in a way that is harmonious with conservation. Evidence suggests that this will frequently be true, but some critics worry that great harm can come from a generalized assumption that it will *always* be true.

Australian legal scholar Harriet Ketley makes this point well, arguing that those who too-closely link cultural diversity and biodiversity tend to make two dangerous and false assumptions: First, that Aboriginal peoples never negatively affected their environments and, second, that contemporary Aboriginal peoples have goals and plans that exactly match those of conservationists. These assumptions ignore the fact that indigenous peoples can and have had negative impacts on their local environments, and even caused extinctions and degradation. It also denies contemporary peoples the capacity to make choices about their own lives. Ketley worries that this attitude "ignores the variety of aspirations of contemporary Aboriginal communities, aspirations which may well include commercial development." It is entirely possible that members of traditional cultures will want to be part of the large-scale, industrialized practices that degrade biodiversity. This would lead to a conflict, a choice between the desire to conserve the variety of life on the one hand and to respect the autonomy and freedom of marginalized peoples on the other.[34]

Conservation biologists Kent Redford and Allyn Stearman also express this concern well: "To expect indigenous people to retain traditional, low-impact patterns of resource use is to deny them the right to grow and change in ways compatible with the rest of humanity."[35] Some of these peoples may well have goals and ideas entirely suited to conservation, but others may not. The central point for Redford and Stearman is that, just like all other cultures and traditions, "indigenous peoples are not a monolithic entity." It is unfair to restrict them to any set of goals or ideals, particularly a conservationist way of life that well-intentioned outsiders might wish to impose on them.[36] Interestingly, Redford and Stearman conclude that supporting indigenous land rights in tropical forests may well be "the best hope" for conserving those ecosystems, but they adamantly remind their readers that giving people the right to control their own land does not necessarily mean it will be conserved.[37]

A similar argument can be made about the case of eagle preservation on the Yankton Sioux reservation in South Dakota. It may well be that the best way to ensure healthy ecosystems in the southeastern part of that state is to allow the Sioux nation complete sovereignty over the land. However, if that sovereignty is based upon a legal treaty, then it should not depend upon conservation to justify it. If the Sioux have the right to hunt on their land without any outside interference, then that right should not depend upon whether they would do so sustainably and carefully. On the other hand, if they are bound by the laws made in Washington, D.C., then it is impossible to claim that their cultural autonomy is fully respected. Even when they might be compatible, it is impossible and irresponsible to claim that cultural diversity and biological diversity are the same thing. It will not always be possible to advocate both with a single agenda.

The Homology between Biodiversity and Cultural Diversity

Clearly there are good reasons to emphasize the connections between biodiversity and cultural diversity but also good reasons to cautiously remember the distinctions between them. It is important to recognize that the variety of human cultures has evolved from the natural world, that the two are connected, and that advocates of each therefore have reason to recognize the importance of both diversities. However, it is also important to emphasize the agency and freedom of human cultures, particularly those indigenous and traditional cultures that have too often been denied control over their own existence, and so it is not appropriate to simplistically claim that cultures should be conserved or that such protection will be necessarily compatible with the conservation of biodiversity.

Given these concerns, perhaps the most helpful way to think about the relationship between cultural and biological diversity is to simultaneously emphasize their links and their distinctions, a dynamic solidified by recognizing a homology between them. In biology a homology is a correspondence in structure that does not necessarily imply a correspondence in function. For example, the five fingers of a human hand are homologous to the five skeletal supports in a whale's flipper; an evolutionary link between these mammals helps to explain this similarity, but it does not detract from the very real differences between whale and human appendages.

A homology implies a similarity in structure and a common evolutionary origin without suggesting an absolute identity between two things. This is exactly the sort of nuance required to think about the relationship between biological and cultural diversity: the two are homologous because both arise from and depend upon natural systems, but they also have important differences. Understanding each one can help us to understand the other, but they should not be collapsed into one category.

In light of the homology between cultural and biological diversity, activists can and should stress the rhetorical importance of diversity as a broad concept, but this should not go so far as the assertion that the protection of cultures always and necessarily overlaps with the protection of ecosystems. Advocates for human beings can stress the importance of agency in cultural preservation, but they should not simplistically assume that the nonhuman systems from which we evolved are unimportant. The common threats to cultural and biological diversity can be opposed by a united front, but this does not mean that marginalized cultures should be simplistically understood as inevitably on the side of conservation. In general there are important distinctions between cultural and biological diversity, but we can still gain a great deal by comparing and linking them. This homology means that an ethics of biodiversity is not always and necessarily also an ethics of cultural diversity, but there are nevertheless reasons for conservationists to pay attention to the related efforts to protect the variety of human systems.

The destruction of cultural diversity, the depletion of the various and intricate views of the world that the human race has developed, is a serious problem and a tragedy. As human languages and ways of life disappear, it makes the human species less adaptable, simultaneously demonstrating and exacerbating our capacity to neglect and abuse one another. The degradation of biological diversity, the depletion of variety throughout the biosphere, is also a serious problem and a tragedy. As genetic, species, and ecosystemic variety disappear, the living world becomes less adaptable, and the dangerous human capacity to carelessly neglect and destroy the world around us expands unchecked. These issues demand urgent, organized, and serious responses. The best responses to these problems may be interrelated; but they are not the same problem, so the solutions will not be identical. Some cultures have a legitimate claim on autonomous rights regardless of whether they will conserve the diversity around them, and some ecosystems should be defended regardless of the impact on human systems that utilize them. If biodiversity and cultural diversity are homologous, we can accept both the commonalities and the differences between them.

An Ethics of Biodiversity amid a Variety of Moral Challenges

Thinking of biodiversity and cultural diversity as homologous does not answer all the challenging questions facing us. It does not offer conclusive answers when tribal sovereignty or religious freedom clash with conservation, as they appear to have clashed in the case of Dwight Dion. However, this perspective at least suggests a language with which to characterize the common grounds and conflicts between competing interests. Tribal sovereignty is frequently, but not always, compatible with the protection of biological diversity. Conservation efforts often help to make space for a variety of human cultures to thrive, but they will not always do so.

This language is useful to characterize the relationship between biological and cultural diversity. It also serves as an example of how an ethics of biodiversity might relate to the many other legitimate moral challenges facing human beings today. Of course, not all problems are as neatly related to the degradation of biodiversity as the destruction of cultural diversity, but it is important to recognize that there are such connections and distinctions between all moral challenges.

This recognition is important, in part, because there are so many social and environmental problems in our world. Indeed, perhaps the greatest challenge facing those of us who hope to conserve the variety of life is that we cannot present this as the only or most urgent moral issue. As much as we should pass laws and change minds about biodiversity, other realities and problems also demand immediate attention. Human beings suffer the cruel fate of abject poverty across the world in shockingly high numbers. Violence, neglect, and genocide are produced by senseless prejudices rooted in differences in race, nationality, gender, sexual orientation, and many other factors. The scourge of war destroys habitats, communities, and lives at an alarming rate. Industrialized civilizations are increasingly warming the climate, fundamentally changing the character of many of Earth's ecosystems. No attentive person in the world today can deny that these and many other problems are real, are serious, and demand a response. An ethics of biodiversity must acknowledge such disturbing realities, neither ignoring their importance nor pretending that it can address them all.

It is far beyond the scope of this book to explore the wide and troubling variety of moral challenges facing the human race today.

However, it is worthwhile to note that the general approach taken to cultural diversity in this chapter can also apply when relating other problems to an ethics of biodiversity. There are, for instance, many connections to be made between the variety of life and human poverty: both reflect the limitations of our current agricultural systems, and both call for privileged peoples to consider sacrificing some comforts and luxuries to help others. However, there are also important differences and potential conflicts: one successful path out of poverty for some communities has been a switch away from subsistence farming to industrialized agriculture and resource extraction, both of which harm the variety of life. Biodiversity and poverty are issues with both common ground and important differences.

The same case could be made about climate change. The atmosphere is changing because of the same careless expansion of human life and industry that degrades biodiversity, and climactic shifts are potentially one of the central threats to many populations, species, and ecosystems in the coming decades and centuries. However, an ethics of climate change would be informed by very different scientific evidence and approaches, and would enter into political and moral debate with a very different status and starting ground, from an ethics of biodiversity. Climate change is widely understood as a very real problem, and there is genuine urgency in the ways many people approach it that far fewer bring to the loss of biodiversity. However, climate change is also frequently understood exclusively as a technological problem that can be solved by engineers without changes in behavior or human attitudes, and so it creates different challenges for moral formation.

The point to be generalized from these brief examples is that biodiversity degradation is intricately connected to other moral challenges, and it should not be understood without reflecting on these connections. Beginning from an ecological perspective, an ethics of biodiversity must recognize and develop the relationships and interconnections between moral issues rather than narrowly exclude them. However, it can be tempting when thinking ecologically to believe that all things are so interconnected that they can always be neatly and completely synthesized. These examples demonstrate that an ethics of biodiversity is not identical to an ethics of poverty, climate change, or cultural diversity: there are important distinctions, crucial limits to the interconnectedness between moral issues and challenges.

The overarching theme of this chapter and the next is that an ethics of biodiversity must be nuanced and flexible enough to recognize other moral challenges and still advocate the conservation of the variety of life. Biodiversity is not the only thing worth saving in this world, and its protection is not the only work to which concerned people are called; other social and environmental challenges are very real and very important. Nevertheless, the variety of life is worth saving, and the work of preserving it remains crucial. To make both these claims requires a delicate balance. As such, it is vital that our ethical approach to biodiversity include a careful and thoughtful approach to analyzing its impact on and implications for other interests, on issues such as cultural diversity, poverty, and climate change. The next chapter builds on this idea by bringing an ethics of biodiversity into conversation with the concerns of Christian liberation theology.

Notes

1. U.S. Congress, The Bald Eagle Protection Act, § a. Perhaps the earliest attention to the plight of the eagle that could be called "environmentalist" in the contemporary sense comes in one of the cornerstones of the movement, Rachel Carson's 1962 classic *Silent Spring*. Carson demonstrates that the rampant insecticides in eagle habitats had "virtually destroyed its ability to reproduce" and calls upon citizens and lawmakers to take drastic action. Carson, *Silent Spring*, 118.

2. *United States v. Dion.* It is important to note, however, that the Court makes no substantive ruling about how the ESA might affect treaty rights. It only notes that, since it finds the right to hunt eagles abrogated in 1940, no claim needs to be made about the relationship between this right and the 1973 act. The Court therefore resolved the narrow case of whether this particular tribal member had the right to hunt eagles but declined to address the question of how the ESA affects tribal sovereignty. See Mary Gray Holt, "Choosing Harmony: Indian Rights and the Endangered Species Act" in Baur and Irvin, *The Endangered Species Act.*

3. Quoted in Wilkinson, "The Role of Bilateralism," 1072. Wilkinson was a participant in the Seattle workshop, as well as the later meetings with the Secretary.

4. Ibid., 1070.

5. Davis, *Light at the Edge of the World*, 5.

6. Ibid., 121–22.

7. Crystal, *Language Death*, 19.

8. Ibid., 33–34.

9. Harmon, *In Light of Our Differences*, 44.

10. Ibid., 8.

11. Davis, *Light at the Edge of the World*, 202.

12. Ibid., 14.

13. Some would argue against this goal, of course. For an important critique against "diversity" as an organizing moral principle, see Michaels, *The Trouble with Diversity*.

14. Crystal, *Language Death*, 32.

15. Davis, *Light at the Edge of the World*, 5.

16. See Terralingua, www.terralingua.org/html/home.html.

17. See Mark Stoll, "Creating Ecology: Protestants and the Moral Community of Creation" in Lodge and Hamlin, *Religion and the New Ecology*, 55.

18. Harmon, *In Light of Our Differences*, xiii.

19. Ibid., chap. 3. Harmon even argues that linguistic diversity, like biodiversity, is best thought of at three hierarchical levels: the structural diversity within a language, the diversity between languages, and the diversity of lineages that link language families, 55–56.

20. Darrell A. Posey, "Biological and Cultural Diversity: The Inextricable, Linked by Language and Politics" in Maffi, *On Biocultural Diversity*, 379. Posey quotes the phrase "inextricable link" from the Declaration of Bélem, which was produced at the First International Congress of Ethnobiology of the International Society of Ethnobiology in 1988.

21. Nabhan, *Cultures of Habitat*.

22. Shiva, *Monocultures of the Mind*, 5.

23. In much of her writing, Shiva expresses this as an explicitly ecofeminist argument: "The logic of diversity is best derived from biodiversity and from women's links to it. It helps to look at dominant structures from below, from the ground of diversity, which reveal monocultures to be unproductive and the knowledge that produces them as primitive rather than sophisticated." Vandana Shiva, "Women's Indigenous Knowledge and Biodiversity Conservation" in Mies and Shiva, *Ecofeminism*, 164–65.

24. Shiva, *Monocultures of the Mind*, 65.

25. Vandana Shiva, "Biodiversity, Biotechnology, and Profits," in Shiva, *Biodiversity*.

26. Shiva, *Monocultures of the Mind*, 73.

27. Shiva, *Tomorrow's Biodiversity*, 127.

28. Shiva, *Monocultures of the Mind*, 25–26.

29. Noss and Cooperrider, *Saving Nature's Legacy*, 14.

30. Ibid.

31. Jürgen Habermas, "Struggles for Recognition in the Democratic Constitutional State," in *Multiculturalism: Examining the Politics of Recognition*, ed. Charles Taylor and Amy Gutmann (Princeton, NJ: Princeton University Press, 1994), 130.

32. Some thinkers challenge Habermas on this assumption—that ecosystems do not have a recognizable agency. See for instance Whitebook, "The Problem of Nature in Habermas."

33. Habermas, "Struggles for Recognition," 130.

34. Ketley, "Cultural Diversity versus Biodiversity," 108, 59.

35. Redford and Stearman, "Forest-Dwelling Native Amazonians," 252.

36. Ibid., 251.

37. Ibid., 254.

Chapter 9

Diversities and Justice

Habitat destruction is a problem for spotted owls, salmon, and polar bears. It is also a problem for human beings, who lose their homes, food sources, and ways of life when the ecosystems around them are degraded and destroyed. Economist Norman Myers has characterized those who lose their homes this way as "environmental refugees," defined as "people who can no longer gain a secure livelihood in their homelands because of drought, soil erosion, desertification, deforestation, and other environmental problems."[1] Myers estimated that there were twenty-five million such refugees in 1995 and that this number would likely double by 2010. In 2008 the United Nations made an even more drastic, longer-term estimate, predicting that because of climate change, soil loss, and desertification, "by 2050 some 200 million people will be displaced by environmental problems."[2] While the UN refers to these persons as "environmental migrants" to avoid the political connotations of the word "refugee," the fact that people are increasingly being driven away from their homes by environmental degradation is widely accepted.

This issue becomes even more complicated when another type of refugees is also considered: those who are displaced not by environmental degradation but rather by efforts to save the variety of life. Sociologist Charles Geisler defines these "conservation refugees" as "people who involuntarily part with their livelihood claims in places set aside for natural protection."[3] A 2008 report from the International Union for Conservation of Nature (IUCN), a global network of conservationists and conservation organizations, estimates that 12 percent of the planet's land is now protected in order to preserve wildlife, and on the vast majority of that land, human habitation is completely forbidden, regardless of who once lived there or how long they and their ancestors had been there.[4] By calculating the average population densities of such protected areas, Geisler projects that the conservation movement has displaced "8.5 to 136 million people," a staggering range that demonstrates the extent of the problems created when human beings are banished from their habitats. If even Geisler's lowest estimate is accurate, it points to a drastic and terrible problem: enormous numbers of people have been made homeless by conservation.[5]

Environmental and conservation refugees are displaced by the decisions of other human beings. The disturbing numbers of both kinds of refugees serve as a vital reminder that an ethics of biodiversity is not only about birds and rain forests but also about human lives. Human beings are creatures alongside all others; just like all other species, our lives are influenced and often harmed by the degradation of the environments upon which we depend and with which we live. The choices that some humans have made about how to develop land, how to grow food, how to extract resources, and how to use our energy supply are making it more difficult for many other humans to live their lives. In Christian terms this serves as a reminder that care for God's creation must include a concern not merely with issues traditionally thought of as environmental, but also with the oppression and abuse that too often characterize human relationships.

The awareness of environmental injustices and the assertion that Christian ecological ethics must include a concern for social justice are strengthened by the lessons of the previous chapters. After defining biodiversity it is impossible to ignore the fact that human beings are one species among many, dependent upon healthy ecosystems, expressions of genetic diversity and therefore intricately a part of the variety of life on Earth. We value biodiversity in large part because it is good for human beings, and we must concern ourselves with its social and economic values because its degradation causes the most harm to those who are marginalized and have few resources. Political efforts to conserve biodiversity, such as the Endangered Species Act, will inevitably affect social structures and human lives, and it is the duty of responsible conservationists to take this into account.

This chapter builds on these ideas and extends them, emphasizing both the importance and complexity of an ethics of biodiversity by stressing that it must include the concerns of those who are poor and oppressed among our own species while offering reminders that this is not an easy or a straightforward task. The reality of environmental injustice challenges ethical thinkers from privileged communities to rethink and question their ideas and actions. After offering a preliminary articulation of the relationship between justice and biodiversity, I will turn to liberation theologians who write about environmental issues from within communities of the marginalized and oppressed—James Cone, Leonardo Boff, and Ivone Gebara. These thinkers develop a vision of what a liberationist program of conservation might look like. They also offer a reminder of this book's limits in the face of the injustices that characterize so much of human society.

Biodiversity as an Issue of Justice

One place to learn that an ethics of biodiversity must attend to humanity and human relationships is the science of ecology. In the 1997 *Science* article "Human Domination of Earth's Ecosystems," the authors conclude that "no ecosystem on Earth's surface is free of pervasive human influence" and that "most aspects of the structure and functioning of Earth's ecosystems cannot be understood without accounting for the strong, often dominant influence of humanity."[6] The article goes on to assert: "The rate and extent of human alteration of Earth should affect how we think about Earth. It is clear that we control much of Earth and that our activities affect the rest."[7] The same point is made by ecologist Steward Pickett and his colleagues: "Ecology is now beginning to unembarrassedly examine human populated areas in the same way that it might approach any ecological system—as an arena to generate new patterns, to examine the structure and function of ecological systems, and to test general theories."[8] Human society is an issue for ecosystems, and so it has become an issue for ecologists.

Conservationists are also increasingly paying attention to human beings as a vital part of their activism. Like ecology, conservation has a heritage that sometimes neglected human beings and human interests. This is well reflected in the 2008 report of the International Union for Conservation of Nature mentioned above, which laments: "When the modern conservation movement started (at the end of the nineteenth century) it tried to protect nature by keeping people away from it in protected areas. People were the problem to which conservation was the response. Such conservation was nothing to do with economic uses of nature, it was an alternative to it."[9] This approach, sometimes called "fortress" or "exclusionary" conservation, created a system of wildlife preserves, protecting the 12 percent of Earth's land surface from which human beings have been largely banished. However, the IUCN now argues, this is no longer a justifiable strategy for two reasons: First, destructive development continues unchecked and relatively unchanged on 88 percent of the planet's land: the attempt to protect certain areas has allowed the degradation of unprotected lands, and has continued the assumption that "economic use" of nature need not be responsible use.

The second problem is that the conservation refugees who once lived on this 12 percent of land were too often driven away from it without attention to their needs, their traditions, or the possibility that they might live sustainably *with* the natural systems that conservationists strove to protect. This is a gross injustice and a missed opportunity. People who could have contributed to the work of protecting biodiversity and wildlife were instead driven away from their homes and given reason to resent the environmental interests that justified their exile. So, the IUCN report argues, "strategies must be crafted that deliver a biodiverse world that includes people, not a world of biodiversity enclaves in a lifeless human landscape."[10]

A Christian ethics of biodiversity must learn from these ecologists and conservationists and must build upon their work by explicitly grappling with justice as a norm of Christian life. Preliminary tools for this were introduced in chapter 5, which discussed the work of three Christian ethicists who each establish a clear commitment to human well-being as well as environmental flourishing. John Hart pays special attention to the native peoples of the Columbia River in developing his ethics of salmon preservation, expressing concern not only for endangered fish species but also for the endangered indigenous cultures and the unjust ways in which they have been treated. Thus, Hart writes, a sacramental consciousness cannot exist without including a "social consciousness" that understands and responds to "social relations, social structures, and social injustices in human communities."[11]

Along similar lines Michael Northcott calls for a prophetic attention to environmental degradation, globalization, and political structures not just for the sake of the nonhuman world but also for the sake of human beings who are poor and oppressed, for whom environmental degradation causes the most problems: "Justice is crucial to an ecological perspective on human society, for as we have seen, the oppression of the poor is intricately connected with the destruction of environments and habitats throughout human history as well as in the contemporary developing world."[12]

Perhaps the most developed perspective on how justice can be incorporated into Christian ecological ethics comes from Larry Rasmussen, who cautions against "apartheid thinking" in order to point out that the forces separating human beings from the nonhuman world also separate us from one another. Rasmussen's project of an Earth ethic affirms the value of all life-forms, including human beings, and so requires rigorous social as well as environmental analysis. Like Northcott, Rasmussen bases this commitment on the prophetic texts of the Hebrew Bible, finding in these a vision of the universe as "a moral one bent by God's own struggle to arch in the direction of redemption and eventual harmony." When this assertion is translated into contemporary environmentalist terms, we learn "that justice pertains to humans and nonhumans alike, as it does in the Bible's inclusive, theocentric understanding of creation."[13]

Rasmussen goes on to offer a more concrete definition: justice "means essentially that we share one another's fate and are obligated by creation itself to promote one another's well-being."[14] Justice for Rasmussen is about mutuality, about a community that encompasses the whole of Earth. In *Earth Community, Earth Ethics*, Rasmussen's primary emphasis is on extending the idea of justice, arguing that Christians must treat the nonhuman world with the same mutuality we extend to one another. In a 2004 article he continues this argument but reverses its emphasis, stressing that the encompassing notion of Earth justice must not ignore the very real needs of oppressed human beings and suggesting that justice should be recast in light of the environmental justice movement. This movement struggles not merely against environmental degradation but also against the unbalanced distribution of environmental harms and the exclusionary nature of environmental decision making, which disproportionately harm and exclude people of color, people who live in poverty, women, and other oppressed groups.

A crucial lesson emerging from this movement, Rasmussen argues, is that environmentalists and ethicists who come from dominant and comfortable social status must be deeply cautious about suggesting that all human beings cause environmental degradation and suffer from the problems it creates. Environmental justice teaches "that not all are being poisoned equally, or even breathing the same air."[15] In light of this lesson, Rasmussen suggests, it is not enough for Christian ethics to "extend moral community to the full community of life," to teach an ideal of justice that includes nonhuman creatures. It is vital also to extend "the same inclusion to the standing of human members," to pay attention to the oppressed human beings who suffer poverty and cruelty.[16] Justice defined this way incorporates *both* human society and the nonhuman world, and the complexities and challenges of each must be recognized.

Perhaps the most important aspect of Rasmussen's argument about justice is the premise of his 2004 article: those of us coming from privileged positions and secure economic standing must learn from those who have been marginalized and oppressed. Justice as Rasmussen defines it is about mutuality for all, but the reality and goal of mutuality cannot be completely understood from the perspective of those who are comfortable in the social systems that currently exist. We must learn about justice from those who have suffered injustices, who have experienced the failures and limitations of current realities.

In other words, it is essential for an ethics of biodiversity to make space for the voices of marginalized persons. For that reason I turn now to the work of three liberation theologians who have developed perspectives on how environmental and ecological issues connect to the concerns of marginalized human communities. By working closely with the texts they have written, I aim to begin learning about justice and diversity from the perspective of the oppressed.

Environmentalism and Racism: James Cone's Question for Ecological Ethics

James Cone, a foundational figure in liberation theology from the United States, writes in his classic text, *A Black Theology of Liberation*, that "any message that is not related to the liberation of the poor in a society is not Christ's message."[17] Cone's theology repeatedly emphasizes that God is on the side of the oppressed, and a central theological proof of this claim is Christological: Jesus came to live among the oppressed and was marginalized by the powers of his time. For Cone this is a sign that "God came, and continues to come, to those who are poor and helpless, for the purpose of setting them free."[18]

Because God is on the side of the oppressed, Cone argues, Christians should be also. Writing out of his own experience as an African American and speaking primarily for and to this community, Cone demands more specifically that Christian theology and ethics in the United States must make sense in light of the legacies of slavery, segregation, and racism that have defined this country. For him there is "no knowledge of God's revelation in the U.S. that did not arise out of the black struggle against white supremacy."[19]

It is crucial to take this argument seriously in the context of an ethics of biodiversity, to ask how a Christian attention to ecology and commitment to conservation can learn from the injustices of the past and present while struggling against injustice in the future. Cone deals with this question most explicitly in a 2001 essay that asked "Whose Earth Is It, Anyway?" which begins by affirming a basic connection between human oppression and environmental degradation. As Cone puts it, "The logic that led to slavery and segregation in the Americas, colonization and apartheid in Africa, and the rule of white supremacy throughout the world is the same one that leads to the exploitation of animals and the ravaging of nature."[20] Thus, the moral challenges of colonization and racism are not cleanly distinct from the challenges of environmental degradation; the two sets of problems are linked by common roots.

In part Cone's essay is an argument to liberation theologians and others involved in struggles for racial justice, encouraging them to take environmental issues seriously. He writes: "Ecology touches every sphere of human existence. It is not just an elitist or a white middle-class issue. A clean, safe environment is a human- and civil-rights issue that affects the lives of poor blacks and other marginalized groups." Activists who care about racism and social justice should also care about environmental degradation. He asks: "What good is it to eliminate racism if we are not around to enjoy a racist-free environment?"[21]

However, the bulk of the critique is directed at environmentalists: "What is absent from much of the talk about the environment in First World countries is a truly radical critique of the culture most responsible for the ecological crisis. . . . There is hardly a hint that perhaps whites could learn something of how we got into this ecological mess from those who have been the victims of white world supremacy."[22] This fact—that European and European-American Christians concerned with the environment have often ignored links between environmental degradation and the history of oppression—is undeniable. The environmental movement has had historically white leadership that has been justly criticized for failing to listen to the concerns of marginalized peoples or to alter its goals in light of their concerns and their histories of oppression.[23]

Cone's particular concern is with Christian theologians and ethicists, who have the tools to do better if only they will attend to liberation theology's radical critiques of inherited traditions. If ecological theologians and ethicists believe in the moral power of diversity and interconnectedness, he asks, "why do most still live in segregated communities? Why are their essays and books about the endangered earth so monological—that is, a conversation of a dominant group talking to itself?"[24] Cone's point is not to dismiss environmentalist concern among Christians but rather to reform it. He therefore urges theologians to "deepen our conversation by linking the earth's crisis with the crisis in the human family." Stressing that environmental degradation is not an excuse to ignore the plight of the oppressed, Cone writes, "If it is important to save the habitats of birds and other species, then it is at least equally important to save black lives in the ghettos and prisons of America."[25]

Human habitats are threatened, just as nonhuman habitats are threatened. When applied to an ethics of biodiversity, this observation demands an attention to the almost 50 million environmental refugees in our world today and the up to 136 million refugees who were driven from their homes by conservationists. This is a deeply troubling legacy, and it must be reversed and decried if conservationists want to stand up for the entirety of the variety of life.

Perhaps the most important lesson to be learned from Cone's essay is revealed in the fact that he defends attention to "black lives in the ghettos and prisons of America" as *at least equally important* as "the habitats of birds and other species." Cone does not simplistically state that the conservation of species is equivalent to the quest for social and racial justice; neither does he suggest that the two concerns will always be mutually compatible and sustaining. Rather, he asserts that they are two related but different goals and leaves room for the reader to place them on equal footing or to lift the goal of social justice above environmentalist conservation. Cone clearly has not dismissed the possibility that these linked problems have different, and perhaps even competing, solutions.

Cone's work offers a vital caution against the assumption that the goals of social justice and environmentalist conservation will be simplistically coherent. Christian ecological ethics may entail an implicit concern for the oppressed, but this should not lead to a categorization of social justice as simply a subset of conservation's broader goals. That move would deny the legacy of racism and colonization *within* the conservation movement and commit the fundamental mistake of assuming that those of us who come from the dominant culture can fully understand the reality of oppression. In *God of the Oppressed* Cone writes: "suggesting that the problem of racism and oppression is only one social expression of a larger ethical concern" is too often simply a strategy by which "white theologians and ethicists simply ignore black people."[26] To suggest that issues of racial and social justice should be subsumed under environmental issues would, in Cone's view, be a dismissal of the needs of the oppressed. Doing so would defy the fundamental basis of Christian life.

Thus, a Christian ethics of biodiversity must do more than simply voice concern about ecological and conservation refugees. It calls Christians to take the side of these refugees, to assert that their plight is unacceptable, and to work actively to change it. Conservationists should not only prevent further destruction of human habitat but also actively advocate on behalf of those who have been made homeless by the protection or destruction of land.

Cone's work poses a profound and challenging question to Christian ecological ethics: How is it related to the liberation of society's poor and marginalized peoples? In the United States this means asking about how the conservation of biodiversity can prevent further harm to the inner city minorities Cone writes about, to the "black lives in the ghettos and prisons of America" as well as to the Latino lives, the poor lives, and all the many other disenfranchised peoples who share those ghettos and prisons. It also means asking what benefit conservation offers to Native American communities like the Yankton Sioux discussed in the previous chapter: how can environmentalists affirm the importance of saving the variety of life while not compromising the sovereignty of native nations? This is a challenge to Christian ethics: it calls people of faith to expand our attention, to attend to the oppressed and marginalized of our own species even as we devote ourselves to the wide variety of life.

The Most Threatened Creatures: Leonardo Boff's Multiscalar Challenge

Like James Cone, Leonardo Boff emphasizes the connections between environmental issues and social justice while maintaining a distinction between them. Boff's theology is written out of a commitment to the poor of the world and of Latin America in particular, emerging from his context as a Brazilian who began his theological career amid horrific political repression and poverty. In a 1978 book he describes "the brutal reality facing the vast majority of people" in Latin America this way: "They are living and dying amid inhuman living conditions: malnutrition; a high infant mortality rate; endemic diseases; low income; unemployment; lack of social security; lack of health care, hospitals, schools, and housing facilities. In short, they lack all the basic necessities that might ensure some minimum of human dignity."[27] In the face of this reality, Boff emphasizes that the fundamental duty of Christians is to liberate human beings from oppression and make it possible for the poor to acquire the genuine agency with which they can build lives of human dignity.

In his recent work Boff has increasingly recognized that human dignity depends on an awareness of its nonhuman context. In the book *Cry of the Earth, Cry of the Poor*, he writes: "We are sons and daughters of Earth. We are the Earth itself in its expression of consciousness, of freedom, and of love."[28] This self-awareness has shaped the ethical dimensions of Boff's theology, turning his attention to environmental degradation and leading him to stress that the moral problems of that degradation are not cleanly separable from the moral problems of human oppression. In his words, these two sets of problems "stem from two wounds that are bleeding. The first, the wound of poverty and wretchedness, tears the social fabric of millions and millions of poor people the world over. The second, systematic aggression against the earth, destroys the equilibrium of the planet, threatened by the depredations made by a type of development undertaken by contemporary societies, now spread throughout the world."[29]

According to Boff, these two "wounds" were inflicted by the same weapon: domination, the use of power over others rather than power employed cooperatively with others: "The logic that exploits classes and subjects peoples to the interests of a few rich and powerful countries is the same as the logic that devastates the Earth and plunders its wealth, showing no solidarity with the rest of humankind and future generations."[30] For Boff this identification of a common logic of domination at the root of two social problems is vital in the process of liberation from both. The solution to environmental degradation is "ecological justice—respect for the otherness of beings and things and their right to continue to exist," and the solution to human oppression is related, a "constant social justice, respect and concern for people, as well as the abrogation of those forms of oppression that are exercised through social relations."[31]

However, Boff is aware of pervasive and persistent social conflicts and violence in the natural world, and so he does not believe that achieving either form of justice will be easy or straightforward. Because of this he has retained his liberationist emphasis on the priority of oppressed peoples, even going so far as to write: "The most threatened creatures are not whales but the poor, who are condemned to die before their time. United Nations statistics indicate that each year fifteen million children die of hunger or hunger-related diseases before they are five days old; 150 million children are under-nourished, and 800 million go hungry all the time."[32] Boff here offers a priority of social over environmental issues. The poor are "the most threatened creatures"; social justice is an even more urgent priority than ecological justice.

This is not an argument that environmental issues should be ignored until social justice is established. Environmental degradation remains a serious wound that must be healed. Boff does not critique the project of Christian ecological ethics as a whole but rather offers an important caution to any ethicist who might ignore social concerns for the sake of the nonhuman world: not all human beings relate to the natural world in the same way. More specifically Boff notes that the privileged have special responsibilities to curtail and repair environmental degradation, while poor people do not. There is "too little consumption by the poor" simultaneous with "too much consumption by the rich."[33] Boff's work develops hope for a more just world in which those who are now poor will have enough resources to survive and thrive as well as the agency to choose to use them well and sustainably.

The inequality and oppression that characterize our world make it inappropriate to suggest that the degradation of the environment or the destruction of biodiversity is caused by human beings as a whole. Instead, Boff argues, wealthy human beings who have chosen to live lives of domination and overconsumption cause these problems. Similarly the costs and burdens of environmental degradation and biodiversity loss are not borne indiscriminately by "humanity," but rest disproportionately on the poorest and least powerful of our species.

While Boff does not use this language explicitly, he is making an argument about the scale of attention required for an ethics of biodiversity. He argues that environmentalist theologians and ethicists cannot see the human species as a single unit but must instead be aware of the diverse groups and communities that make it up; they must write in light of our differences as well as our common ground as humans and creatures. Boff does at times refer to the human species as a united category: "Humans are made for participation and creation," and "We are sons and daughters of Earth."[34] However, he balances such sweeping claims with others that acknowledge the diversity among human communities, lamenting the historic, social, economic, and cultural inequities that divide our species. His central argument is that those who are starving and oppressed should be empowered to assert their agency more fully in the world around them, while those who are rich and overconsumptive should learn to give up power and better appreciate their dependence upon the natural world around them. This reflects a balance between the global level of attention and a more detailed analysis of the differences between rich and poor peoples.

Boff's perspective is still remarkably broad—generalizing "the poor" and "the rich" of the world—but it nevertheless attends to the diversity *within* the human species. In this way he moves downward toward the level of communities, emphasizing the vital distinctions between poor and rich communities in our world today. Learning from Boff, Christian ethics must attend to the variety of life within our species and must not casually suggest that "we" human beings are a single category in every sense, with a single relationship to and power over the natural world. There is unity to humanity, and there are justifications for speaking of the entire species in the first person plural. But it is vital to also note that the human species is not always an undifferentiated unit, and it is important to think at levels that reveal the important differences between people. Attention to these differences quickly reveals that any discussion of human domination over this planet is really a discussion of domination by the wealthy and empowered among us. Privileged peoples will have an ethics of biodiversity that calls for reductions in consumption with an attitude of humility and respect. Peoples and communities that are poor and oppressed, on the other hand, may well steward the variety of life best by taking more control over their own lives and environments.

Unity in Diversity: Ivone Gebara's Ecofeminist Epistemology

An additional perspective on the relationship of justice to conservation is developed in the work of another Brazilian, Ivone Gebara. She offers an ecofeminist liberation theology that emphasizes the importance of recognizing the limitation of what any human being of human culture can know. Like Cone and Boff, Gebara begins from a concern for the poor and oppressed people of her own land. Indeed, at the beginning of the book *Longing for Running Water*, she admits that her own concern for ecological issues is often constrained "by the struggle for survival in which innumerable people in my country, especially women and children, continue to be immersed."[35] Reflecting on these people's experiences, she notes: "It is hard to try to save the earth when your relationship with it is marked by conflict, and when you spend your time just wishing for a piece of it—an urban lot or a patch of land in the countryside on which you can live." Gebara chastises theologians and ethicists who write about the environment without "any awareness of the extreme inadequacy of the food the poor eat, of their unhealthy housing situations, and of the very bad water and air, especially in the outlying areas of large cities."[36]

For Gebara paying attention to people who are poor and oppressed requires Christians to think differently, and so she begins her articulation of this new theology with an extensive discussion of epistemology, of how theological knowledge is constructed. She asks: "In what ways do the feminist and ecological issues change our understanding of our own reality?"[37] Her answer is that ecofeminist knowledge about the world must be fundamentally different from those that have dominated the western tradition, which "were profoundly androcentric—centered on male interest and points of view—and anthropocentric—centered on human values and experiences."[38] Such bias has led to a desire for eternal, unquestionable, and universal truths, but Gebara argues that no human being can have access to truly eternal and absolute truth. For centuries men have believed their truths—which largely ignored the interests and insights of women—to be unquestioningly applicable to all people; this was a mistake that should not be repeated.

Gebara argues that it is more productive and more liberating to accept human limitation, to acknowledge that no woman or man can ever claim to have absolute and universal truth, and to instead embrace the limits of human knowledge and the wide diversity of what humans know and believe. Her epistemology is, above all, contextual. It reminds human beings "that we cannot absolutize our present way of knowing; rather, we need to admit its historical and provisional character and the importance of always being open to the new referents that history—and life in general—will propose."[39] This means that no human community should seek to overpower others but rather that all should understand and celebrate the variety of perspectives available within our species. Christians should not claim to know the salvific path for all people but should lift up the wide array of beliefs within Christianity and the even wider array of religious attitudes throughout the world. For Gebara truth and justice are not about who has the singular correct answer but rather about how to participate in a mutual exchange across inevitable differences.

However, this does not mean that she has dismissed *all* universality. On the contrary, the differences in the manner and content of human knowledge are themselves universal and so offer a genuine common ground on which to build:

> It is precisely this local character, this quality of being spatiotemporally limited, that opens out into universality. Universality does not mean that a concrete knowing is valid for all human groups but rather that all knowing has a universal localness about it. What is most universal about knowing is not the type of content that is learned but the 'located' way in which we learn the universality that marks us all. In the final analysis, it is on this basis that the human world discovers its universal identity.[40]

What we have in common is the fact of our differences. Our diversity unites us. All knowledge comes from a particular place; it is located and therefore limited. Another way Gebara makes this point is to emphasize that knowledge comes from local places on Earth: human beings are "of the planet Earth" but primarily "of earth, in the sense of the soil that makes it possible for seeds, plants, and trees to grow: the earth that feeds us and allows us to live and share in life."[41] Human beings are creatures of particular places; we share nourishment from particular soil on this planet. We can understand one another only when we recognize that we come from different places.

Perhaps the most helpful demonstration of this point comes in

Gebara's extensive discussion of biodiversity, which begins from the premise that human beings are a part of and a reflection of the variety of life. Human biodiversity is as local as the family "in the way each child is different, in the variety of like and dislikes in food, in affinities, in temperaments."[42] It is also as global as the differences between "Whites, blacks, indigenous peoples, Asiatics and *mestizos*, all with different languages, customs, statures, and sexes," which "make up the awesome and diverse human symphony."[43] Most important to Gebara's argument is what she calls "religious biodiversity," which summarizes her argument that the variety of spiritual traditions "goes along with the biodiversity of the cosmos and the earth, and with the diversity of cultures." Those who acknowledge and appreciate all these diversities, Gebara argues, will adopt "an attitude of humility, which means that there cannot be absolute powers that regulate and dictate the meaning of life, or the art of weaving meaning."[44]

Gebara's perspective suggests the same caution and multiscalar attention to human differences as did Cone's and Boff's. Her liberationist perspective reminds theologians and ethicists to be cautious about speaking for all people or all life without qualification, to never make carelessly universal statements that leave out the vital differences between peoples and ignore the particular plight and insight of the oppressed and marginalized. This is a crucial reminder for an ethics of biodiversity.

In addition Gebara adds a liberationist ecofeminist perspective that emphasizes the opportunity presented by diversity. Diversity, for Gebara, is a chance to learn from those who are different from us by approaching them with humility. When understood without any attempt at domination, diversity is a universal that can unite us. Gebara's perspective leaves open the possibility that an ethics of biodiversity can be about bringing peoples together by embracing the differences between us. However, this is only possible in the context of the humility that she has emphasized; it is only appropriate to celebrate our connections after our differences have been acknowledged. Gebara especially reminds those of us who come from relative comfort and power that we must learn from those who are suffering and oppressed. An ethics of biodiversity that takes her ecofeminist perspective seriously cannot ignore the realities of poverty, patriarchy, and pain that exist throughout the world. As Gebara notes, when we locate our ethics and our theology in a particular place on Earth, we will inevitably recognize the reality of oppression and suffering there. Ours is an Earth "of refugees, prisoners, and the homeless, of those who are hungry for love and for bread. An earth that is burned, robbed, exhausted, devastated, divided up, and poorly loved."[45] Unless it responds to this reality, unless it makes sense in light of such suffering, an ethics of biodiversity is incomplete.

The Complexity of an Ethics of Biodiversity

By this standard, the ethics of biodiversity presented in this book is incomplete. This book is not itself a work of liberation theology in the sense meant by authors like James Cone, Leonardo Boff, and Ivone Gebara. A liberation perspective emerges from poor and marginalized people themselves and is written and tested in community with them. As Boff writes with his brother, Clodovis: "In liberation, the oppressed come together, come to understand their situation through the process of conscientization, discover the causes of their oppression, organize themselves into movements, and act in a coordinated fashion." Later, they add, "if we are to understand the theology of liberation, we must first understand and take an active part in the real and historical process of liberating the oppressed."[46] Boff has lived out this commitment, developing his ideas in conversation with Latin American base communities and remaining committed to the poor of his own country. Similarly Gebara and Cone have committed themselves to speaking from and for oppressed communities and testing their ideas within such communities.

This book has not been written in direct and explicit community with people who are poor and oppressed; its author is a white, heterosexual, middle-class male with economic security in the United States of America. To claim that I could fully comprehend the realities of human suffering and oppression that inspire liberation theology would be ridiculous, and to claim that I can outline a perspective on biodiversity that fully reflects the realities and needs of oppressed peoples would be the height of hubris. Thus, while I work as a scholar and a concerned human being to understand and respond to the plight of those who suffer under sexism, classism, racism, and multifaceted other forms of oppression, I cannot speak for or even fully with the oppressed. The work of an ethics of biodiversity remains incomplete in the sense that it must continue to develop in open dialogue with people made homeless by environmental degradation, communities driven away from their homes by conservation efforts, and those who suffer starvation, war, and oppression.

To say that this work is incomplete, however, is not to say that it is worthless. Rather, it is to embrace the humility that the thinkers discussed in this chapter urge. Ivone Gebara's ecofeminist epistemology emphasizes that all knowing is partial, and it follows that all proposals about how human beings should relate to the variety of life will be limited and incomplete. To some extent this lesson of humility is similar to the lesson already learned from scientists who continue to find more questions than answers about the variety of life, who remind students of biodiversity that there is so much we do not know and that there will always be limits to what we can say with certainty.

However, there is an important difference between the humility learned from biodiversity science on the one hand and the humility asserted by liberation theology on the other. In response to the vast array of things we do not yet know about biodiversity, we human beings should be humble but must nevertheless do our best to manage the variety of life, to act as stewards who conserve as much of the variety of life as possible. In contrast, when responding to the vast amount that people of privilege and comfort do not understand about the lives of the poor and marginalized, Christian ecological ethicists must be humble in a way that prevents privileged individuals from managing other human lives and deciding other human fates. The proper response to threatened peoples is not to seek to manage their world for them but rather to find a way to empower them to manage themselves, to affirm their agency as human beings and their power to decide their own fate. Those of us who have not suffered racism should not tell those who have how to live. Those of us who have consumed too many of the Earth's resources should not now tell those who have consumed too few what they should do next.

Larry Rasmussen defines justice as an affirmation of mutuality between all people and all creatures. The work of James Cone, Leonardo Boff, and Ivone Gebara helps to enrich and explore this definition, emphasizing that mutuality cannot mean simplistic unity. Rather, mutuality should mean acknowledging the long history of injustices between human beings, recognizing that different peoples relate to the variety of life in vastly different ways, and calling for very different responses from different human communities.

For comfortable and privileged Christians in the United States,

Christian ecological ethics calls for careful and extensive commitment to conserving the variety of life. It also calls for a commitment never to conserve biodiversity at the expense of marginalized human communities—the urban poor, women and children in Latin America, traditional peoples in Africa, Native Americans within the borders of the United States still struggling to maintain their sovereignty. An ethical approach to protecting biodiversity must not create conservation refugees, it must not abrogate the rights of native and traditional peoples, and it must not ignore the vital work of feeding the hungry and advocating for the marginalized.

This set of commitments makes an ethics of biodiversity an incredibly complicated and challenging project. The laws that we Christians advocate and the moral formation we nurture must incorporate social justice as well as environmental concern, recognizing the links between the two but not simplistically assuming that they are the same. Multiscalar attention must differentiate not only between small and large temporal and spatial awareness but also between different kinds of human communities, specifying when it is appropriate to talk about the human species as a united community and when it is important to differentiate the cultures, races, and classes into which we have become divided. It is not enough to ask why biodiversity is valuable or whether it is sacramental. It is also vital to ask who values biodiversity in what ways and which communities can be helpfully shaped by a sacramental attitude to the variety of life.

Despite these complications and qualifications, the clear message from the liberation theologians discussed here is that the variety of life is relevant not merely to the rich and comfortable but also to people who are poor and marginalized. Cone, Boff, and Gebara clearly all value the variety of life and support the conservation of biodiversity in addition to and as part of their advocacy on behalf of the human beings threatened by social oppression and environmental degradation. This means that however incomplete and limited all ethical perspectives might be, the central message of an ethics of biodiversity can be asserted boldly and without qualification: Christians are called to care for the poor and oppressed of our world, and this includes all the threatened creatures of God's Earth.

Notes

1. Myers, "Environmental Refugees," 609.

2. Institute for Environment and Human Security, "Environmental Migrants," 1.

3. Geisler, "A New Kind of Trouble," 69.

4. Adams and Jenrenaud, "Transition to Sustainability."

5. Geisler, "A New Kind of Trouble," 71. For the most detailed description of conservation refugees and the conditions that create them, see Dowie, *Conservation Refugees*.

6. Vitousek et al., "Human Domination of Earth's Ecosystems," 494.

7. Ibid., 498–99.

8. Steward Pickett, V. Thomas Parker, and Peggy Fiedler, "The New Paradigm in Ecology: Implications for Conservation Biology Above the Species Level" in Fiedler and Jain, *Conservation Biology*, 73.

9. Adams and Jenrenaud, "Transition to Sustainability," 53.

10. Ibid., 54.

11. Hart, *Sacramental Commons*, 62.

12. Northcott, *Environment and Christian Ethics*, 314.

13. Rasmussen, *Earth Community, Earth Ethics*, 259.

14. Ibid., 260.

15. Rasmussen, "Environmental Racism and Environmental Justice," 8.

16. Ibid., 22.

17. Cone, *A Black Theology of Liberation*, vii.

18. Cone, *God of the Oppressed*, 126.

19. Ibid., x.

20. James H. Cone, "Whose Earth Is It, Anyway?" in Hessel, *After Nature's Revolt*, 23.

21. Ibid., 29.

22. Ibid., 30.

23. For a discussion of this critique and a compelling alternative story about diverse contemporary and historical expressions of environmentalism, see Gelobter et al., "The Soul of Environmentalism," www.rprogress.org/soul/soul.pdf.

24. Cone, "Whose Earth?" 31.

25. Ibid., 32

26. Cone, *God of the Oppressed*, 184.

27. Leonardo Boff, *Jesus Christ Liberator*, 268.

28. Boff, *Cry of the Earth, Cry of the Poor*, 14.

29. Leonardo Boff, "Liberation Theology and Ecology: Alternative, Confrontation, or Complementarity?" in Boff and Elizondo, *Ecology and Poverty*, 67.

30. Boff, *Cry of the Earth*, xi.

31. Boff, *Ecology and Liberation*, 77.

32. Boff, *Cry of the Earth*, 111–12.

33. Boff's central contrast is between the "rich" of the industrialized so-called first world and the "poor" of the developing world. It would be a different matter to consider whether there is "too little consumption" by the poor in the industrialized world, such as the urban poor in my own nation. Without a doubt, however, such persons share with the "poor" Boff addresses the fate of having too little ability to influence the social structures that shape their lives.

34. Boff, *Cry of the Earth*, 9, 14.

35. Gebara, *Longing for Running Water*, 1.

36. Ibid., 5, 12.

37. Ibid., 21. She explains why her liberationist theology begins with epistemology this way: "Reflecting on my Latin American experience, I have come to see epistemological issues first and foremost as practical ones, directly related to our work among poor people. In other words, beginning to think in a different way requires us to take different positions on the subject of knowing: to open up spaces for new ways of thinking and to consider our own thinking in terms of how our goals affect our perceptions."

38. Ibid., 22.

39. Ibid., 61.

40. Ibid., 62.

41. Ibid., 89.

42. Ibid., 207.

43. Ivone Gebara, "The Trinity and Human Experience: An Ecofeminist Approach" in Ruether, ed., *Women Healing Earth*, 17.

44. Gebara, *Longing for Running Water*, 205, 209.

45. Ibid., 213–14.

46. Boff and Boff, *Introducing Liberation Theology*, 5, 9.

Conclusion

The Work of Conserving Biodiversity

This book offers an ethics of biodiversity developed from a Christian perspective in dialogue with scientific ecology, and its foundation is a set of data about the variety of life. These data are endlessly complex and intricate, but it is nevertheless worth trying to summarize with a few numbers: for more than three billion years, life has evolved on the planet Earth, with countless births and deaths leading to the 10 million or so distinct species on the planet today, 350,000 of which are beetles. Our own single species—which evolved less than two hundred thousand years ago—has almost 7 billion members, and each of us carries approximately 400 distinct species of microbes inside our mouths.

A second set of numbers is as disturbing as the first is amazing: Today, species are going extinct at one hundred to one thousand times their natural rate because of human activity. One-quarter of mammals are currently endangered. By the year 2060, one in twenty of all currently existing species may be extinct, and uncounted populations within species and ecosystems that support them will likely be gone as well. The Brazilian rain forest, one of the most richly diverse biomes on our planet, has been cut down by 20 percent in the last twenty years. By 2050, 200 million people may well be driven from their homes because of such environmental destruction, and as many as 136 million may have already been made refugees by conservation efforts. For related but not identical reasons, fully half of the six thousand human languages currently spoken are likely to disappear in this century, one indicator of the traditional and indigenous cultures endangered by the expansion of industrialized and homogenized ways of life.

This information is disturbing, and it is amazing. Above all, it is deeply important to anyone who seeks to live morally in our complicated, diverse, and troubled world. For Christians who recognize the Earth as God's good creation and accept the responsibility to steward life on this planet as advocates for the oppressed and marginalized, these data are a call to attention and to action. *An Ethics of Biodiversity* has developed a particularly Christian response to these data by reflecting on five questions that, in review, can summarize the book's basic argument about how Christians should approach conservation.

The first step for any ethics is to understand what is being studied, and so the foundational question is *What is biodiversity?* Biodiversity is most basically the variety of life, most technically a multiscalar subject of careful scientific study, and theologically the variety of creatures in God's creation that manifests God's glory. Biodiversity is a basic characteristic of the world we live in and of which we are a part, a sign of the richness and endless mystery of the creation. The variety of life can best be understood when we pay attention to it, learning from the scientists who study it, carefully observing and appreciating the myriad creatures with which we share life on Earth.

Implied in these definitions are some answers to the second question: *Why does biodiversity matter?* Scientists, politicians, and economists have developed a long list of reasons, noting that the variety of life is valuable to human beings as the basis of ecosystem functioning, improves human well-being, and can inspire and educate. In addition many argue that biodiversity is intrinsically valuable, worthy of conservation regardless of its contribution to human flourishing. To these ideas I add a particularly Christian argument: biodiversity is valuable for its sacramentality, because it serves as a sign of and connection to the mysteries and workings of God. Christians who wish to know the creator and live as the creator intends must study creation, which is characterized by the variety of life.

As a sacramental sign of God, biodiversity's importance comes in part from its sheer complexity: it offers a sign of the mystery of creation because it does not exist in any single place, at any single scale, and it cannot be quantified in any single way. This is emphasized in the third question: *How and at what level should we pay attention to biodiversity?* No single answer to this question could be adequate because life exists on multiple scales and in myriad ways, and so our moral and theological responses to it must be as multiscalar, nuanced, and cautious as are scientific perspectives. It is vital to develop an ethics of biodiversity that can respond to and conserve the variety of life locally, regionally, and globally. When choices between these scales are necessary, it is equally vital that moral agents be thoughtful, deliberate, and honest about the foci of our attention.

Scalar thinking reminds us that there are trade-offs inherent in this work, a point also emphasized by the fourth question: *How should politics and moral formation be balanced in the conservation of biodiversity?* Again, there is no one final answer because the goal of human society that can live sustainably with the variety of creation will be reachable only if both social institutions and personal attitudes are reformed in an ongoing dialogue with one another. However, conservationists must still decide how we will balance our energy between changing laws and changing hearts, whether we believe that we can better protect biodiversity by enforcement or inspiration. Christian churches have an established role as sites of moral formation, and those of us within these communities must use them to change the ways people think about biodiversity. Some among us must also be challenged to take political stands and reshape the institutional structures by which conservation will be sustained.

As answers to the first four questions have demonstrated, biodiversity is at the mercy of human beings. This power of our species over biodiversity must not blind us to the fact that we are, ourselves, a part of and an expression of the variety of life. Neither can it disguise the fact that "we" as human beings are deeply diverse internally, and the differences between us matter deeply. The fifth question—*What does the conservation of biodiversity have to do with human diversity and with social justice?*—emphasizes differences between human beings that emerge from our different cultures and from our varying degrees of power and agency in the world today. Biodiversity is related to the diversity of human cultures, and so the conservation of the variety of life should also attend to the homologous task of ensuring that traditional, indigenous, and minority communities are empowered to sustain the ways of life they inherit. Conservation cannot be an excuse to ignore justice. Indeed, attention to the injustices of mainstream society broadly and environmentalism in particular will help conservationists to advocate for all the marginalized on God's Earth, including the marginalized members of our own species.

To live out this ethics of biodiversity will not be easy. It calls for Christians to conserve the variety of God's creation as a sacrament at multiple scales, through both political and morally formative work, with deliberate attention to the connections and tensions to marginalized human beings. However, Christian faith suggests that this challenge is what we were made for: to live with and as the variety of life on God's Earth.

In the course of addressing these five questions, I have offered a number of moral arguments. I argued that U.S. citizens concerned about biodiversity should support the Endangered Species Act, advocate ratification of the Convention on Biodiversity, and work for even stronger national and international conservation legislation. I also argued that Christians should shape the moral attitudes of believers in churches by using feast days, biblical interpretations, and theological arguments to help people of faith appreciate the marvels of the non-human world and humanity's place within it. I argued that environmentalists should balance the goals of subsidiarity and socialization, attending to bioregional and community issues while not ignoring local and global concerns. I argued that we human beings must accept our place as the dominant species on Earth by taking on the responsibility of stewardship but that this must not blind us to the crucial differences between and among us.

I also argued that conservationists should ascribe an intrinsic value to the variety of life without ignoring its importance to human economies and human survival, and that concerned people should attend not only to the degradation of biodiversity but also to the injustices facing marginalized peoples. Drawing on the work of three liberation theologians, I have embraced the theological claim that Christians have a particular responsibility to those who are poor and oppressed, a claim that includes but cannot be reduced to nonhuman species marginalized by the development of industrial society directed by privileged human beings.

An Ethics of Spotted Owls

Some readers may be frustrated that these arguments are all somewhat abstract. I have not advocated a list of concrete actions individuals can take to conserve biodiversity, and I have not developed a comprehensive program for social change. This ethics cannot serve as a practical and straightforward guide to saving the variety of life. The work of conservation is too complicated for such clarity, too difficult and too particular to think that there are a few simple actions, a straightforward guidebook, or a universal blanket statement about how the variety of life can be saved. Readers who are inspired to conserve biodiversity have work yet to do to determine the most urgent issues in their own neighborhoods and bioregions, to discern what their churches and communities could be doing to spread information and passion about biodiversity, and to channel their energies into national and global change. However, it is worth at least briefly providing a more specific example, and for this I will return to the case from my own region that began this text: the northern spotted owl.

Based on the ethics developed in this book, I believe it is a moral responsibility for those of us who are Christian in the Pacific Northwest to do all we can to preserve the subspecies of northern spotted owls. These birds are important subjects of scientific study, and there is much left to learn about and from them. What's more, these owls have become a symbol of the old-growth forests that define this region and a legal means by which the rest of the old-growth forest is protected. By virtue of the Endangered Species Act, the northern spotted is a surrogate for all the many birds, insects, rodents, trees, and shrubs that depend upon this habitat. What is more, my theology asserts that these owls have intrinsic value as creations of God and sacramental value as signs of their creator. The northern spotted owl is worth conserving for theological and ecological reasons.

This simple assertion must be expanded upon, however, because any careful ethics of biodiversity must reflect the complications of conservation. It is first vital to notice the scale of my claim: I believe that the northern spotted owl should be preserved as a subspecies in its own right, but my primary justification works at a broader scale, calling for protection of the owl as a means to protect the ecosystems of which it is a part. This reveals the relatively broad scale of my attention. Indeed, in this book I have used the spotted owl as a stand-in for all endangered species, and so as a symbol for biodiversity as a whole. This is part of why the spotted owl matters: it symbolizes conservation and so stands for countless species, populations, and ecosystems. The spotted owl is a small subspecies, but it matters because of all it represents for its habitat and for conservation more broadly.

I have not argued that individual spotted owls must be conserved. My primary moral interest is broader, and so particular birds are important to me mainly as indicators of the health of the subspecies and the forest broadly. While I believe that each individual owl is a creature of God, I do not believe we have special responsibilities to ensure that each one survives. It is for this reason that I can support the proposal to capture and kill barred owls in order to assist the spotted owl population, which is what the Fish and Wildlife Service hopes to do as of this writing. This is not a decision to take lightly, and there are good reasons to be cautious about managing a forest by killing birds within it. However, the health of the spotted owl population is crucial for many reasons, and lamentable sacrifices must be made to preserve it.

For the same reason, it is not enough to simply follow the Fish and Wildlife Service's recommendation unquestioningly, because that agency's suggestion to kill barred owls is not accompanied by serious considerations of what other sacrifices might be necessary to ensure survival of northern spotted owls.[1] While the barred owl is a real threat, I am not convinced that it is a bigger danger than the limits of the protected critical habitat that has been established, and I believe that even more land should be given over to preserving this ecosystem. Furthermore, if spotted owls are more threatened by fires and extreme weather conditions because of a changing climate, then perhaps they offer a sign of even more drastic shifts that must take place in our society. Part of protecting the spotted owl involves questioning the patterns of economic development in the Northwest and questioning the international habits of consumption that lead to climate change. If Christians take seriously the call to protect this one species, then we must take seriously the substantial social change required to make a world in which these owls can survive.

Such shifts would have costs to human beings, as existing efforts at spotted owl conservation already have. A moral approach to this work cannot ignore the human lives that have been changed and hurt by conservation already. Indeed, many of those who oppose spotted owl conservation argue that it degrades cultural diversity, viewing the loggers of the Pacific Northwest as a culture unto themselves, a culture with a close relationship to its natural surroundings that understood how to extract resources and livelihood from it. Journalist William Dietrich chronicles this argument in his book *The Final Forest,* telling the stories of men and women who feel that the conservation of the forest is destroying their culture. For instance, a timber mill owner in Forks, Washington, who was closing down his business told Dietrich: "For us to lose everything, that's not what is really the worst. . . . To have a whole way of life destroyed, that's the worst."[2]

Others have argued that spotted owl conservation cannot be blamed for the loss of logging jobs,[3] but the ethics this book has developed emphasizes the importance of understanding people's own definitions of their own cultures, so I refuse to dismiss the claims of loggers who blame the owl and environmentalists for the loss of their way of life. Instead, I believe it vital to acknowledge that something real has been lost, to mourn that fact, and to nevertheless argue that the most just and responsible action is to conserve the owls and their habitat even when it alters these particular human lives. It is equally important to notice the human interests that have *not* taken a prominent place in public discussion of spotted owls, most particularly the indigenous inhabitants of this region, many of whom were driven away, killed off, or marginalized and separated from the forest habitat with which they lived for centuries long before conservation became an issue. No ethics of spotted owls is complete without acknowledging that the old growths of the Pacific Northwest were inhabited and in a very real way managed by human beings long before people of European descent arrived.

Today the political work of conserving the northern spotted owl is fueled by the Endangered Species Act, which protects the subspecies and requires the U.S. government to do whatever is necessary to save it. An even better political structure would be another law, with at least as much enforceable strength, that allowed for the protection of old-growth forests and other ecosystems regardless of the demonstrated existence of endangered species within them. Ideally, this law would be developed in dialogue with another that honored the rights of this region's indigenous peoples, setting aside land to be given over to these cultures for their own unimpeded use, in no way managed by federal or state governments. Concerned citizens of the Pacific Northwest and the United States should call for such laws from our leaders.

However, because a workable, if imperfect, law already exists to protect the spotted owl, perhaps even more energy should be devoted to the work of moral formation. The northern spotted owl has been the occasion for so much controversy and so much emotion that perhaps the first task is to teach people about it, to educate the public about these birds and the forests in which they make their nests. Those who dismiss the owl as unimportant should be taught about its intricate relationship to the entirety of the old-growth forest. Those who are Christian should be encouraged to recognize the theological importance of all creatures and the relevance of the command to "keep them alive with you." All who live near their habitat should learn to think of the spotted owl as an expression of the majestic variety of life, an intricate and crucial reality of which we ourselves are a part.

The Work of Hope

I am personally committed to conserving the old-growth forests of my region, to defending the laws that ensure this conservation, and to educating people about their importance every chance I get. However, I am not certain that these efforts will be successful. I am not certain that the spotted owl will survive this century, and I fear for what will happen to the forests it has come to represent. I am not sure that my own efforts or those of other conservationists will succeed, and I remain cautious about the implications of these efforts upon critical issues of human justice.

Given these fears and uncertainties, it is vitally important to find a reason to work for conservation and justice, to believe that these efforts could succeed and that it is reasonable to hope for a diverse and healthy world. An ethics of biodiversity should end with hope.

One source of such hope is biodiversity itself: the evolution of life over three billion years is a clear sign that the life on this planet is resilient—collectively if not individually—and some remnant of life on Earth today is very likely to endure for billions of years more. Biodiversity is not a lost cause because the variety of life remains older and more pervasive even than the threats we have created for it.

This hope may not be enough for most conservationists, however, because while some biodiversity is likely to endure, it is less certain that the life remaining will be recognizable to us, healthy by our current standards, or capable of supporting human civilization as we know it. To find hope for a human future on this planet, for life as we want it to survive, we must believe that people in the industrialized world can learn and adapt quickly, that we can find ways to live with rather than against the creatures with whom we share this planet. We must believe that privileged and powerful human beings will care enough to address the complex problems of how to conserve the variety of life. I gain significant hope along these lines from the scientists and other authors cited in this book, so many of whom have committed their lives to understanding and conserving biodiversity. Of course, these sources represent only one small part of a far broader movement, which also includes many scientists, managers, activists, and community members not cited here. I draw even more hope from the knowledge that so much is being done for conservation beyond my awareness.

Despite this hope, however, another common theme emerging from work about biodiversity is that the problem remains very real and very serious, and more must be done by more people if human society is to coexist living sustainably with the rest of life's variety. The degradation of biodiversity continues and will likely increase unless fundamental attitudes, behaviors, and institutions are changed. We cannot be certain that we have the tools we need to solve this enormous problem. We cannot be sure that enough people will make the changes required to truly conserve biodiversity.

For this reason I conclude with a reminder of the basis of this particular ethics of biodiversity: faith in God the creator as revealed in the incarnation of Christ and taught by Christian traditions. Hope in this context arises not only from the variety of life and the behavior of human beings but also from the belief that a God who is love created both. God did not make a world in which we can trust that things will work out if we simply have faith and do nothing; the contemporary degradation of biodiversity is clear evidence that action is necessary. Neither did God make a world where there are perfect and straightforward solutions to any problem; the necessity of killing barred owls to save spotted owls is clear evidence of that. Nevertheless, there is room in the context of faith to hope that God made a world in which human beings can do better, can conserve more life than is being conserved today, and can find a way to survive and thrive with and as the variety of life.

This is a hope that the God of the Hebrew Bible who told Noah to "keep them alive with you" will help contemporary human beings find the tools to do the same, to keep the variety of this Earth alive alongside us. The future of biodiversity depends upon whether this is a realistic hope, on whether enough people care enough and work hard enough to make it a reality.

Notes

1. An analysis released by the Society for Conservation Biology explicitly states that "far too much emphasis is placed on the adverse effects of barred

owl range expansion" in the Fish and Wildlife Service plan, and called for a more serious consideration of the spotted owl's habitat requirements. See Noss and Fitzgerald, "Society for Conservation Biology," www.conbio.org/sections/namerica/SCB-NA%20Comments%20to%20FWS%20Northern%20Spotted%20Owl.pdf.

2. Dietrich, *Final Forest*, 237.

3. See Freudenburg and Wilson, "Forty Years of Spotted Owls?"

Bibliography

Adams, W. M., and S. J. Jenrenaud. "Transition to Sustainability: Towards a Humane and Diverse World." Gland, Switzerland: International Union for the Conservation of Nature, 2008.

Allen, T. F. H., and T. W. Hoekstra. *Toward a Unified Ecology.* New York: Columbia University Press, 1992.

Angermeier, Paul L. "Does Biodiversity Include Artificial Diversity?" *Conservation Biology* 8, no. 2 (1994): 600–602.

Aquinas, Thomas. *Summa Theologiae.* New York: Blackfriars, 1964.

Attfield, Robin. "Evolution, Theodicy, and Value." *Heythrop Journal* 41, no. 3 (2000): 281–96.

Baur, Donald C., and William Robert Irvin. *The Endangered Species Act: Law, Policy, and Perspectives.* Chicago: American Bar Association, 2002.

Bean, Michael J., Melanie J. Rowland, Environmental Defense Fund, and World Wildlife Fund (U.S.). *The Evolution of National Wildlife Law.* 3rd ed. Westport, CT: Praeger, 1997.

Beattie, Andrew, and Paul R. Ehrlich. *Wild Solutions: How Biodiversity Is Money in the Bank.* New Haven, CT: Yale University Press, 2001.

Beckley, Harlan, and Charles M. Swezey. *James M. Gustafson's Theocentric Ethics: Interpretations and Assessments.* Macon, GA: Mercer University Press, 1988.

Black, Richard. "Nature Loss 'Dwarfs Bank Crisis.'" BBC News, http://news.bbc.co.uk/2/hi/science/nature/7662565.stm.

Boff, Leonardo. *Cry of the Earth, Cry of the Poor.* Maryknoll, NY: Orbis Books, 1997.

———. *Ecology and Liberation: A New Paradigm.* Translated by John Cumming. Maryknoll, NY: Orbis Books, 1995.

———. *Jesus Christ Liberator: A Critical Christology for Our Times.* Translated by Patrick Hughes. Maryknoll, NY: Orbis Books, 1978.

———. "Liberation Theology and Ecology: Alternative, Confrontation, or Complementarity?" In *Ecology and Poverty: Cry of the Earth, Cry of the Poor,* edited by Leonardo Boff and Virgil Elizondo. Maryknoll, NY: Orbis Books, 1995.

———. *Saint Francis: A Model for Human Liberation.* Translated by John W. Diercksmeier. New York: Crossroad, 1982.

Boff, Leonardo, and Clodovis Boff. *Introducing Liberation Theology.* Translated by Paul Burns. Maryknoll, NY: Orbis Books, 1987.

Bouma-Prediger, Steven. *For the Beauty of the Earth: A Christian Vision for Creation Care.* Grand Rapids, MI: Baker Academic, 2001.

Bouma-Prediger, Steven, and Virginia Vroblesky. *Assessing the Ark: A Christian Perspective on Non-Human Creatures and the Endangered Species Act.* Wynnewood, PA: Crossroads, 1997.

Brooks, Thomas M., Ana S. L. Rodrigues, and Gustavo A. B. da Fonseca. "Protected Areas and Species." *Conservation Biology* 18, no. 6 (2004): 616–18.

Bullard, Robert D., Paul Mohai, Robin Saha, and Beverly Wright. *Toxic Wastes and Race at Twenty: 1987–2007.* Cleveland, OH: The United Church of Christ Justice and Witness Ministries, 2007.

Burgess, Bonnie B. *Fate of the Wild: The Endangered Species Act and the Future of Biodiversity.* Athens: University of Georgia Press, 2001.

Callicott, J. Baird. *In Defense of the Land Ethic.* Albany: State University of New York Press, 1989.

Carroll, Ronald, Carol Augspurger, Andy Dobson, Jerry Franklin, Gordon Orians, Walter Reid, Richard Tracy, David Wilcove, and John Wilson. "Strengthening the Use of Science in Achieving the Goals of the Endangered Species Act: An Assessment by the Ecological Society of America." *Ecological Applications* 6, no. 1 (1996): 1–11.

Carson, Rachel. *Silent Spring.* New York: Houghton Mifflin, 1994.

Center for Biological Diversity. "Saving the Polar Bear: Background." www .biologicaldiversity.org/species/mammals/polar_bear/background .html.

Chivian, Eric, and Aaron Bernstein, eds. *Sustaining Life: How Human Health Depends on Biodiversity.* New York: Oxford University Press, 2008.

Chryssavgis, John. *Beyond the Shattered Image.* Minneapolis, MN: Light & Life Publishing, 1999.

Cone, James H. *A Black Theology of Liberation.* 2nd ed. Maryknoll, NY: Orbis Books, 1986.

———. *God of the Oppressed.* Rev. ed. Maryknoll, NY: Orbis Books, 1997.

Costanza, Robert, Ralph d'Arge, Rudolf de Groot, Stephen Farber, Monica Grasso, Bruce Hannon, Karin Limburg, et al. "The Value of the World's Ecosystem Services and Natural Capital." *Nature* 387, no. 6630 (1997): 253–60.

Crystal, David. *Language Death.* New York: Cambridge University Press, 2000.

Curran, Charles E. *The Catholic Moral Tradition Today: A Synthesis.* Washington, DC: Georgetown University Press, 1999.

Daily, Gretchen C., ed. *Nature's Services: Societal Dependence on Natural Ecosystems.* Washington, DC: Island Press, 1997.

Daly, Herman E., and John B. Cobb Jr. *For the Common Good: Redirecting the Economy toward Community, the Environment, and a Sustainable Future.* 2nd ed. Boston: Beacon Press, 1994.

Darwin, Charles. *The Origin of Species: Complete and Fully Illustrated.* New York: Random House, 1979.

Davis, Wade. *Light at the Edge of the World: A Journey through the Realm of Vanishing Cultures.* Vancouver, BC: Douglas & McIntyre, 2007.

DeLong, Don C. "Defining Biodiversity." *Wildlife Society Bulletin* 24, no. 4 (1996): 738–49.

DeWitt, Calvin B., Richard A. Baer Jr., Thomas Sieger Derr, Vernon J. Ehlers, James W. Skillen, and Luis E. Lugo. *Caring for Creation: Responsible Stewardship of God's Handiwork.* Grand Rapids, MI: Baker Books, 1998.

Dietrich, William. *The Final Forest: The Battle for the Last Great Trees of the Pacific Northwest.* New York: Simon & Schuster, 1992.

Dillard, Annie. *Pilgrim at Tinker Creek.* New York: HarperCollins, 1974.

Doremus, Holly. "The Purposes, Effects, and Future of the Endangered Species Act's Best Available Science Mandate." *Environmental Law* 34 (2004): 397–450.

Dowie, Mark. *Conservation Refugees: The Hundred Year Conflict between Global Conservation and Native Peoples.* Cambridge, MA: MIT Press, 2009.

Dunlap, Thomas R. *Saving America's Wildlife: Ecology and the American Mind, 1850–1990.* Princeton, NJ: Princeton University Press, 1988.

Dwyer, Lynn E., Dennis D. Murphy, and Paul R. Ehrlich. "Property Rights Case Law and the Challenge to the Endangered Species Act." *Conservation Biology* 9, no. 4 (1995): 725–41.

Egan, Timothy. "Strongest U.S. Environment Law May Become Endangered Species." *The New York Times,* May 26, 1992, A1, A11.

Ehrlich, Paul R. "Biodiversity and Ecosystem Function: Need We Know More?" In *Biodiversity and Ecosystem Function,* edited by E. D. Schulze and Harold A. Mooney. New York: Springer-Verlag, 1993.

———. "Bioethics: Are Our Priorities Right?" *BioScience* 53, no. 12 (2003): 1207–16.

Ehrlich, Paul R., and Anne H. Ehrlich. *Extinction: The Causes and Consequences of the Disappearance of Species.* New York: Random House, 1981.

———. *One with Nineveh: Politics, Consumption, and the Human Future.* Washington, DC: Island Press, 2004.

Eilperin, Juliet. "Endangered Species Act Changes Give Agencies More Say." *Washington Post,* August 12, 2008.

Eldredge, Niles. *Life in the Balance: Humanity and the Biodiversity Crisis.* Princeton, NJ: Princeton University Press, 1998.

Evernden, Neil. *The Natural Alien: Humankind and Environment.* Toronto: University of Toronto Press, 1985.

Fiedler, Peggy L., and Subodh K. Jain. *Conservation Biology: The Theory and Practice of Nature Conservation, Preservation, and Management.* New York: Chapman and Hall, 1992.

Folke, Carl, C. S. Holling, and Charles Perrings. "Biological Diversity, Ecosystems, and the Human Scale." *Ecological Applications* 6, no. 4 (1996): 1018–24.

Forman, Richard T. T. *Land Mosaics: The Ecology of Landscapes and Regions.* New York: Cambridge University Press, 1995.

Freudenburg, William R., and Lisa J. Wilson. "Forty Years of Spotted Owls? A Longitudinal Analysis of Logging Industry Job Losses." *Sociological Perspectives* 41, no. 1 (1998): 1–26.

Gardner, Robert H., W. Michael Kemp, Victor S. Kennedy, and John E. Peterson, eds. *Scaling Relations in Experimental Ecology.* New York: Columbia University Press, 2001.

Gaston, Kevin J., and John I. Spicer. *Biodiversity: An Introduction.* 2nd ed. Malden, MA: Blackwell, 2004.

Gebara, Ivone. *Longing for Running Water: Ecofeminism and Liberation.* Translated by David Molineaux. Minneapolis, MN: Fortress Press, 1999.

Geisler, Charles. "A New Kind of Trouble: Evictions in Eden." *International Social Sciences Journal* 55, no. 175 (2003): 69–78.

Gelobter, Michel, Michael Dorsey, Leslie Fields, Tom Goldtooth, Anuja Mendiratta, Richard Moore, Rachel Morello-Frosh, Peggy M. Shepard, and Gerald Torres. "The Soul of Environmentalism: Rediscovering Transformational Politics in the 21st Century." Position paper, Redefining Progress, Oakland, CA, 2005.

Gore, Albert. *An Inconvenient Truth: The Planetary Emergency of Global Warming and What We Can Do about It.* Emmaus, PA: Rodale, 2006.

———. *Earth in the Balance: Ecology and the Human Spirit.* New York: Houghton Mifflin, 1992.

Gustafson, James M. *Ethics from a Theocentric Perspective: Theology and Ethics.* Vol. 1. Chicago: University of Chicago Press, 1981.

Habermas, Jürgen. "Struggles for Recognition in the Democratic Constitutional State." In *Multiculturalism: Examining the Politics of Recognition,* edited by Charles Taylor and Amy Gutmann, 107–48. Princeton, NJ: Princeton University Press, 1994.

Habgood, John. "A Sacramental Approach to Environmental Issues." In *Liberating Life: Contemporary Approaches to Ecological Theology,* edited by Charles Birch, William Eakin, and Jay B. McDaniel, 46–53. Maryknoll, NY: Orbis, 1991.

Hamer, Thomas E., Eric D. Forsman, and Elizabeth M. Glenn. "Home Range Attributes and Habitat Selection of Barred Owls and Spotted Owls in an Area of Sympatry." *The Condor* 109, no. 4 (2007): 750–68.

Hamilton, Lawrence S., Helen F. Takeuchi, and East-West Center. *Ethics, Religion and Biodiversity: Relations between Conservation and Cultural Values.* Cambridge, UK: White Horse, 1993.

Harmon, David. *In Light of Our Differences: How Diversity in Nature and Culture Makes Us Human.* Washington, DC: Smithsonian Institution Press, 2002.

Hart, John. *Sacramental Commons: Christian Ecological Ethics.* Lanham, MD: Rowman & Littlefield, 2006.

Haught, John F. *The Promise of Nature: Ecology and Cosmic Purpose.* New York: Paulist Press, 1993.

Hay, Peter. *Main Currents in Western Environmental Thought.* Bloomington, IN: Indiana University Press, 2002.

Hessel, Dieter T., ed. *After Nature's Revolt: Eco-Justice and Theology.* Minneapolis, MN: Fortress Press, 1992.

Hessel, Dieter T., and Larry L. Rasmussen, eds. *Earth Habitat: Eco-Injustice and the Church's Response.* Minneapolis, MN: Fortress Press, 2001.

Hessel, Dieter T., and Rosemary Radford Ruether, eds. *Christianity and Ecology: Seeking the Well-Being of Earth and Humans.* Cambridge, MA: Harvard University Press, 2000.

Heywood, V. H., ed. *Global Biodiversity Assessment.* New York: Cambridge University Press, 1995.

Houck, Oliver. "On the Law of Biodiversity and Ecosystem Management." *Minnesota Law Review* 81 (1997): 869–979.

Hughes, Jennifer B., Gretchen C. Daily, and Paul R. Ehrlich. "Population Diversity: Its Extent and Extinction." *Science* 278, no. 5338 (1997): 689–92.

Institute for Environment and Human Security. "Environmental Migrants: Conference Aims to Build Consensus on Their Definition, Support, and Protection." Tokyo: United Nations University, 2008.

Irwin, Kevin W. "The Sacramentality of Creation and the Role of Creation in Liturgy and Sacraments." In *Preserving the Creation: Environmental Theology and Ethics*, edited by Kevin W. Irwin and Edmund D. Pellegrino, 67–111. Washington, DC: Georgetown University Press, 1994.

Jefferson, Thomas. *Notes on the State of Virginia.* New York: Penguin Books, 1999.

John Paul II. "The Ecological Crisis: A Common Responsibility." The Vatican, www.vatican.va/holy_father/john_paul_ii/messages/peace/documents/hf_jp-ii_mes_19891208_xxiii-world-day-for-peace_en.html.

Johnson, Elizabeth A. *Women, Earth, and Creator Spirit.* New York: Paulist Press, 1993.

Kearns, Laurel. "Saving the Creation: Religious Environmentalism." PhD diss., Emory University, 1994.

Kearns, Laurel, and Catherine Keller, eds. *Ecospirit: Religions and Philosophies for the Earth.* New York: Fordham University Press, 2007.

Ketley, Harriet. "Cultural Diversity Versus Biodiversity." *Adelaide Law Review* 16 (1994): 99–160.

Kinzig, Ann P., Stephen W. Pacala, and David Tilman. *The Functional Consequences of Biodiversity: Empirical Progress and Theoretical Extensions.* Princeton, NJ: Princeton University Press, 2001.

Kohák, Erazim. *The Green Halo: A Bird's-Eye View of Ecological Ethics.* Chicago: Open Court, 2000.

Kohm, Kathryn A., ed. *Balancing on the Brink of Extinction: The Endangered Species Act and Lessons for the Future.* Washington, DC: Island Press, 1991.

Kunin, William E., and John H. Lawton. "Does Biodiversity Matter? Evaluating the Case for Conserving Species." In *Biodiversity: A Biology of Numbers and Difference,* edited by Kevin J. Gaston, 283–308. London: Blackwell, 1996.

Leakey, Richard E., and Roger Lewin. *The Sixth Extinction: Patterns of Life and the Future of Humankind.* New York: Doubleday, 1995.

Leopold, Aldo. *A Sand County Almanac, with Essays on Conservation from Round River.* New York: Ballantine Books, 1966.

Levin, Simon A. "The Problem of Pattern and Scale in Ecology: The Robert H. Macarthur Award Lecture." *Ecology* 73, no. 6 (1992): 1943–67.

Lodge, David M., and Christopher Hamlin. *Religion and the New Ecology: Environmental Responsibility in a World in Flux.* Notre Dame, IN: University of Notre Dame Press, 2006.

Loreau, Michel, Shahid Naeem, and Pablo Inchausti. *Biodiversity and Ecosystem Functioning: Synthesis and Perspectives.* New York: Oxford University Press, 2002.

Loreau, Michel, and Alfred Oteng-Yeboah. "Diversity without Representation." *Nature* 442 (2006).

Lovejoy, Thomas E. "Changes in Biological Diversity." In *The Global 2000 Report to the President, Vol. 2 (Technical Report),* edited by G. O. Barney. New York: Pergamon Press, 1980.

Maffi, Luisa. *On Biocultural Diversity: Linking Language, Knowledge, and the Environment.* Washington, DC: Smithsonian Institution Press, 2001.

Maguire, Daniel C. *Death by Choice.* Garden City, NY: Image Books, 1984.

Martin, Edward Thomas. *Thomas Jefferson: Scientist.* New York: H. Schuman, 1952.

May, Robert M. *Stability and Complexity in Model Ecosystems.* Princeton, NJ: Princeton University Press, 2001.

McFague, Sallie. *The Body of God: An Ecological Theology.* Minneapolis, MN: Fortress Press, 1993.

———. *Life Abundant: Rethinking Theology and Economy for a Planet in Peril.* Minneapolis, MN: Fortress Press, 2001.

———. *Super, Natural Christians: How We Should Love Nature.* Minneapolis, MN: Fortress Press, 1997.

Michaels, Walter Benn. *The Trouble with Diversity: How We Learned to Love Identity and Ignore Inequality.* New York: Metropolitan Books, 2006.

Mies, Maria, and Vandana Shiva. *Ecofeminism.* New York: Zed Books, 1993.

Miller, James R. "Biodiversity Conservation and the Extinction of Experience." *TRENDS in Ecology and Evolution* 20, no. 8 (2005): 430–34.

Myers, Norman. "Environmental Refugees: A Growing Phenomenon of the

21st Century," *Philosophical Transactions of the Royal Society of London B* 357, no. 1420 (2002): 609–13.

Myers, Norman, Russel A. Mittermeler, Cristina G. Mittermeler, Gustavo A. B. da Fonseca, and Jennifer Kent. "Biodiversity Hotspots for Conservation Priorities." *Nature* 403 (2000): 853–58.

Nabhan, Gary Paul. *Cultures of Habitat: On Nature, Culture, and Story.* Washington, DC: Counterpoint, 1997.

Naeem, Shahid, F. Stuart Chapin, Robert Costanza, Paul Ehrlich, Frank B. Golley, David U. Hooper, John H. Lawton, et al. "Biodiversity and Ecosystem Functioning: Maintaining Natural Life Support Processes." In *Issues in Ecology.* Washington, DC: The Ecological Society of America, 1999.

Naeem, Shahid, L. J. Thompson, S. P. Lawler, J. H. Lawton, and R. M. Woodfin. "Declining Biodiversity Can Alter the Performance of Ecosystems." *Nature* 368 (1994): 734–37.

Nash, James A. "The Bible vs. Biodiversity: The Case against Moral Argument from Scripture." *Journal for the Study of Religion, Nature, and Culture* 3, no. 2 (2009): 213–37.

———. *Loving Nature: Ecological Integrity and Christian Responsibility.* Nashville, TN: Abingdon Press, 1991.

Newsom, Carol A. "The Moral Sense of Nature: Ethics in Light of God's Speech to Job." *The Princeton Seminary Bulletin* 15, no. 1 (1994): 9–27.

Norse, E. A., and R. E. McManus. "Ecology and Living Resources: Biological Diversity." In *Environmental Quality 1980: Eleventh Annual Report of the Council on Environmental Quality.* Washington, DC: Council on Environmental Quality, 1980.

Northcott, Michael S. *The Environment and Christian Ethics.* New York: Cambridge University Press, 1996.

———. "From Environmental U-Topianism to Parochial Ecology: Communities of Place and the Politics of Sustainability." *Ecotheology* 8 (2000): 71–85.

———. *A Moral Climate: The Ethics of Global Warming.* Maryknoll, NY: Orbis Books, 2007.

Northern Spotted Owl v. Hodel, 716 F. Supp. 479 (W.D. Wash. 1988).

Northern Spotted Owl v. Lujan, 758 F. Supp. 621 (W.D. Wash. 1991).

Norton, Bryan G. *Searching for Sustainability: Interdisciplinary Essays in the Philosophy of Conservation Biology.* New York: Cambridge University Press, 2003.

———. *Sustainability: A Philosophy of Adaptive Ecosystem Management.* Chicago: University of Chicago Press, 2005.

———. *Toward Unity among Environmentalists.* New York: Oxford University Press, 1991.

———. *Why Preserve Natural Variety?* Princeton, NJ: Princeton University Press, 1987.

Noss, Reed F., and Allen Cooperrider. *Saving Nature's Legacy: Protecting and Restoring Biodiversity.* Washington, DC: Island Press, 1994.

Noss, Reed, and John Fitzgerald. "Society for Conservation Biology North American Section Comments on Proposed Critical Habitat Exemptions for the Northern Spotted Owl." www.conbio.org/sections/namerica/SCB-NA%20Comments%20to%20FWS%20Northern%20Spotted%20Owl.pdf.

Novacek, Michael J. *The Biodiversity Crisis: Losing What Counts.* New York: The American Museum of Natural History, 2001.

O'Brien, David J., and Thomas A. Shannon. *Catholic Social Thought: The Documentary Heritage.* Maryknoll, NY: Orbis Books, 1992.

O'Brien, Kevin J. "Ecology." In *The Encyclopedia of Sustainability*, edited by Willis Jenkins. Great Barrington, MA: Berkshire, 2009.

Olson, Gail S., Robert G. Anthony, Eric D. Forsman, Steven H. Ackers, Peter J. Loschl, Janice A. Reid, Katie M. Dugger, Elizabeth M. Glenn, and William J. Ripple. "Modeling of Site Occupancy Dynamics for Northern Spotted Owls, with Emphasis on the Effects of Barred Owls." *Journal of Wildlife Management* 69, no. 3 (2005): 918–32.

Orians, Gordon H., Gardner M. Brown, William E. Kunin, and Joseph E. Swierzbinski, eds. *The Preservation and Valuation of Biological Resources.* Seattle: University of Washington Press, 1990.

Orr, David. "Orr's Laws." *Conservation Biology* 18 (2004): 1457–60.

Petersen, Shannon. *Acting for Endangered Species: The Statutory Ark.* Lawrence: University Press of Kansas, 2002.

Peterson, David L., and V. Thomas Parker. *Ecological Scale: Theory and Applications.* New York: Columbia University Press, 1998.

Pimm, Stuart L., and Peter Raven. "Extinction by Numbers." *Nature* 403, no. 6772 (2000): 843–45.

Rasmussen, Larry L. "Drilling in the Cathedral." *Dialog: A Journal of Theology* 42, no. 3 (2003): 202–25.

———. *Earth Community, Earth Ethics.* Maryknoll, NY: Orbis Books, 1996.

———. "Environmental Racism and Environmental Justice: Moral Theory in the Making?" *Journal of the Society of Christian Ethics* 24, no. 1 (2004): 3–28.

Reaka-Kudla, Marjorie L., Don E. Wilson, and Edward O. Wilson, eds. *Biodiversity II: Understanding and Protecting Our Biological Resources.* Washington, DC: Joseph Henry Press, 1997.

Redford, Kent H., and Brian D. Richter. "Conservation of Biodiversity in a World of Use." *Conservation Biology* 13, no. 6 (1999): 1246–56.

Redford, Kent H., and Allyn Maclean Stearman. "Forest-Dwelling Native Amazonians and the Conservation of Biodiversity: Interests in Common or in Collision?" *Conservation Biology* 7, no. 2 (1993): 248–55.

Reid, Walter V., and Kenton Miller. *Keeping Options Alive: The Scientific Basis for Conserving Biodiversity.* Washington, DC: World Resources Institute, 1989.

Rhoads, David, ed. *Earth and Word: Classic Sermons on Saving the Planet.* New York: Continuum, 2007.

Rolston, Holmes. *Environmental Ethics: Duties to and Values in the Natural World.* Philadelphia, PA: Temple University Press, 1988.

Ruether, Rosemary Radford. "Theological Resources for Earth Healing: Covenant and Sacrament." In *The Challenge of Global Stewardship: Roman Catholic Responses,* edited by Maura A. Ryan and Todd David Whitmore, 54–66. Notre Dame, IN: University of Notre Dame Press, 1997.

———, ed. *Women Healing Earth: Third World Women on Ecology, Feminism, and Religion.* Maryknoll, NY: Orbis Books, 1996.

Sagan, Carl, Hans Bethe, Elise Boulding, M. I. Budyko, S. Chandrasekhar, Paul J. Crutzen, Margaret Davis, et al. "An Open Letter to the Religious Community." In *Ecology and Religion: Scientists Speak,* edited by John E. Carroll and Keith Warner, ii–vi. Quincy, IL: Franciscan Press, 1998.

Santmire, H. Paul. "The Genesis Creation Narratives Revisited: Themes for a Global Age." *Interpretation* 45, no. 4 (1991): 366–79.

———. *The Travail of Nature: The Ambiguous Ecological Promise of Christian Theology.* Minneapolis, MN: Fortress Press, 1985.

Sarkar, Sahotra. *Biodiversity and Environmental Philosophy: An Introduction.* New York: Cambridge University Press, 2005.

Schumacher, E. F. *Small Is Beautiful: Economics as If People Mattered.* New York: Harper & Row, 1973.

Secretariat of the Convention on Biological Diversity. "Convention on Biological Diversity." Montreal: United Nations Environment Programme, 1992.

———. "Global Biodiversity Outlook 2." Montreal: United Nations Environment Programme, 2006.

Shinn, Roger L. "The Mystery of the Self and the Enigma of Nature." In *Christianity in the 21st Century,* edited by Deborah A. Brown. New York: Crossroad, 2000.

Shiva, Vandana. *Biodiversity: Social & Ecological Perspectives.* London; Atlantic Highlands, NJ: Zed Books, 1991.

———. *Monocultures of the Mind: Perspectives on Biodiversity and Biotechnology.* London: Zed Books, 1993.

———. *Tomorrow's Biodiversity.* New York: Thames & Hudson, 2001.

Shrader-Frechette, Kristin. "Throwing out the Bathwater of Positivism, Keeping the Baby of Objectivity: Relativism and Advocacy in Conservation Biology." *Conservation Biology* 10, no. 3 (1996): 912–14.

Sideris, Lisa H. *Environmental Ethics, Ecological Theology, and Natural Selection.* New York: Columbia University Press, 2003.

Soper, Kate. *What Is Nature? Culture, Politics, and the Non-Human.* Cambridge, MA: Blackwell, 1995.

Soulé, Michael E. "What Is Conservation Biology? A New Synthetic Discipline

Addresses the Dynamics and Problems of Perturbed Species, Communities, and Ecosystems." *BioScience* 35, no. 11 (1985): 727–34.

Species Survival Commission. "State of the World's Species." International Union for the Conservation of Nature, http://cmsdata.iucn.org/downloads/state_of_the_world_s_species_factsheet_en.pdf.

Spencer, Daniel T. *Gay and Gaia: Ethics, Ecology, and the Erotic.* Cleveland, OH: Pilgrim Press, 1996.

Stokstad, Erik. "What's Wrong with the Endangered Species Act?" *Science* 309 (2005): 2150–52.

Sukhdev, Pavan. *The Economics of Ecosystems & Biodiversity: An Interim Report.* Brussels: European Union Commission for the Environment, 2008.

Swingland, Ian R. "Definition of Biodiversity." In *Encyclopedia of Biodiversity,* edited by Simon A. Levin, 377–91. San Diego, CA: Academic Press, 2001.

Takacs, David. *The Idea of Biodiversity: Philosophies of Paradise.* Baltimore, MD: Johns Hopkins University Press, 1996.

Tal, Alon. *Speaking of Earth: Environmental Speeches That Moved the World.* New Brunswick, NJ: Rutgers University Press, 2006.

Tennessee Valley Authority v. Hill, 437 U.S. 153 (1978).

Tennyson, Alfred. *In Memoriam: Authoritative Text & Criticism.* 2nd ed. New York: W. W. Norton, 2004.

Tilman, David, and Joel E. Cohen. "Biosphere 2 and Biodiversity—the Lessons So Far." *Science* 274, no. 5290 (1996): 1150–51.

Toolan, David. *At Home in the Cosmos.* Maryknoll, NY: Orbis Books, 2001.

Tracy, C. Richard, and Peter F. Brussard. "The Importance of Science in Conservation Biology." *Conservation Biology* 10, no. 3 (1996): 918–19.

Tucker, Mary Evelyn, and John A. Grim. *Worldviews and Ecology: Religion, Philosophy, and the Environment.* Maryknoll, NY: Orbis Books, 1994.

Union of Concerned Scientists. "A Letter from Biologists to the United States Senate Concerning Science in the Endangered Species Act." http://www.ucsusa.org/scientific_integrity/restoring/biologists-letter-on.html.

United States Conference of Catholic Bishops. "Renewing the Earth: An Invitation to Reflection and Action on Environment in Light of Catholic Social Teaching." United States Conference of Catholic Bishops, http://www.usccb.org/sdwp/ejp/bishopsstatement.htm.

United States v. Dion, 476 U.S. 734 (1986).

U.S. Congress. "The Bald Eagle Protection Act." Washington, DC: U.S. Government Printing Office, 1940.

———. "The Endangered Species Act of 1973." Washington, DC: U.S. Government Printing Office, 1973.

U.S. Department of the Interior. "Salazar Retains Conservation Rule for Polar Bears." www.doi.gov/news/09_News_Releases/050809b.html.

———. "Secretary Kempthorne Announces Decision to Protect Polar Bears under Endangered Species Act: Rule Will Allow Continuation of Vital Energy Production in Alaska." http://www.doi.gov/news/08_News_Releases/080514a.html.

U.S. Fish and Wildlife Service. "Final Recovery Plan for the Northern Spotted Owl (Strix Occidentalis Caurina)." Portland, OR: U.S. Fish and Wildlife Service, 2008.

U.S. Fish & Wildlife Service. "Summary of Listed Species." http://ecos.fws.gov/tess_public/Boxscore.do.

Vitousek, Peter M., Harold A. Mooney, Jane Lubchenco, and Jerry M. Melillo. "Human Domination of Earth's Ecosystems." *Science* 277 (1997): 494–99.

Walker, Brian H. "Biodiversity and Ecological Redundancy." *Conservation Biology* 6, no. 1 (1992): 18–23.

Wardle, David A., Michael A. Huston, J. Philip Grime, Frank Berendse, Eric Garnier, William K. Lauenroth, Heikki Setälä, and Scott D. Wilson. "Biodiversity and Ecosystem Function: An Issue in Ecology." *Bulletin of the Ecological Society of America* 81, no. 3 (2000): 235–39.

Wardle, David A., Olle Zackrisson, Greger Hörnberg, and Christiane Gallet. "The Influence of Island Area on Ecosystem Properties." *Science* 277 (1997): 1296–99.

White, Lynn Jr. "The Historical Roots of Our Ecologic Crisis." In *Western Man and Environmental Ethics: Attitudes toward Nature and Technology*, edited by Ian G. Barbour. Reading, MA: Addison-Wesley, 1973.

Whitebook, Joel. "The Problem of Nature in Habermas." In *Minding Nature: The Philosophers of Ecology*, edited by David Macauley, 283–316. New York: Guilford Press, 1996.

Wilkinson, Charles. "The Role of Bilateralism in Fulfilling the Federal-Tribal Relationship: The Tribal Rights-Endangered Species Secretarial Order." *Washington Law Review* 72 (1997): 1063–88.

Wilson, Edward O. *Consilience: The Unity of Knowledge*. New York: Knopf, 1998.

———. *The Creation: An Appeal to Save Life on Earth*. New York: Norton, 2006.

———. *The Diversity of Life*. Cambridge, MA: Harvard University Press, 1992.

———. *The Future of Life*. New York: Vintage, 2002.

Wilson, Edward O., and Frances M. Peter. *Biodiversity*. Washington, DC: National Academy Press, 1988.

Wood, Bernard, and Paul Constantino. "Human Origins: Life at the Top of the Tree." In *Assembling the Tree of Life*, edited by Joel Cracraft and Michael J. Donoghue, 517–35. New York: Oxford University Press, 2004.

Worster, Donald. *Nature's Economy: A History of Ecological Ideas*. 2nd ed. New York: Cambridge University Press, 1994.

Index